Hedges, Screens & Espaliers

How to Select, Grow & Enjoy

by Susan Chamberlin

HPBooks

HPBooks

Publishers
Bill and Helen Fisher

Executive Editor
Rick Bailey

Editorial Director
Randy Summerlin

Editor
Scott Millard

Art Director
Don Burton

Book Design
Kathleen Koopman

For Horticultural Publishing Co., Inc.

Executive Producer
Richard M. Ray

Editor
Michael MacCaskey

Production Editor
Kathleen S. Parker

Associate Editor
Lance Walheim

Illustrations
Roy Jones

Major Photography
Michael Landis

Additional Photography
William Aplin
Susan Chamberlin
Pamela Harper

Cover photo
by Gill Kenny

Published by HPBooks
P.O. Box 5367
Tucson, AZ 85703
602/888-2150
ISBN: 0-89586-190-9
Library of Congress Catalog
Card Number: 82-83306
©1983 Fisher Publishing Inc.
Printed in U.S.A.

About the Author

Susan Chamberlin received her degree in Landscape Architecture from the University of California. She is a practicing Landscape Architect in Santa Cruz, California, specializing in designing landscapes that are functional as well as attractive.

Acknowledgments

Dane Anderson, Wayside Gardens, Hodges, SC
The Avant Gardener, New York, NY
Russell A. Beatty, A.S.L.A., Department of Landscape Architecture, University of California, Berkeley, CA
Robert Boro, Landscape Architect, Fresno, CA
Brooklyn Botanic Garden, Brooklyn, NY
Mrs. Ralph Brown, Vancouver, British Columbia
Richard Casale, USDA Soil Conservation Service, Santa Cruz County, CA
Barrie D. Coate, Saratoga Horticultural Foundation, Saratoga, CA
Bob Cowden, Nurseryman, Walnut Creek, CA
Walter Doty, Horticulturist, Los Altos, CA
Lucy Erickson, Horticulturist, Filoli Center, Woodside, CA
John E. Ford, Curator, Secrest Arboretum, Wooster, OH
Mary A. Gamble, Founding Member, Boxwood Society of the Midwest
Melvin Gum, San Gabriel, CA
W. Richard Hildreth, Director, State Arboretum of Utah, University of Utah, Salt Lake City, UT
Michael Hopping, Landscape Designer, Baton Rouge, LA
Joe Larkin, Morton Arboretum, Lisle, IL
Henry Leuthardt Nurseries, Inc., Long Island, NY
Charles Lewis, Morton Arboretum, Lisle, IL
George Lewis, Garden Superintendent, Descanso Gardens, La Canada, CA
Frank Mackiness, Horticulturist, Corbett, OR
Richard D. Mahone, Director of Landscape Construction & Maintenance, Colonial Williamsburg, VA
Henry McLaren, Vancouver, British Columbia
Hugh Martin, Vancouver, British Columbia
Joel Michaelsen, Berkeley, CA
Joy Mintz, Horticulturist, Longue Vue Gardens, New Orleans, LA
Harold Newfeldt, Vancouver, British Columbia
Julius Nuccio, Nuccio's Nursery, Altadena, CA
Mr. and Mrs. Jonathan Parker, Vancouver, British Columbia
Mrs. George E. Penhale, Boxwood Society of the Midwest
Mrs. P. Percheson, Vancouver, British Columbia
Janet Pollock, Landscape Architect, Santa Cruz, CA
Mark Primack, Santa Cruz, CA
William A. P. Pullman, Lake Forrest, IL.
Pat Resine, Conrad Pyle Nursery, Westgrove, PA
A. W. Robertson, Vancouver, British Columbia
Robert and Shirley Roos, Hillsboro, CA
Roy Rydell, A.S.L.A., Santa Cruz, CA
Dr. Robert Stebbins, Corvalis, OR
Richard Steinfeld, Santa Cruz, CA
Roy Taylor, University of British Columbia, Vancouver
R.L. Ticknor, Northern Willamette Experiment Station, Aurora, OR
Carl A. Totemeier Jr., Director, Old Westbury Gardens, Long Island, NY
Mr. Valance, Vancouver, British Columbia
Dennis White, Saratoga Horticultural Foundation, Saratoga, CA
Mrs. Whitthall, Vancouver, British Columbia

Contents

1

INTRODUCTION

Hedges, screens and espaliers are the basic, *practical plants* of the landscape. Planted in the right location, they reduce heating and cooling costs, and increase privacy and outdoor space. Edible hedges, screens and espaliers perform triple duty, supplying beauty, landscape function and fresh produce.

On a large scale, hedgerow and screen plantings provide cover to wildlife. Barrier plants can often be substituted for fences wherever practical on large properties for increased security. On a small scale, property owners in residental areas can plant screens and hedges in a common effort to screen eyesores or channel breezes. Such unified plantings create a real sense of elegance and harmony, and regional identity is achieved.

Some hedges and screens produce flowers. Some are deciduous after a brilliant burst of fall color. Some make thorny barriers. Screens are excellent for gardeners who want minimum maintenance, or a natural

effect. Espalier is a surprisingly efficient training method that dates back centuries.

CHEAPER THAN FENCES
Walls and fences provide privacy, protection and wind control, but plants do these things at less cost. Plants do require a period of time before they are able to serve their purpose, but substantial results are usually obtained within three years.

Growing plants is a rewarding experience in other ways. It is satisfying to watch seedlings increase in size and beauty each year, while also increasing the value of your property. And the natural qualities of seasonal change, leaf texture, flower color and fragrance cannot be duplicated by human-built objects.

HOW TO USE THIS BOOK
The following pages will show you how to put these functional plant forms to work for you. On pages 17 to

53, the principles of using hedges, screens and espaliers in the landscape are described. Plants are organized into dozens of lists according to special functions or qualities. These lists make it simple to select the right plant for the task you have in mind. For example, there are lists on such subject areas as fast-growing plants for privacy, drought-tolerant plants, plants for windbreaks, plants that require little pruning and plants for security barriers.

If you are interested in growing plants espalier-fashion, refer to pages 55 to 71. Step-by-step, illustrated instructions show you how to train certain plants to espalier patterns.

To find out how to grow a particular plant, refer to pages 93 to 172. This section is an encyclopedia of hedge, screen and espalier plants, listed in alphabetical order by botanical name. Plants are described, including growth habits, cultural requirements and recommended climate zones.

Left: Home landscape features a narrow hedge of *Taxus* species, yew. It functions as a privacy screen and as a backdrop for mixed shrubbery inside. Above: Same location as at left but from a streetside view. Hedge and retaining wall with a feathery base of *Picea,* spruce, gives a softer effect than a solid screen of tall foliage.

Hedges

A hedge is a neat, living wall, usually composed of one kind of plant for a simple, pleasing effect. Shearing produces elegant formality but is by no means necessary. Informal hedges consist of plants that grow in a natural form, requiring only periodic shaping. Hedges form part of the garden framework by defining edges and spaces. They also give a sense of movement to paths by transforming flat, two-dimensional lines of direction into functional channels.

Hedges are categorized by size. *Borders* fall below the knee. They edge flowerbeds and paths. *Low hedges* are knee- to waist-high. They keep people in or out of areas by serving as visual or actual barriers. *Medium hedges* are waist- to chest-high. They provide privacy for seated people and form true barriers. They also make excellent backdrops for flowers and sculpture when dark-green, fine-textured foliage is used. *Tall hedges*—6 to 8 feet high—provide privacy and enclosure, and make suitable backdrops. *Informal* tall hedges move into the screen category.

Large-scale *hedgewalls* reach stately proportions from 8 to 50 feet high or more. They are used for grand architectural effects and complete privacy. Plants that have the potential to last for centuries are the best choice if large-scale hedgewalls or stately effects are desired.

Hedgerow describes a line of plants or a large-scale installation of mixed varieties. Hedgerows have been used in Great Britain since the Middle Ages to define field ownership lines and contain livestock. Hedgerows form complex ecological relationships with the land and give regional identity to the landscapes where they appear. They may or may not be pruned.

Precisely shaped hedge of *Buxus microphylla* var. *japonica,* Japanese boxwood, creates an interesting pattern.

A border planting of *Nandina domestica* 'Nana', dwarf nandina, helps prevent shortcuts across walkway.

Manicured hedge of *Thuja* species frames driveway and makes an impressive entry.

Spacious landscape allows for spectacular use of low hedges and tall hedgewall of *Taxus x media,* intermediate yew.

Medium-size hedge and juniper ground cover serve as an evergreen buffer zone between house and street.

Closely sheared hedgewall makes front yard private and helps to reduce noise slightly from nearby street traffic.

Screens

Anything that blocks a view is a screen. Chain-link fence covered with vines or espaliers, and hedges six feet or more high are screens. In this book, however, a *screen* is defined as a row of tall plants in their natural form.

Screens perform many of the same functions as tall hedges but are generally broader and take up more space. They also have fewer maintenance requirements. Screens composed of unclipped, low-branching trees or shrubs require only periodic shaping. They are always suitable for a casual, natural effect, and have great flower and fruit potential. Screens are usually less expensive than hedges because individual plants are spaced farther apart.

Natural forms of plants vary. *Fastigiate* plants, those that are tall and narrow, are quite useful for screens. They take little space and require no shaping. *Columnar* plants, which are slightly wider, also make excellent screens. Columnar and fastigiate forms do not always have branches at their base, so planting shrubs may be necessary to make a solid screen. If space is not at a premium, use round, arching and pyramidal plants for their flowers, fruit or low-maintenance requirements. Deciduous plants allow for maximum penetration of winter sun.

A canopy tree is a screen in an umbrella form. See photo, page 16. Widespreading branches block views of tall buildings and elevated highways overhead, while providing a sense of enclosure. Canopies also block the view of people looking down into private gardens. Deciduous trees out of leaf provide a light, twiggy canopy, and most winter sun penetrates to help warm your home.

Screens are typically used to conceal unattractive views, such as highways, business signs or telephone wires. They also work well to offset crowded effects of suburbanization. Houses, condominiums and gardens can be blended with the regional landscape by screening with native plants.

Screens with regular gaps lend a different quality to a landscape than a solid line of plants. A rhythm is created, especially when tall, narrow trees are used. People can catch glimpses in or out of a garden scene. Widely spaced plantings are still effective as windbreaks.

Similarly, a curtain or *scrim* of delicate greenery serves as a partial veil to create interest in the view. Use these curtains of plant material when screening is necessary, but when some light and air penetration is desired.

Ilex 'Foster's No. 2' is excellent for large-scale screening.

Plants in wooden containers are movable screens. Here they substitute for railing along edge of raised deck.

Many screens provide colorful displays of flowers or fruit. *Ilex cornuta* 'D'Or' produces large, yellow berries in abundance.

Tall bamboo screen provides shade to cool patio and house. Plants at base are *Nandina domestica,* nandina.

Hibiscus rosa-sinensis, tropical hibiscus, produces large, colorful flowers if plants are not sheared.

Azaleas create a mass of color, and serve as a low, protective screen on this slope.

Espaliers

Espalier—pronounced *ess-PAL-yeah* or *ess-PAL-yer*—is an ancient method of training plants to grow flat against a support. You may wonder why anyone would want to shape plants into unnatural forms. But espaliers have many advantages. Most important, they save space. This feature alone makes them worth growing, especially in today's smaller gardens. More leaf surface captures light for higher and more efficient fruit yield. Heat radiated from a south wall permits growth of flowering shrubs or fruit in marginal climate areas. The small stature of espaliers makes them easy to protect against frost damage or marauding birds. Espaliers are well suited to windy sites because they are supported. In humid climates, their open form tends to reduce mildew problems. Espaliers are vinelike, but lack a vine's rampant and sometimes destructive growth. They can be used to reduce home heating and cooling bills by insulating the walls they are trained against.

Espaliers create a dramatic and decorative architectural effect. In essence, they are living, sculptural forms in tailored, formal, natural or informal patterns. The most basic form is the *cordon,* a single, straight stem, with many, shortened side shoots. Hedge effects are obtained by staking single cordons in rows or by training multiple cordons along wires.

Espaliers have many uses. They make excellent screens on trellises or wire supports. A container-grown espalier on a frame makes a handy, space-saving, movable screen. Espaliers soften blank stretches of wall or chain-link fence. They make living, space-saving fences. Cordon fences are both ornamental and productive when fruit trees are used. A *Belgian fence* is a special lattice pattern that makes an attractive espalier screen. Border espaliers are often used to edge paths and vegetable plots.

A simple way to get started with espaliers is to buy them pretrained from the nursery. Early shaping that is critical to the plant's form is done by specialists. This makes it easy for today's gardener to adapt ancient espalier principles to produce fruit on balconies, rooftops and small, city lots. By growing espaliers, it is possible and practical to raise mini-orchards without sacrificing outdoor gardening and living space.

Formal apple espalier trained as a horizontal T is gorgeous in spring and productive in fall. Major limbs have been carefully pruned to produce maximum amounts of fruit.

Formal espalier is a pear formed in a Verrier palmette pattern. This traditional form originated centuries ago.

Informal pyracantha espalier decorates a wall. These are spring flowers; berries will follow in fall.

Espalier-fence of 'Golden Delicious' apples. It provides tasty fruit, and adds beauty and privacy to the landscape.

An Inside Look

It is sometimes difficult to understand the value of hedges, screens and espaliers. Much of their usefulness is their *utility*—screening and dividing to increase privacy and livability. To best show this aspect, we took a bird's-eye vantage point to photograph some exceptional examples of hedges and screens in use.

Right: From the street, passers-by can only imagine what lies behind this massive, evergreen screen. Dark-green foliage shows off ornately designed fence. For a look inside the screen, see photos below.

Below: High above ground level, the camera looks into an expansive, secluded landscape. The double rows of evergreens perform their screening function well.

Below right: Inside, it's a flower-lover's world. The same evergreens that served as streetside screens are excellent backdrops for flowering annuals and perennials.

Above: Hedge of *Prunus laurocerasus,* English laurel, was planted to extend code-imposed fence height. Impatiens add a bright row of color.

Above right: Beyond this gate is a courtyard, formed by fence-hedge combination. It creates a transition zone between public street and private home.

Right: Inside, the garden courtyard is quiet and private, with a formal yet relaxed feeling. Views of neighboring houses and street traffic are screened out. Dark-green hedge is a nice backdrop for flowers.

Below: The owners of this home wanted a pool, but the best exposure to the sun was in the front yard, which faced a busy street. A pool was installed and enclosed by an evergreen hedge and bamboo screen. Seldom used previously, area is now private for swimming and sunbathing. Inside, sunbathers see only leafy greenery.

Right: Streetside view of home reveals nothing of the pool inside. Stone retaining wall, wooden fence and evergreens combine nicely as a privacy screen, yet are not obtrusive.

Above: This home is located at a busy city intersection. Tall, dense screen helps reduce street noise slightly, but more importantly, it blocks views of passing automobiles and tall busses.

Right: Without a tall screen, front yard would not be a desirable place to spend time. See page 21 for additional photos of same site.

FUNCTIONAL FORMS

2

Hedges, screens and espaliers are plants that can serve you. Before you buy plants to grow into one of these forms, you should decide on the function you want them to perform. Use this chapter for planning. After you know your landscape needs, choose plants to suit your purposes from the lists included in the following pages. Refer to the individual descriptions provided on pages 96 to 172 to find out if a particular plant will grow in your area.

Be realistic about the amount of care you want to give plants. All require various levels of maintenance, from low to high. Most screens require only occasional shaping and care. Hedges require anything from yearly shaping to weekly shearing. The faster the growth, the more often shearing is required. Espaliers need intensive care for three years and regular care thereafter.

A plan is important. Shrubs and trees planted at random have little impact except as clutter. Grouped into screens and hedges, the same plants define spaces and create visual lines. There is no reason why these lines must be straight. A curved hedge softens the corners at a square lot.

Use plants to solve functional problems before you concentrate on aesthetics or style. The Planning Process on the following page will help you arrive at logical and pleasing designs. It is best to start with a basic framework of plants that are chosen for screening, privacy and definition of functional areas.

Informal landscape styles depend on *contrasts* for their qualities. Lines are loose. Formal styles depend on symmetry, order and restraint for their qualities. Lines are tailored. You can strive for an architectural, sculptural, natural, classic, picturesque or Oriental effect. Or you may create your own style. Keep it simple in the beginning.

Hedges of dark-green, fine-textured foliage are the most basic of these plants. The more tightly they are sheared, the less space they require.

Homeowners are often advised to envision their property as outdoor rooms, with hedges for walls, ground covers for floors and trees for ceilings. Outdoor rooms can transform flat, open sites into interesting spaces that appear larger, and have a direct connection to the existing architecture. But avoid limiting the use of hedges and screens to the role of a living wall. Use them to break up small, roomlike yards by rounding out corners, or position them to "borrow scenery." See page 18.

DIRECT MOVEMENT AND ADD INTEREST
Using hedges and screens to direct movement is a useful design technique. Lines of plants, combined with human curiosity, tend to draw people through outdoor spaces.

Left: Branches of canopy-shaped trees interweave to make a solid, overhead screen. This kind of planting is useful to create privacy if tall buildings stand over your lot. Hedge in background further encloses area, helping to complete the feeling of an outdoor room. Above: Windbreak of tall, evergreen trees produces a sheltered microclimate and serves as backdrop for small, sunny terrace.

A path leads the eye. Borders, hedges and screens create a sense of movement by turning flat paths into channels. Tall screens or crisply sheared hedges of any size heighten this effect. Lower hedges define areas without blocking vision. Use them to separate pedestrian and vehicular traffic. Thorny material discourages wandering and shortcuts across lawn and planting areas.

Curve a path behind a hedge or screen, and curiosity will motivate people to explore. Turn flat, open space into interesting areas with hedges. As people move through the garden, spaces are concealed then revealed to create a sense of anticipation. Contrast bright, large expanses with shady, narrow corridors. Allow a glimpse of view, then force people to follow an indirect route to make the objective or vista seem more worthwhile.

SCREEN AND DIRECT VIEWS

One of the most important functions of a hedge or screen is to selectively block objects from view. Use either to screen a tennis court, a distant view of a smoke-belching factory, a single, local eyesore or the small corner where the garbage cans are stored.

Canopy-shaped trees screen views from above and below. Short baffle sections of hedge can be positioned to screen front windows from headlight glare and neighbors' eyes.

Hedges and screens are also used to direct views. One or two bold lines of plants call attention to the feature to which they point. A great vista may be overwhelming or lost without proper framing. If a feature in the landscape is worth noticing but is surrounded by distractions, frame the feature and screen the rest.

BORROWED SCENERY

This is an ancient design principle attributed to the Japanese. Hedges and screens are artfully arranged to obliterate every trace of straight property lines and surrounding neighbors. Attention is directed to a feature in the distance—a tree, mountain or temple. The garden, however small, becomes part of a greater landscape picture, and the feature is "borrowed" to become part of the garden. The result is a feeling of spaciousness and a connection to nature. Straight, square, property lines disappear so the garden seems to expand.

Home entry is designed to intrigue. After visitors enter wrought-iron gate, green passageway and walk disappear behind leafy screen. This creates an urge to find out "what's around the corner?" See photos opposite.

The Planning Process

Go outside and take a long look at your property. Divide it into areas by asking yourself these questions:

1. *What needs to be screened?*
2. *What edges need definition for a visual line or a boundary barrier?*
3. *Which views should be accentuated or hidden?*
4. *Is privacy needed?*
5. *Who will use the space or spaces, and what are their activities?*
6. *Should microclimates be modified?*
7. *Are there winds to block, breezes to capture, windows to shield from glare or sun?*
7. *Will various areas be unified in a design? Should they be?*
8. *How will people move through the garden or property? Where will paths lead?*

The answers to these eight questions will help you determine what spaces you need and their size. Next, ask yourself some practical questions that will affect your choice of plants and the form they will take: hedge, screen or espalier.

1. *Should plants have dense foliage to block a view or ensure privacy?*
2. *Is fast cover a necessity?*
3. *How much maintenance and pruning time do you have on a weekly, monthly or yearly basis? Be realistic.*
4. *How much space is available?*

Are there limits on the height and width of plants? Will shearing be required?
5. *Should corner intersections or driveways be kept clear so drivers will have unobstructed views of oncoming traffic?*
6. *Is snow-removal equipment used in your neighborhood? If so, place hedges or screen 3 or 4 feet back from sidewalks to allow snow banks to form.*
7. *Will neighbors cooperate in trimming property-line hedges? It is best to include two or three feet of path behind a hedge for ease in pruning.*
8. *Do you live where plants should be fire retardant or drought tolerant?*
9. *Do you want to attract birds or bees with fruit, flowers, seasonal color or berries?*

Keep the cultural requirements of plants in mind. Consider the following:

1. *Is climate particularly harsh? Are winters severe? Is the area subject to high winds or coastal salt spray?*
2. *Is it sunny or shady?*
3. *What is the soil like?*
4. *How is the soil drainage? Is the soil soggy or dry?*
5. *Are tree roots nearby that will compete with hedge, screen and espalier plants?*
6. *Do you have any microclimates that can be used to your plant's advantage?*

Simple turn in the path is crucial to create interesting sequence between entry gate and front door. The hedges enclose and screen house from view, while creating the green passageway effect.

Path turns then continues to front door. Contrast of closed-in entry walk and open, spacious garden makes walkway sequence from gate seem longer and more interesting than a straight line.

Here are some other classic tricks for using hedges and screens for design effects. But do not try them all at once.

• Create several small gardens in one by enclosing areas with hedges. Fill each area with colorful, seasonal plants—spring-flowering bulbs in one, summer perennials in another. For maximum color impact, plant color plants with framework and backdrop hedges.

• Use color to create effects. Dark, cool hues seem to retreat into the background. Light, warm hues seem to advance.

• Experiment with forcing perspective. The eye moves quickly along sheared hedge lines. To create an illusion of greater distance, make two apparently parallel hedges converge slightly at one end. A similar effect can be created by slanting the tops of sheared hedges slightly up or down a few inches at one end.

• Create interesting contrasts by combining crisply sheared hedges with loose, flowery screens or borders.

• Use light-green or yellow-green foliage plants or variegated varieties with white or yellow leaf markings to brighten dark corners. Screens with white flowers accomplish the same thing. Or use any dark-green hedge or screen as a backdrop for a low, white-flowering border.

• Several species of plants growing together and sheared into one multi-patterned and multicolored unit create a striking *mosaic hedge*. Choose plants with similar growth habits and growth rates.

• Arrange hedges or screens in a labyrinth pattern to create a maze.

PRIVACY

Wherever you might need a fence, plant a hedge or screen. They are cheaper and their use is rarely restricted by ordinances. Screens, hedges, short baffle sections of hedge or aerial hedges can be used if your front windows look directly onto the street, but local codes prohibit fences more than three feet high. Canopy trees provide privacy to city dwellers whose gardens are situated below tall buildings.

An *aerial hedge* stretches a fence. This is when lower branches are gradually pruned from the trunks over several growing seasons until the leaves begin clearing the fence top. Regular hedge forms can then be created, with the screening effect extended to the height desired.

Six feet is the typical maximum fence height allowed by zoning regulations in area yards and side yards. But six feet is just above eye level and creates an awkward visual line. It is also inadequate when second-story windows look down into your property. An aerial hedge can solve problems of privacy and aesthetics. Use them in conjunction with low fences or walls.

Another privacy solution for low walls is to place planter boxes along the wall top. Let plants grow as high as necessary. A strong, architectural effect is obtained by constructing boxes the width of the wall, painting them the same color and then shearing plants to the same width. Select species recommended for container planting. Installation can be permanent. Or remove the boxes in winter to allow more sun to shine on the area or to protect cold-tender plants, like citrus, from frost. For more on container planting and movable screens, see page 22.

Le Corbusier and Pierre Jeanneret devised what is probably the ultimate use of movable screens in their 1931 design of the De Beistegui penthouse roof garden. Clipped hedges were set into electrically operated sliding boxes. One had only to flip a switch for complete privacy or a fabulous view of Paris.

FAST PLANTS FOR PRIVACY

A fast-growing screen or hedge has advantages and disadvantages. The more rapid the growth rate, the more you have to shear. Plants that grow quickly tend to be short-lived. A fast variety is useful planted behind a slow-growing, permanent variety. Remove the fast plant when it has passed its prime or when the permanent planting has matured.

Acacia longifolia .... Sydney golden wattle
Acer ginnala .... Amur maple
Bambusa .... Bamboo species
Berberis koreana .... Korean barberry
Berberis thunbergii .... Japanese barberry
Carissa grandiflora .... Natal plum
Chamaecyparis lawsoniana .... Port Orford cedar
Cornus stolonifera .... Red-osier dogwood
Cupressocyparis leylandii Cupressocyparis
Cupressus glabra .... Arizona cypress

Dodonea viscosa .... Hopbush
Escallonia rubra .... Escallonia
Eucalyptus .... Eucalyptus species
Euonymus fortunei .... Wintercreeper
Hibiscus rosa-sinensis ..... Tropical hibiscus
Ilex cassine .... Dahoon holly
Ilex 'Nellie R. Stevens' .... Holly
Ilex opaca .... American holly
Ligustrum .... Deciduous privets
Lonicera korolkowii 'Zabeli' .... Zabel's honeysuckle
Lonicera tatarica .... Tatarian honeysuckle
Malus baccata 'Columnaris' .... Columnar Siberian crabapple
Nerium oleander .... Oleander
Philadelphus x virginalis .... Mock orange
Photinia x fraseri .... Photinia
Picea abies .... Norway spruce
Picea glauca .... White spruce
Pinus eldarica .... Mondell pine
Pittosporum crassifolium .... Karo
Pittosporum undulatum .... Victorian box

Plumbago auriculata .... Plumbago
Populus alba 'Bolleana' .... Bolleana poplar
Populus nigra 'Italica' .... Lombardy poplar
Populus simonii 'Fastigiata' .... Pyramidal Simon's poplar
Potentilla fruticosa .... Potentilla
Prunus caroliniana .... Cherry laurel
Prunus ilicifolia .... Hollyleaf cherry
Prunus laurocerasus .... Laurel cherry
Pseudotsuga menziesii .... Douglas fir
Pyracantha .... Pyracantha
Raphiolepis indica .... Indian hawthorn
Rhamnus alaternus .... Italian buckthorn
Rhamnus cathartica ...... Common buckthorn
Rhamnus frangula 'Columnaris' .... Tallhedge buckthorn
Salix purpurea .... Purple-osier willow
Sequoia sempervirens .... Coast redwood
Spiraea .... Spiraea species
Syzygium paniculatum .... Eugenia
Tamarix aphylla .... Tamarisk
Tsuga heterophylla .... Western hemlock

Prunus laurocerasus, English laurel, is a fast-growing hedge or screen.

Syzygium paniculatum is a fast-growing, narrow hedge plant. It requires frequent clipping to keep it neat and narrow.

PROTECTION FROM OUTSIDE ANNOYANCES

Hedges and screens can protect you from many other nuisances besides wind or inquisitive eyes. Position hedges to shield your yard and windows from headlight glare or the glare from streetlights. Locate movable screens according to season to block sunlight and glare reflected from paved surfaces, swimming pools, glass or light-colored walls. This strategy also reduces heat gain indoors.

Hedges and screens reduce dust more than fences or walls. In addition to deflecting dust, leaf surfaces capture and trap dust as it adheres. This principle applies equally well to salty ocean spray.

A dense, wide, evergreen hedge also reduces noise levels slightly. Hedges and screens composed of certain plant species can act as firebreaks in combination with bare soil or fire-retardant ground covers.

NOISE BUFFERS

Plants absorb and refract sound. Hedges and screens reduce noise slightly. You may not even be able to notice a difference in noise levels. If the source of the noise is blocked from view, the sound *seems* to be reduced. It also helps to plant noise buffers with lawns or ground covers adjacent to noise source.

Earth mounds called *berms* are effective noise buffers. A hedge or screen on top of an earth mound is more effective than berms alone. Broadleaf evergreens may be the most sound-absorbing plants.

Calocedrus decurrens .... California incense cedar
Carpinus betulus ....Hornbeam
Ceratonia siliqua ....Carob
Chamaecyparis lawsoniana ....Port Orford cedar
Citrus ....Citrus
Cupressocyparis leylandii Cupressocyparis
Cupressus ....Cypress species
Eucalyptus globulus 'Compacta' ....Dwarf blue gum

Eucalyptus lehmannii ....Bushy yate
Euonymus kiautschovica 'Manhattan' ....Euonymus
Fagus sylvatica ....Beech
Ilex .... Holly
Juniperus .... Juniper species
Ligustrum lucidum .... Glossy privet
Picea abies ....Norway spruce
Picea glauca .... White spruce
Pinus eldarica ....Mondell pine
Pinus nigra .... Austrian pine
Pinus strobus ....White pine
Pittosporum eugenioides .... Lemonwood
Pittosporum undulatum .... Victorian box
Podocarpus gracilior ..Podocarpus fern pine
Podocarpus macrophyllus .... Yew pine
Prunus caroliniana .... Cherry laurel
Prunus ilicifolia ....Hollyleaf cherry
Pseudotsuga menziesii .... Douglas fir
Sequoia sempervirens ....Coast redwood
Syzygium paniculatum ....Eugenia
Tamarix aphylla ....Tamarisk
Taxus ....Yew
Thuja occidentalis ....American arborvitae
Tsuga canadensis ....Canadian hemlock
Tsuga heterophylla ....Western hemlock

Bird's-eye view shows hedge-enclosed yard. Busy intersection is just outside. Inside, view of city street is eliminated. Lawn and other plantings create a relaxing retreat. Fence with low planting breaks wall effect of hedge and helps reduce noise.

INCREASE LIVABLE OUTDOOR SPACE

The front yard of most homes is often a patch of lawn and some driveway. This useful outdoor area is much more inviting for adults and safer for children when it is enclosed. Where zoning ordinances prohibit fences in front, plant a hedge. Neighbors find walls of living greenery much less objectionable than wooden fences or walls of masonry.

Another way to increase outdoor space is to make an outdoor "closet" by planting double walls of plants around the periphery of your property. These double walls might be two hedges or screens spaced 5 to 10 feet apart, a screen and hedge combination or two rows of edible fruit espaliers on fence supports. Into this closet place barbeque grills, the dog house, compost pile, extra garden furniture, pool equipment and metal storage sheds. The same area could also serve as a dog run or children's play area. An illusion of greater space in the garden outside the screen is achieved by removing clutter. Noise from outside is slightly reduced, and one sees only fresh greenery. This added quiet and simplicity expands the perception of space, even though actual outdoor space has been slightly reduced.

MOVABLE SCREENS

A line of boxed plants makes a movable screen. Because of their shape, sheared hedges or certain espaliers grown in boxes are especially suited to narrow spaces. They can be used where paved surfaces or balconies make it impossible to grow plants in the earth.

Container plants make terrific temporary screens. They are inexpensive and versatile, and the results are almost instant. They create privacy on roof gardens, and it is simple to move them aside if views are desired. Boxed canopy trees produce instant shade and screening. Use deciduous species or move canopies in winter if shade is not wanted.

Plants can be grown in containers if the soil is not suitable. Use a special soil mix that allows for good drainage. Many commercial potting soil mixes are available. Generally, plants require more water and fertilizer when grown in containers. Check soil moisture content frequently, and apply weak, liquid fertilizer regularly during the growing season.

Evergreen screens block view of city street, and enable these homeowners to expand their living space by installing a pool in the front yard.

Small-lot jumble of fruit trees, vegetables and odd shrubs is concealed and protected in outdoor "closet" formed by patio wall and streetside hedge.

MOVABLE SCREENS AND CONTAINER ESPALIERS

Almost any plant will grow in a container. The plants listed here are particularly well suited because of their compact size, or ability to thrive without elaborate care. For minimum maintenance, select a plant with a loose, screen form. Sheared hedges, espaliers and topiary in containers should be given the same pruning as their free-growing counterparts. However, plants in containers can move when you do, which means your efforts will not be wasted should you relocate.

A container built as a short section of hollow, free-standing fence with planting pockets is called a *fedge*. Plant strawberries, ivy or trailing annuals in these fence-hedge combination screens for quicker results than provided by newly planted boxed shrubs. Position fedges wherever movable screens are needed. Or, use them as a permanent, garden feature like the baffles described on page 30. They are easy to build. You can buy them prefabricated from nurseries and by special order under the brand name Living Wall. Built-in drip-irrigation systems save time and water.

Abelia x grandiflora .... Glossy abelia
Arbutus unedo 'Compacta' .. Strawberry tree
Bambusa .... Bamboo species
Buxus .... Boxwood
Camellia japonica .... Camellia
Camellia sasanqua .... Sasanqua camellia
Carissa grandiflora .... Natal plum
Citrus .... Citrus—most species
Eriobotrya japonica .... Loquat
Euonymus fortunei .... Wintercreeper
Feijoa sellowiana .... Pineapple guava
Gardenia jasminoides .... Gardenia
Hibiscus rosa-sinensis ..... Tropical hibiscus
Ilex .... Holly—dwarf cultivars
Ilex crenata .... Japanese holly
Ilex vomitoria .... Yaupon holly
Juniperus .... Juniper species
Laurus nobilis .... Grecian laurel
Ligustrum japonicum .... Japanese privet
Ligustrum lucidum .... Glossy privet
Ligustrum texanum .... Waxleaf privet
Malus pumila .... Apple
Myrtus communis .... Myrtle
Nandina domestica .... Nandina
Nerium oleander .... Oleander

Osmanthus heterophyllus .... False holly
Osmanthus fragrans .... Sweet osmanthus
Photinia x fraseri .... Photinia
Pinus mugo mugo .... Mugo pine
Pittosporum crassifolium 'Nana' .... Dwarf karo
Pittosporum tobira .... Tobira mock orange
Pittosporum undulatum .... Victorian box
Plumbago auriculata .... Plumbago
Podocarpus gracilior ..Podocarpus fern pine
Podocarpus macrophyllus .... Yew pine
Prunus .... European plum
Prunus .... Japanese plum
Prunus caroliniana .... Cherry laurel
Psidium .... Strawberry guava
Punica granatum 'Chico' .... Dwarf pomegranate
Pyrus communis .... Pear
Pyrus hybrid .... Pear-apple
Raphiolepis indica .... Indian hawthorn
Rosa .... Rose
Rosmarinus officinalis .... Rosemary
Syzygium paniculatum .... Eugenia
Taxus .... Yew
Viburnum tinus .... Laurustinus

Screens in containers can be moved wherever needed to create privacy. Here they soften the starkness of solid masonry walls and paving, and divide space into more usable sections.

Movable screens can be created with espaliers in containers. This is *Citrus reticulata,* mandarin, supported by a simple wire-and-wood frame.

PLANTS TO PLEACH

Pleach means to weave and interlace branches. In pleached hedges, the branches of individual plants are grafted together to form an impenetrable living fence that may be sheared. *Crataegus* and *Tilia* are classic subjects for pleaching.

Carpinus betulus .... Hornbeam
Crataegus .... Hawthorn
Fagus sylvatica .... Beech
Malus pumila .... Apple
Pyrus communis .... Pear
Pyrus hybrid .... Pear-apple or Asian pear
Pyrus kawakamii .... Evergreen pear
Tilia cordata .... Littleleaf linden

BARRIERS FOR SECURITY

Thorny or prickly shrubs or trees planted closely together make an impenetrable barrier. Osage orange, *Maclura pomifera,* was used on American rangeland before the invention of barbed wire. In the Middle Ages, hedgerows made stock-proof fences in Great Britain. See *Crataegus,* page 114.

Space any of the following plants 6 inches apart to keep children and dogs in or out. Spacing 12 inches apart keeps adults and larger animals out. If deer are a problem, hedge or screen should reach at *least* 8 feet high. Be sure to choose plants that deer do not like to eat.

Low, thorny hedges beneath windows may discourage burglars, but few plant barriers can keep out a determined professional. The ultimate barrier is a secured metal or barbed-wire fence hidden within a thorny hedge.

Slow-growing barrier plants normally last decades longer than wood fences. Weave chicken wire through stems as a temporary barrier. The wire need not be removed after plants are mature.

Berberis ....Barberry
Carissa grandiflora ....Natal plum
Carpinus betulus .... Hornbeam
Chaenomeles speciosa .... Flowering quince
Citrus ....Citrus
Crataegus .... Hawthorn
Elaeagnus angustifolia ....Russian olive
Elaeagnus pungens ....Silverberry
Escallonia rubra ....Escallonia
Ilex .... Holly
Mahonia aquifolium .... Oregon grape
Pseudotsuga menziesii .... Douglas fir
Punica granatum ....Pomegranate
Pyracantha .... Pyracantha
Rhamnus cathartica ......Common buckthorn
Rosa .... Rose
Taxus .... Yew

Leaves of *Ilex cornuta* 'Rotunda' are spiny, good for barriers.

Berberis thunbergii, Japanese barberry, for barrier.

Crataegus phaenopyrum, Washington thorn, has sharp thorns.

The Right Size

Border plants, low, medium and high hedges, screens and large-scale hedgewalls serve various purposes in the landscape. One of the easiest ways to reduce maintenance chores is to use plants that do not exceed a specific, desired height.

Classics, as indicated in the following, are plants that have proved their popularity and value for a century or more. Many classics live for 100 years or more. It is best to choose plants that last for generations if stately effects are desired.

BORDERS

Border plants are those that stay in the below-the-knee range. Artemisia, dwarf box, apple and pear horizontal cordons, Japanese holly, rosemary, lavender and myrtle are classics. Those marked with an asterisk * require little shaping. Others need pinching or shearing to keep them dense, neat and border-size.

Artemisia abrotanum .... Southernwood
Baccharis pilularis .... Dwarf coyote brush
Berberis thunbergii .... Dwarf Japanese barberry
Buxus .... Dwarf boxwood
Caragana pygmaea .... Dwarf pea shrub
Carissa grandiflora 'Boxwood Beauty' .... Dwarf natal plum
Chaenomeles japonica 'Alpina' .... Dwarf quince
Euonymus fortunei .... Wintercreeper
Euonymus japonica .... Evergreen euonymus
Forsythia x intermedia 'Arnold Dwarf' .... Forsythia
Ilex cornuta .... Dwarf Chinese holly cultivars
Ilex crenata .... Japanese holly
Ilex vomitoria .... Yaupon holly
Ilex vomitoria 'Nana', 'Stokes' .... Dwarf yaupon cultivars
Lagerstroemia indica ..... Dwarf crape myrtle
Lavandula .... Lavender

Ligustrum japonicum .... Japanese privet
Ligustrum ovalifolium .... California privet
Ligustrum 'Suwanee River' .... Privet
Ligustrum texanum .... Waxleaf privet
Lonicera xylosteum ......Dwarf honeysuckle
Malus pumila .... Apple—single horizontal cordon
Myrtus communis .... Dwarf myrtle
Nandina domestica .... Dwarf nandina
Nerium oleander .... Dwarf oleander
Physocarpus opulifolius ....Dwarf ninebark
Pinus mugo mugo .... Mugo pine
Pittosporum crassifolium .... Dwarf karo
Pittosporum tobira 'Wheeler's Dwarf' ....Dwarf tobira
Potentilla fruticosa .... Potentilla
Punica granatum 'Chico' .... Dwarf pomegranate
Pyracantha .... Dwarf pyracantha
Raphiolepis indica 'Ballerina' .... Ballerina Indian hawthorn
Pyrus communis .... Pear—shaped horizontal cordon
Pyrus hybrid .... Apple-pear—single horizontal cordon
Ribes alpinum ....Alpine currant
Rosa .... Rose—see list page 160
Rosmarinus officinalis 'Collingwood Ingram' ....Rosemary
Salix purpurea ....Dwarf blue arctic willow
Spiraea japonica 'Alpina' .....Daphne spiraea
Viburnum opulus ...... Dwarf cranberry bush

A border of unclipped, dwarf *Ilex cornuta,* Chinese holly, accentuates a graceful curve adjacent to walk.

Border planting of *Ilex vomitoria,* yaupon, helps guide pedestrian traffic around turn in sidewalk.

LOW HEDGES

A low hedge—from knee to waist high—is one of the most versatile landscape forms. Here are some of the best. Many of these are held low by pruning. Those marked with an asterisk * stay low on their own and require little pruning.

Berberis buxifolia .... Magellan barberry
*Buxus .... Dwarf boxwood
Buxus microphylla
   var. japonica ....Japanese boxwood
*Buxus microphylla
   var. koreana .... Korean littleleaf box
*Caragana pygmaea .... Dwarf peashrub
*Carissa grandiflora ....Natal plum
Chaenomeles speciosa .... Flowering quince
Cornus mas ...... Cornealian cherry dogwood
Cotoneaster lucidus .... Hedge cotoneaster
*Escallonia .... Escallonia
*Euonymus fortunei .... Wintercreeper
*Euonymus japonica .. Evergreen euonymus cultivars
*Forsythia x intermedia
   'Arnold Dwarf' ....Forsythia
*Forsythia ovata 'Ottawa' ... Ottawa forsythia
*Ilex cornuta ....Chinese holly
*Ilex crenata .... Japanese holly
Lagerstroemia indica ..... Dwarf crape myrtle
*Lavandula .... Lavender
Ligustrum japonicum .... Japanese privet
Ligustrum ovalifolium .... California privet
Ligustrum texanum .... Waxleaf privet
Mahonia aquifolium
   'Compacta' ....Compact Oregon grape

Matus pumila .... Apple—horizontal cordon
*Myrtus communis .... Myrtle
*Nandina domestica 'Nana' ... Dwarf nandina
*Nerium oleander ....Dwarf oleander
*Physocarpus opulifolius 'Nanus',
   'Dart's Gold' ....Dwarf ninebark
*Pinus mugo mugo .... Mugo pine
*Pittosporum crassifolium .... Dwarf karo
Pittosporum tobira
   'Wheeler's Dwarf' .... Dwarf pittosporum
Plumbago auriculata .... Plumbago
Podocarpus macrophyllus .... Yew pine
Potentilla fruticosa ....Potentilla
Prunus caroliniana .... Cherry laurel
Prunus laurocerasus ....Laurel cherry
Prunus lusitanica ....Portugal laurel
*Punica granatum .... Dwarf pomegranate
Pyracantha .... Pyracantha
Pyrus communis .....Pear horizontal cordons
Pyrus hybrid Pear-apple horizontal cordons
Rhododendron .... Southern indica and kurume hybrid azaleas
*Ribes alpinum ....Alpine currant
*Rosa .... Rose—see list page 160
Rosmarinus officinalis ....Rosemary
Salix purpurea .... Dwarf blue arctic willow
Spiraea x bumalda ....Bumalda spiraea
Spiraea japonica .... Japanese spiraea
Syringa patula .... Dwarf Korean lilac
Syzygium paniculatum .... Eugenia
Taxus cuspidata .... Japanese yew
*Viburnum opulus
   'Nanum' .... Dwarf cranberry bush
Xylosma congestum ....Shiny xylosma

MEDIUM HEDGES

Waist-high to chest-high hedges define and enclose space without blocking vision, so they are rarely categorized as screens. Not all have to be sheared, although many can be held to the desired height by pruning. Those marked with an asterisk * stay at medium height without clipping.

*Abelia x grandiflora
   'Edward Goucher' ....Glossy abelia
*Arbutus unedo 'Compacta' ....Compact strawberry tree
*Arctostaphylos densiflora
   'Howard McMinn' .... Manzanita
*Atriplex lentiformis 'Breweri' ....Brewer saltbush
Berberis buxifolia .... Magellan barberry
Berberis darwinii ....Darwin barberry
Berberis koreana ....Korean barberry
Berberis x mentorensis ....Mentor barberry
Berberis thunbergii .... Japanese barberry
*Buxus microphylla
   var. japonica ....Japanese boxwood
*Buxus microphylla
   var. koreana .... Korean littleleaf box
Buxus sempervirens .... English box
Camellia japonica .... Camellia
Camellia sasanqua .... Sasanqua camellia
Caragana arborescens ..... Siberian pea tree
Carissa grandiflora ....Natal plum
Carpinus betulus .... Hornbeam
Chaenomeles speciosa .... Flowering quince
Chamaecyparis lawsoniana .... Port Orford cedar

Podocarpus macrophyllus, yew pine, separates path from lawn. It is held to this size by pruning.

Ilex crenata 'Helleri', Japanese holly, combine with azaleas in background.

MEDIUM HEDGES, CONTINUED

*Citrus .... Citrus—see lists page 111
Cornus mas .... Cornelian cherry dogwood
Cotoneaster lucidus .... Hedge cotoneaster
Cupressocyparis leylandii Cupressocyparis
Dodonea viscosa ....Hopbush
Elaeagnus angustifolia .... Russian olive
Elaeagnus pungens .... Silverberry
Escallonia rubra .... Escallonia
*Euonymus alata .... Winged burning bush
*Euonymus fortunei .... Wintercreeper
*Euonymus japonica .. Evergreen euonymus
Feijoa sellowiana .... Pineapple guava
Fontanesia fortunei ....Fontanesia
*Forsythia ovata 'Ottawa' ....Forsythia
*Gardenia jasminoides .... Gardenia
Hibiscus syriacus ....Rose of Sharon
Ilex .... Holly cultivars
*Lagerstroemia indica ....Crape myrtle
Laurus nobilis .... Grecian laurel
Ligustrum ....Deciduous privet
Ligustrum japonicum .... Japanese privet
Ligustrum lucidum .... Glossy privet
*Ligustrum obtusifolium
  regelianum .... Regal privet
Ligustrum texanum .... Waxleaf privet
*Lonicera x xylosteum
  'Clavey's Dwarf' ....Lonicera
*Mahonia aquifolium .... Oregon grape
Malus pumila .... Apple cordon fence
Malus sargentii ....Sargent crabapple
Myrica californica .... Pacific wax myrtle
Myrtus communis .... Myrtle

*Nandina domestica ....Nandina
Nerium oleander .... Oleander
Osmanthus fragrans .... Sweet osmanthus
Osmanthus heterophyllus ....False holly
Photinia x fraseri .... Photinia
Pinus strobus ....White pine
Pittosporum crassifolium ....Karo
Pittosporum eugenioides .... Lemonwood
Pittosporum tenuifolium ....Black-
  stemmed pittosporum
Pittosporum tobira .... Tobira mock orange
Pittosporum undulatum .... Victorian box
Plumbago auriculata .... Plumbago
Podocarpus gracilior ..Podocarpus fern pine
Podocarpus macrophyllus .... Yew pine
*Potentilla fruticosa
  'Jackmanii' ... Potentilla Jackman's variety
Prunus ....European plum
Prunus ....Japanese plum
Prunus caroliniana .... Cherry laurel
Prunus ilicifolia ....Hollyleaf cherry
*Prunus laurocerasus ....'Otto Luykens'
Prunus lusitanica ....Portugal laurel
Prunus maritima ....Beach plum
Punica granatum ....Pomegranate
*Pyracantha coccinea .... Pyracantha
Pyrus communis .... Pear—cordon fence
Pyrus hybrid .... Pear-apple—cordon fence
*Raphiolepis indica .... Indian hawthorn
Rhamnus alaternus ....Italian buckthorn
Rhamnus cathartica ...... Common buckthorn
Rhamnus frangula
  'Columnaris' .... Tallhedge buckthorn

Rhododendron .... Southern indica
  hybrid azaleas
Rhododendron maximum ....Rosebay
  rhododendron
Rhododendron obtusum ....Kurume azalea—
  a Classic
Rhododendron PJM ....Hybrid
  rhododendrons
*Rosa ....Rose—see list page 160
*Rosmarinus officinalis ....Rosemary
Sequois sempervirens .... Coast redwood
Spiraea prunifolia plena .... Bridal-wreath
  spiraea
Syringa x chinensis ....Chinese lilac
*Syringa patula .... Dwarf Korean lilac
Syringa vulgaris .... Lilac
Syzygium paniculatum .... Eugenia
Tamarix aphylla .... Tamarisk
Taxus ....Yew
Thuja occidentalis ....American arborvitae
Tsuga canadensis ....Canadian hemlock
Tsuga heterophylla ....Western hemlock
Vaccinium ashei ....Rabbiteye blueberry
Vaccinium corymbosum .... Blueberry
Viburnum dentatum ....Arrowwood
Viburnum japonicum .... Viburnum
Viburnum lantana ....Wayfaring tree
Viburnum
  opulus ....European highbush cranberry
Viburnum suspensum ....Sandankwa
Viburnum tinus .... Laurustinus
Xylosma congestum ....Shiny xylosma

Natural form of *Nandina domestica*, nandina, works well as an easy-care, medium-size hedge.

Taxus species make some of the finest clipped hedges. Form and maximum height vary with the cultivar. Medium height is ideal for separating and defining an area without producing a closed-in feeling.

HIGH HEDGES AND SCREENS

Many of the most popular, classic hedge and screen plants are listed under Large-Scale Hedges and Screens, but they can be held to eye level or lower by pruning. The plants listed here rarely exceed 6 to 8 feet. Shape them into hedges or leave them natural as screens where space allows. Those marked with an asterisk * should not be sheared.

Abelia x grandiflora ....Glossy abelia
Acer circinatum .... Vine maple
Atriplex lentiformis
   'Breweri' ....Brewer saltbush
*Bambusa glaucescens
   riviereorum .... Chinese goddess bamboo
Berberis buxifolia .... Magellan barberry
Berberis darwinii .... Darwin barberry
Berberis koreana ....Korean barberry
Berberis x mentorensis ....Mentor barberry
Berberis thunbergii .... Japanese barberry
Buxus microphylla
   var. japonica ....Japanese boxwood
Buxus sempervirens ....English box
*Camellia japonica .... Camellia cultivars
Camellia sasanqua .... Sasanqua camellia
Caragana arborescens ..... Siberian pea tree
Carissa grandiflora ....Natal plum
Chaenomeles speciosa .... Flowering quince
Citrus .... Citrus—see list page 111
*Cornus stolonifera .... Red-osier dogwood
Cotoneaster lucidus .... Hedge cotoneaster
Escallonia .... Escallonia
*Eucalyptus spathulata .... Swamp malee
Euonymus alata .... Winged burning bush
Euonymus fortunei 'Sarcoxie' ....Sarcoxie
   wintercreeper
Euonymus kiautschovica
   'Manhattan' ....Euonymus
*Forsythia x intermedia .... Forsythia

*Gardenia jasminoides
   'Mystery' ....Mystery gardenia
Hibiscus rosa-sinensis ..... Tropical hibiscus
Ilex .... Holly
Juniperus .... Juniper
*Lagerstroemia indica ....Crape myrtle
Ligustrum japonicum .... Japanese privet
Ligustrum texanum .... Waxleaf privet
Ligustrum x vicaryi ....Vicary golden privet
Malus sargentii ....Sargent crabapple
Mahonia aquifolium .... Oregon grape
Myrtus communis .... Myrtle—a Classic
*Nandina domestica ....Nandina
Nerium oleander .... Oleander
*Philadelphus x virginalis ....Mock orange
Plumbago auriculata .... Plumbago
Prunus laurocerasus ....Laurel cherry
Punica granatum .... Pomegranate
Pyracantha .... Pyracantha
Raphiolepis indica .... Indian hawthorn
Rhododendron .... Rhododendron hybrids
*Rhododendron maximum .... Rosebay
   rhododendron
Rosa ....Rose—see list page 160
Rosmarinus officinalis
   'Tuscan Blue' .... Rosemary
Spiraea prunifolia plena .... Bridal-wreath
   spiraea
Syringa x chinensis ....Chinese lilac
Syringa vulgaris ....Lilac—some cultivars
*Vaccinium ashei ....Rabbiteye blueberry
*Vaccinium corymbosum .... Blueberry
Viburnum japonicum .... Viburnum
*Viburnum lantana ....Wayfaring tree
*Viburnum opulus 'Compactum' .....Compact
   European highbush cranberry
Viburnus tinus
   'Spring Bouquet' ....Spring bouquet
   laurustinus
*Weigela .... Weigela
Xylosma congestum 'Compacta'   Compact
   shiny xylosma

LARGE-SCALE HEDGES AND SCREENS

Large screens and hedgewalls from 8 feet to 50 feet high are useful for privacy, noise control and definition of space on a grand scale. Those marked with an asterisk * should not be sheared. Most can be clipped and held to a much lower height. Classics are time-honored plants that will live for a century or more.

Acacia longifolia ....Sydney golden wattle
Acer campestre .....Hedge maple—a Classic
Acer ginnala ....Amur maple
Arbutus unedo .. Strawberry tree—a Classic
Bambusa .... Bamboo—a Classic
Buxus sempervirens English box—a Classic
Calocedrus decurrens .... California
   incense cedar
Camellia japonica .... Camellia—a Classic
Camellia sasanqua ....Sasanqua
   camellia—a Classic
Caragana arborescens ..... Siberian pea tree
Carissa grandiflora ....Natal plum
Carpinus betulus .... Hornbeam—a Classic
Ceratonia siliqua ....Carob
Chamaecyparis lawsoniana .... Port
   Orford cedar
Citrus .. Citrus—see lists page 111. Classics
Cocculus laurifolius ....Cocculus
Cornus mas .... Cornelian cherry dogwood
*Cornus stolonifera ....Red-osier
   dogwood
Corylus avellana .... Filbert—a Classic
Crataegus .... Hawthorn—a Classic
Cupressocyparis leylandii Cupressocyparis
*Cupressus glabra .... Arizona cypress
*Cupressus sempervirens
   'Stricta' ....Italian cypress—a Classic
Dodonea viscosa ....Hopbush
Elaeagnus angustifolia ....Russian olive
Elaeagnus pungens .... Silverberry

'Heitzii' juniper, with its blue-gray color and interesting texture, makes an imposing high screen.

LARGE-SCALE HEDGES AND SCREENS, CONTINUED

Eriobotrya japonica .... Loquat
Escallonia rubra .... Escallonia
*Eucalyptus .... Eucalyptus—See lists, page 118
Euonymus alata .... Winged burning bush
Euonymus japonica .... Evergreen euonymus
Fagus sylvatica .... Beech—a Classic
Feijoa sellowiana .... Pineapple guava
Fontanesia fortunei .... Fontanesia
*Forsythia x intermedia .... Forsythia
Hibiscus rosa-sinensis ..... Tropical hibiscus
Ilex .... Holly—a Classic
Juniperus chinensis .... Chinese juniper—a Classic
Juniperus scopulorum .... Rocky Mountain juniper
Juniperus virginiana .... Eastern red cedar
*Lagerstroemia indica .... Crape myrtle
Laurus nobilis ...... Grecian laurel—a Classic
Ligustrum amurense .... Amur privet
Ligustrum x ibolium .... Ibolium privet
Ligustrum japonicum .... Japanese privet—a Classic
Ligustrum lucidum Glossy privet—a Classic
Ligustrum ovalifolium .... California privet
Lonicera korolkowii 'Zabeli' .... Zabel's honeysuckle
Lonicera tatarica .... Tatarian honeysuckle
Malus baccata 'Columnaris' .... Columnar Siberian crabapple
Malus pumila .... Apple espalier—a Classic
Malus sargentii .... Sargent crabapple
Nerium oleander .... Oleander—a Classic
Osmanthus fragrans .... Sweet osmanthus
Osmanthus heterophyllus .... False holly— a Classic
Photinia x fraseri .... Photinia
Picea abies .... Norway spruce

Picea glauca .... White spruce
*Pinus eldarica .... Mondell pine
*Pinus nigra .... Austrian pine
Pinus strobus .... White pine
Pittosporum crassifolium .... Karo
Pittosporum eugenioides .... Lemonwood
Pittosporum tenuifolium .... Black- stemmed pittosporum
Pittosporum tobira .... Tobira mock orange
Pittosporum undulatum .... Victorian box— a Classic
Podocarpus gracilior .... Podocarpus fern pine—a Classic
Podocarpus macrophyllus .... Yew pine— a Classic
*Populus alba 'Bolleana' ...... Bolleana poplar
*Populus nigra 'Italica' .... Lombardy poplar—a Classic
Prunus .... European plum
Prunus .... Japanese plum
Prunus caroliniana .... Cherry laurel
Prunus ilicifolia ....Hollyleaf cherry
Prunus laurocerasus .... Laurel cherry— a Classic
Prunus lusitanica .... Portugal laurel— a Classic
*Prunus maritima ....Beach plum
Prunus serrulata 'Amanogawa' .... Columnar Japanese flowering cherry
Pseudotsuga menziesii .... Douglas fir
Punica granatum ..Pomegranate—a Classic
Pyracantha .... Pyracantha
Pyrus communis .... Pear espalier— a Classic
Pyrus hybrid ....Pear-apple espalier
Raphiolepis indica .... Indian hawthorn
Rhamnus alaternus ....Italian buckthorn
Rhamnus cathartica ...... Common buckthorn
Rhamnus frangula 'Columnaris' .... Tallhedge buckthorn

Rhododendron .... Southern indica hybrid azaleas
*Rhododendron maximum ....Rosebay rhododendron
Rosa .... Rose—see list page 160. Classics
Salix purpurea .... Purple-osier willow
Sequoia sempervirens .... Coast redwood
*Spirea x vanhouttei .... Vanhoutte spiraea
Syringa x chinensis ....Chinese lilac
Syringa vulgaris .... Lilac
Syzygium paniculatum . Eugenia—a Classic
Tamarix aphylla .... Tamarisk
Taxus .... Yew—Classics
Thuja occidentalis ....American arborvitae—a Classic
Tilia cordata .... Littleleaf linden— a Classic
Tsuga canadensis .... Canadian hemlock— a Classic
Tsuga heterophylla ....Western hemlock
Viburnum dentatum ....Arrowwood
*Viburnum lantana ....Wayfaring tree
Viburnum lentago ....Nannyberry
*Viburnum opulus .... European highbush cranberry
Viburnum tinus .... Laurustinus
Weigela florida .... Weigela
Xylosma congestum .... Shiny xylosma

Pittosporum eugenioides, lemonwood, grows to 40 feet high but can be kept much lower by pruning.

Podocarpus macrophyllus, yew pine, is excellent as a large-scale hedge for narrow spaces.

Altering Climate

Few climates cannot be improved. Manipulating the *microclimates,* small climates around your property, within your general climate zone, can make both your outdoor and indoor living areas more comfortable. Using microclimates to your advantage also saves money by reducing heating and cooling bills. Air movement, solar radiation, humidity and air temperatures are factors you can alter with hedges, screens and espaliers. The first step is to decide your needs so you can manage climate elements to your benefit.

If you examine your property carefully, you will notice outdoor areas that would be more livable if they were warmer, cooler or sheltered from winds. Use the planting tricks described in the following pages to insulate, cast shade, provide wind protection, create breezeways or add humidity. Supplement, modify or remove existing plantings that do not suit your needs.

WINDBREAKS
Properly planned and positioned windbreaks can cut winter heating bills by as much as 30%. Windbreaks may be a hedge, a single row of trees or shrubs or an elaborate combination of plants calculated according to formula. The latter is called a *shelterbelt,* discussed on page 35.

Most people want wind to flow over their houses so that outdoor areas are sheltered. Use a simple, semicircular hedge to extend a house wall and create a sheltered spot. Use the opposite principle—trapping winds—to stir breezes in hot, still air. Thin screens can be used to shelter outdoor areas while allowing some mild wind to enter windows of buildings for increased air circulation.

It may not be possible to plant a windbreak without casting shade where it is not wanted. In many areas, shade is desirable. Common sense is important in planning.

Winter gales and summer breezes usually originate from different sources. Determine the direction of the prevailing wind and sunshine in each season. Existing plantings, adjacent buildings and the slope of the land affect airflow patterns. Cold air flows downhill on still nights.

Most winds blow predictably from the same direction during winter seasons or storms. Windbreaks are positioned perpendicular to the prevailing wind. There is a calm area just behind the break. Just beyond this is an area of shelter called the *wake* that receives some turbulence or moving air. Wind force gradually returns to normal as it moves beyond the wake.

Length of the calm and wake areas depends on windbreak height and density. Sparse plants allow more wind through, but the wake extends for a greater distance behind the break. With dense plants, the calm area just behind the break extends a distance approximately equal to twice the height of the windbreak. The sheltered area extends a distance approximately equal to 10 to 15 times the height of the break.

Dense, evergreen plants with almost vertical sides placed perpendicular to the wind make the most effective windbreak. Foliage must reach the ground or wind speed can increase as air is forced down through the bottom of the break in a funnel effect. Plant low, dense shrubs in front of thin windbreaks to bolster them.

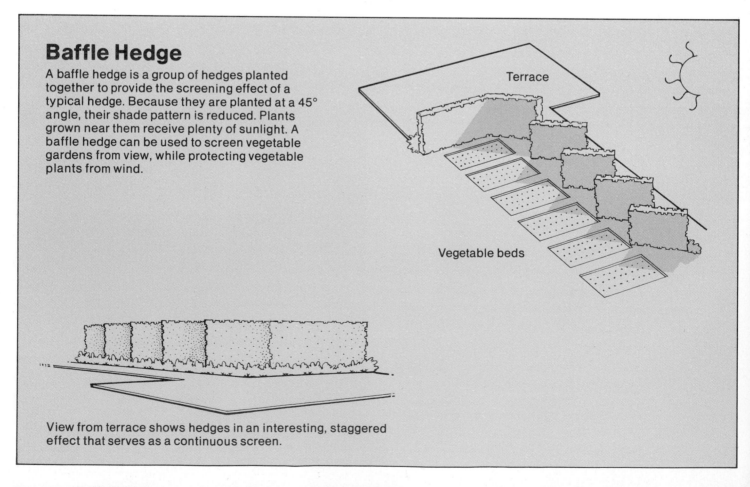

Baffle Hedge

A baffle hedge is a group of hedges planted together to provide the screening effect of a typical hedge. Because they are planted at a 45° angle, their shade pattern is reduced. Plants grown near them receive plenty of sunlight. A baffle hedge can be used to screen vegetable gardens from view, while protecting vegetable plants from wind.

Terrace

Vegetable beds

View from terrace shows hedges in an interesting, staggered effect that serves as a continuous screen.

Deciduous species and sparse evergreens, or plantings with gaps between plants, also make useful windbreaks. They produce less turbulence, and their effectiveness increases as wind velocity increases.

In urban areas where tall buildings send wind rushing through canyonlike avenues, it is often impossible to predict wind direction. Gardens in such areas must be enclosed for protection. Use plants in boxes or other containers on roof gardens and balconies to create sheltered areas. Unfortunately, many species that do well rooted in the earth suffer when exposed to the constant, harsh, drying winds found high above street level. Choose tough, compact varieties.

SHADING

When planning windbreaks, hedges and screens, consider what a solid line of tall plants will do to the amount of sunlight reaching the windows of your home and outdoor areas. What will the shade patterns be?

If shade is not wanted in an area, locate the hedge or screen at a distance equal to twice the expected mature height of plant. For example, if the

Bamboo is fast growing, and serves as a suitable windbreak where adapted. Use *clumping* species instead of *running* species to avoid invasive spreading.

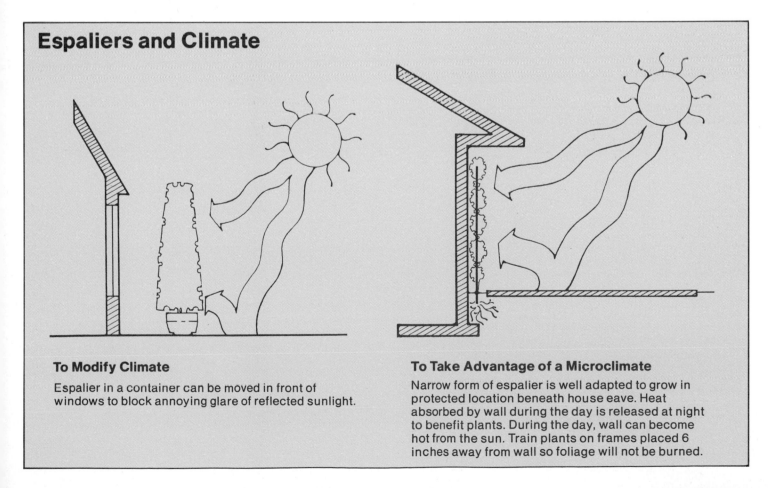

Espaliers and Climate

To Modify Climate

Espalier in a container can be moved in front of windows to block annoying glare of reflected sunlight.

To Take Advantage of a Microclimate

Narrow form of espalier is well adapted to grow in protected location beneath house eave. Heat absorbed by wall during the day is released at night to benefit plants. During the day, wall can become hot from the sun. Train plants on frames placed 6 inches away from wall so foliage will not be burned.

mature height is 15 feet, place plants 30 feet away from the area. You can also control hedge height by planting plants that naturally stay low or by regular pruning.

COOLING

Use hedges, screens and espaliers to reduce summer cooling costs. Cooling is achieved through shading, blocking reflected heat, channeling breezes, lowering air temperature and insulating.

The shady side of a line of plants is distinctly cooler than the sunny side. This is because the sun's rays are blocked, and plants are absorbing moisture from the air and releasing it. This is the process known as *evapo-transpiration*.

A living wall is more effective in cooling dry air than a wood or canvas shade. Put this principle to work on the south and west sides of buildings where the sun's heat is most intense. In humid climates, the cooling effect of added moisture is minimal, but shade and breezes are always welcome.

Use loose, deciduous species to block summer sun. When plants drop their leaves in fall, the winter sun is able to penetrate to add its warmth. Choose plants with sparse or dense foliage to regulate the penetration of sun or wind.

Rows of plants can be used to block the wind or channel it for cooling purposes. Use hedges and screens to capture breezes and funnel them where they are needed. A shady tunnel lowers the air temperature. Position a plant tunnel to take advantage of the prevailing breezes, and the cooler air can be directed to a patio or terrace. One word of caution: Be sure to funnel summer breezes, not cold winter winds.

To make a tunnel, plant two rows of hedges or screens. Shear the sides or prune out the inside branches of the screens. Allow foliage to meet overhead, or plant two rows of canopy-shaped trees to form the ceiling. You can also use espaliers on a pergola framework for a fruiting tunnel like the one pictured on page 111. Use these dramatic features as an approach to an entry, and the cool air can be channeled directly inside your home.

Allées and *pleached allées* are two ancient landscape forms that can be used for cooling purposes. An allée is parallel rows of trees traditionally used to direct views, but allées can be positioned to channel breezes.

Pleaching is a grafting method. Branches from separate trees are interwoven until their tissues have bonded and grown together. Pleach allées along their length and overhead to form tunnels. See list, page 24.

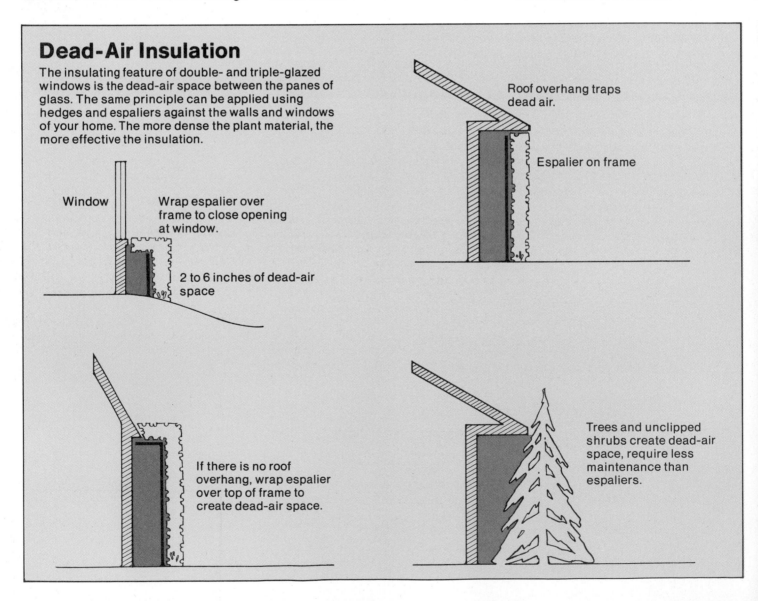

Dead-Air Insulation

The insulating feature of double- and triple-glazed windows is the dead-air space between the panes of glass. The same principle can be applied using hedges and espaliers against the walls and windows of your home. The more dense the plant material, the more effective the insulation.

Window

Wrap espalier over frame to close opening at window.

2 to 6 inches of dead-air space

Roof overhang traps dead air.

Espalier on frame

If there is no roof overhang, wrap espalier over top of frame to create dead-air space.

Trees and unclipped shrubs create dead-air space, require less maintenance than espaliers.

PLANTS FOR WINDBREAKS

Any hedge or screen provides wind protection. These plants are for persistent, harsh wind conditions.

Acer ginnala ....Amur maple
Calocedrus decurrens .... California incense cedar
Caragana arborescens ..... Siberian pea tree
Ceratonia siliqua ....Carob
Chamaecyparis lawsoniana .... Port Orford cedar
Cotoneaster lucidus .... Hedge cotoneaster
Cupressocyparis leylandii Cupressocyparis
Cupressus glabra .... Arizona cypress
Cupressus sempervirens
 'Stricta' .... Italian cypress
Dodonea viscosa ....Hopbush
Elaeagnus angustifolia ....Russian olive
Elaeagnus pungens ....Silverberry
Escallonia rubra ....Escallonia
Eucalyptus ....Eucalyptus species
Juniperus ....Juniper
Ligustrum lucidum ....Glossy privet
Ligustrum texanum .... Waxleaf privet
Lonicera korolkowii
 'Zabeli' ....Zabel's honeysuckle
Lonicera tatarica .... Tatarian honeysuckle

Nerium oleander ....Oleander
Philadelphus x virginalis ....Mock orange
Picea abies ....Norway spruce
Picea glauca ....White spruce
Pinus eldarica ....Mondell pine
Pinus nigra .... Austrian pine
Pittosporum .... Pittosporum species
Populus alba 'Bolleana' ....Bolleana poplar
Populus nigra 'Italica' ....Lombardy poplar
Populus simonii 'Fastigiata' ....Pyramidal Simon poplar
Prunus caroliniana .... Cherry laurel
Prunus ilicifolia ....Hollyleaf cherry
Prunus laurocerasus ....Laurel cherry
Prunus lusitanica ....Portugal laurel
Prunus maritima ....Beach plum
Pseudotsuga menziesii .... Douglas fir
Punica granatum ....Pomegranate
Pyracantha .... Pyracantha
Rhamnus alaternus ....Italian buckthorn
Rhamnus frangula
 'Columnaris' ....Tallhedge buckthorn
Sequoia sempervirens .... Coast redwood
Syringa x chinensis ....Chinese lilac
Syringa vulgaris ....Lilac
Tamarix aphylla ....Tamarisk
Thuja occidentalis ....American arborvitae
Tilia cordata .... Littleleaf linden

An *allée*, a walk or passage created by rows of closely spaced trees, creates a cool, shady tunnel. Use allées to direct views or funnel cooling breezes.

Windbreaks and Shelters

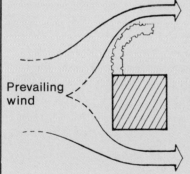

To Make a Sheltered Eddy

Sites buffeted by wind benefit from plantings that force or direct wind away, creating a sheltered area.

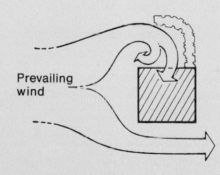

To Trap Breezes

Where wind is rare and appreciated, position plants in a hook pattern facing the wind. This captures and circulates cooling breezes.

Windbreak Height and Placement

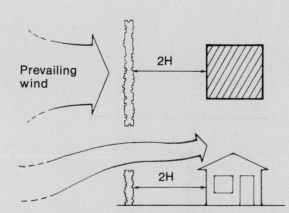

When distance from windbreak to home is equal to *twice the height* of windbreak (2H), wind is lifted over area. Area is very protected.

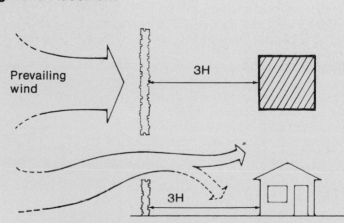

When distance from windbreak to home is equal to *three times the height* of windbreak (3H), most wind is lifted over area, but not all. Area is somewhat protected.

If you live in a hot, arid climate, you can adapt a trick used by the Moors in their 16-century Spanish gardens. They cut windows in garden walls to permit cooling breezes to enter. The breezes distribute sprays of moisture from fountains in the garden. Glimpses of the desert outside heighten the sense of the cool oasis inside. Similarly, windows can be cut in hedges to create the same effect.

Instead of using fountains, place a sprinkler between the prevailing breeze and a loose screen or hedge to create a similar air-conditioning effect. With planning, you can use this sprinkler trick for watering a vegetable plot on one side of a hedge while cooling a patio on the other side.

HEAT CONTROL
Espaliers or hedges placed directly against walls are excellent for heat control. They dramatically reduce temperatures by absorbing solar radiation and reflected heat, while cooling through evapo-transpiration. Vines are usually suggested for these purposes, but their rampant growth can be difficult to control. Many vines cover windows, cause damage to wood and mortar surfaces and invade indoors. Espaliers and wall hedges are far better choices. Plant deciduous species. They drop their leaves in fall to allow winter sun to warm walls. Plant evergreen species for surprisingly effective insulation.

Boxed plants can be positioned to shield windows and walls from solar and reflected heat gain. See Movable Screens, page 22.

INSULATION
The space between the walls of buildings and plants loses and gains heat slowly, preventing substantial heat loss and gain indoors. Set evergreen hedges or espaliers on frames close to walls to create a few inches of "dead-air" insulation. This affects home heating and cooling requirements.

Roof overhangs help to trap dead air. Trees and shrubs should clear the overhang. Or, follow a regular pruning program. Where there is no overhang, wrap espaliers over the top of their frames or train hedge branches back to trap dead air. Seal openings at windows and corners to prevent dead air from escaping. Wrap espaliers around the end of their frames or train hedge branches back. See illustrations, page 32.

PLANTS FOR INSULATION
The key to using dead-air space to insulate your home is keeping plants under control. Sheared, espaliered and naturally compact, evergreen plants are the most effective subjects. Here are some of the best.

Needled Evergreens
Cupressocyparis leylandii	Leyland cypress
Cupressus	Cypress species
Juniperus	Juniper species
Picea	Spruce species
Pinus strobus	White pine
Taxus	Yew species
Thuja	Arborvitae species
Tsuga canadensis	Canadian hemlock

Broadleaf Evergreens
Berberis	Barberry
Buxus sempervirens	English box
Camellia japonica	Camellia species
Carissa grandiflora	Natal plum
Cocculus laurifolius	Cocculus
Elaeagnus pungens	Silverberry
Escallonia rubra	Escallonia
Euonymus kiautschovica 'Manhattan'	Euonymus
Ilex	Holly evergreen species
Laurus nobilis	Grecian laurel
Ligustrum japonicum	Waxleaf privet
Ligustrum lucidum	Glossy privet
Osmanthus fragrans	Sweet osmanthus
Osmanthus heterophyllus	False holly
Pittosporum tenuifolium	Black-stemmed pittosporum
Podocarpus gracilior	Podocarpus fern pine
Podocarpus macrophyllus	Yew pine
Prunus caroliniana	Carolina cherry
Pyracantha	Pyracantha
Rhamnus alaternus	Italian buckthorn
Syzygium paniculatum	Eugenia
Viburnum tinus	Viburnum
Xylosma congestum	Shiny xylosma

Evergreen Espaliers
Camellia	Camellia species
Citrus	Citrus—see lists page 111
Eriobotrya japonica	Loquat
Ilex	Holly species—see lists page 124
Magnolia grandiflora	Southern magnolia
Podocarpus gracilior	Podocarpus fern pine
Pyracantha	Pyracantha
Pyrus kawakamii	Evergreen pear
Rosa banksiae	Lady Banks' rose
Rosmarinus officinalis 'Tuscan Blue'	Rosemary
Taxus	Yew species

Hedgewall of *Cocculus* is used for heat control by shading and insulating this window.

COLD-AIR DRAINAGE

Cold air flows downhill on still nights. It drains down slopes into low spots and valleys like water running off after a storm. If your house is situated on a slope, you can obstruct or divert cold-air flow around houses and outdoor living areas with hedges and screens. Damming is not as effective as diverting, but diverting usually requires more space. Dense, evergreen plants are most effective. Low hedges divert cold air as effectively as tall hedges.

People who live in hot climates can position hedge or screen obstructions on the downslope of their dwellings. This traps the cold-air flow for cooling purposes. There should not be diverters upslope. Loose, deciduous plants are best so cold air can pass through unimpeded during winter months.

SHELTERBELTS AND SNOWCATCHES

Shelterbelts and snowcatches are special screens for large-scale properties. Shelterbelts are windbreaks consisting of numerous rows of trees and shrubs. They protect farms, livestock, agricultural soils and highways. Snowcatches are planted in conjunction with shelterbelts to trap windblown snow. They also serve as substitutes for snowfences along highways and at ski resorts. Check with your local cooperative extension agent for planting recommendations.

Snowcatch Design—Wind deposits snow particles where turbulence occurs, such as in front of and behind windbreaks. Density and height of snowcatch has an effect on how the snow is deposited. The most efficient snowcatch is short in stature and 50% permeable. Deciduous shrub species are usually recommended for snowcatches.

To make a snowcatch, plant two staggered rows close together 40 to 60 feet in front of windbreaks. Species native to your area are recommended.

Shelterbelt Design—A shelterbelt should last at least 70 years and provide food and cover for wildlife. It should also serve as a windbreak, reducing home heating costs by as much as 30%.

Position shelterbelts perpendicular to the prevailing winter wind. Use fast-growing, deciduous plants to provide protection until evergreen species are established. Shelterbelts often consist of 8 to 10 rows of trees and shrubs. They should face the wind in the following order: snowcatch shrubs, 40 to 60 feet open space, deciduous trees in rows, evergreen trees in rows, protected area. There is evidence that a dense, vertical block is more effective than rows that slope up like a peaked roof.

Space rows far enough apart to allow maintenance and cultivating equipment to pass through. Stagger rows. Space evergreen trees far enough apart within rows to prevent crowding when ultimate size is reached. Use shrubs to fill in gaps at tree bases. Remove deciduous rows as necessary as evergreen trees mature.

Acer ginnala, amur maple, can be used in a shelterbelt design planting.

PLANTS FOR SNOWCATCHES

Berberis	Berberis
Caragana	Dwarf peashrubs
Elaeagnus angustifolia	Russian olive
Lonicera korolkowii 'Zabeli'	Zabel's honeysuckle
Lonicera tatarica	Tatarian honeysuckle
Prunus	Some deciduous species
Rosa multiflora	Japanese rose
Rosa rugosa	Rugosa rose
Salix purpurea	Purple-osier willow
Salix purpurea 'Gracilis'	Dwarf blue arctic willow
Syringa	Lilac
Viburnum	Viburnum—deciduous species

PLANTS FOR SHELTERBELTS

Acer ginnala	Amur maple
Caragana arborescens	Siberian pea tree
Elaeagnus angustifolia	Russian olive
Lonicera korolkowii 'Zabeli'	Zabel's honeysuckle
Lonicera tatarica	Tatarian honeysuckle
Picea abies	Norway spruce
Picea glauca	White spruce
Populus nigra 'Italica'	Lombardy poplar
Populus alba 'Bolleana'	Bolleana poplar
Populus simonii 'Fastigiata'	Pyramidal Simon's poplar
Prunus	Deciduous species
Pseudotsuga menziesii	Douglas fir
Rosa multiflora	Japanese rose
Rosa rugosa	Rugosa rose
Salix purpurea	Purple-osier willow
Syringa	Lilac
Viburnum	Viburnum—deciduous species

Plants for Problem Sites

It is essential to know something about your soil, climate and available water supply before you plant. Drought-tolerant plants are smart choices where water is limited. Wet, boggy conditions pose a different problem. Alkaline soils and dry, sandy, nutrient-poor soils are acceptable to certain plants. Keep these factors in mind when you make your plant choices.

The USDA Soil Conservation Service has free information on soil types throughout the United States. If you are investing a lot of time and money in installing a large-scale hedge or screen, it is a good idea to have your soil tested. Most states have soil-testing facilities. Look in the phone book under "county extension agent," "cooperative extension service" or contact your state university to determine the soil-testing laboratory nearest you. In California and Illinois, consult the Yellow Pages for a listing of private soil laboratories.

DROUGHT-TOLERANT PLANTS

Acacia longifolia .... Sydney golden wattle
Acer campestre .... Hedge maple
Arbutus unedo .... Strawberry tree
Arctostaphylos densiflora
  'Howard McMinn' .... Manzanita
Artemisia abrotanum .... Southernwood
Baccharis pilularis .... Coyote brush
Calocedrus decurrens .... California
  incense cedar
Eucalyptus .... Eucalyptus
Feijoa sellowiana .... Pineapple guava
Fontanesia fortunei .... Fontanesia
Ilex x altaclarensis 'Wilsonii' .... Wilson's
  holly
Ilex x aquipernyi .... Holly
Ilex crenata .... Japanese holly cultivars
Ilex cornuta ....Chinese holly
Ilex cornuta 'Burfordii' ....Burford holly
Ilex 'Lydia Morris' .... Holly
Ilex 'Nellie R. Stevens' .... Holly
Ilex pernyi ....Perny holly
Ilex vomitoria .... Yaupon
Juniperus .... Juniper species
Lagerstroemia indica ....Crape myrtle
Laurus nobilis .... Grecian laurel
Lavandula ....Lavender
Ligustrum ....Deciduous privet
Ligustrum lucidum .... Glossy privet
Mahonia aquifolium .... Oregon grape

Myrtus communis .... Myrtle
Nandina domestica ....Nandina
Nerium oleander .... Oleander
Osmanthus fragrans .... Sweet osmanthus
Osmanthus heterophyllus ....False holly
Photinia x fraseri .... Photinia
Picea glauca .... White spruce
Pinus eldarica ....Mondell pine
Pinus mugo mugo .... Mugo pine
Pittosporum .... Pittosporum species
Plumbago auriculata ....Plumbago
Podocarpus macrophyllus .... Yew pine
Prunus caroliniana .... Cherry laurel
Prunus ilicifolia ....Hollyleaf cherry
Prunus lusitanica .... Portugal laurel
Pseudotsuga menziesii .... Douglas fir
Punica granatum ....Pomegranate
Pyracantha .... Pyracantha
Pyrus kawakamii .... Evergreen pear
Raphiolepis indica .... Indian hawthorn
Rhamnus alaternus ....Italian buckthorn
Rhamnus cathartica ......Common buckthorn
Ribes alpinum ....Alpine currant
Rosmarinus officinalis ....Rosemary
Syringa x chinensis ....Chinese lilac
Syringa persica ....Persian lilac
Syringa vulgaris .... Lilac
Syzygium paniculatum .... Eugenia
Tamarix aphylla .... Tamarisk
Viburnum lantana ....Wayfaring tree
Xylosma congestum ....Shiny xylosma

Punica granatum, pomegranate, is reliable despite drought, poor soil or neglect, making it a useful roadside hedge or screen.

TOUGH PLANTS

Plants that require little pruning, watering, spraying or fussing are often referred to as *low maintenance*. They do need attention, care and regular water during their first year after planting. Unsheared screen forms require more garden space but less pruning time. After they are established, these plants can fend for themselves.

Abelia x grandiflora ....Glossy abelia
Acacia longifolia ....Sydney golden wattle
Acer ginnala ....Amur maple
Arctostaphylos densiflora
  'Howard McMinn' .... Manzanita
Atriplex lentiformis
  'Breweri' ....Brewer saltbush
Berberis buxifolia .... Magellan barberry
Berberis x mentorensis ....Mentor barberry
Berberis thunbergii .... Japanese barberry
Camellia japonica .... Camellia
Camellia sasanqua .... Sasanqua camellia
Carissa grandiflora ....Natal plum
Ceratonia siliqua ....Carob
Chaenomeles speciosa .... Flowering quince
Chamaecyparis lawsoniana ....Port Orford cedar
Cocculus laurifolius ....Cocculus
Cornus stolonifera .... Red-osier dogwood
Cotoneaster lucidus .... Hedge cotoneaster
Cupressus glabra .... Arizona cypress

Cupressus sempervirens
  'Stricta' .... Italian cypress
Dodonaea viscosa ....Hopbush
Elaeagnus pungens ....Silverberry
Eriobotrya japonica .... Loquat
Escallonia rubra ....Escallonia
Eucalyptus ....Eucalyptus
Euonymus alata .... Winged burning bush
Feijoa sellowiana .... Pineapple guava
Hibiscus syriacus ....Rose of Sharon
Ilex cornuta ....Chinese holly
Ilex cornuta 'Burfordii' ....Burford holly
Ilex crenata ....Japanese holly
Ilex meserveae 'Dragon Lady' .... Blue holly
Ilex vomitoria ....Yaupon
Juniperus .... Juniper species
Lavandula ....Lavender
Ligustrum lucidum .... Glossy privet
Ligustrum obtusifolium
  regelianum .... Regal privet
Lonicera .... Honeysuckle
Malus sargentii ....Sargent crabapple
Mahonia aquifolium .... Oregon grape
Myrica californica .... Pacific wax myrtle
Myrtus communis .... Myrtle
Nandina domestica ....Nandina
Nerium oleander ....Oleander
Osmanthus fragrans .... Sweet osmanthus
Osmanthus heterophyllus ....False holly
Philadelphus x virginalis ....Mock orange
Photinia x fraseri ....Photinia
Pinus eldarica ....Mondell pine
Pittosporum .... Pittosporum species

Plumbago auriculata ....Plumbago
Podocarpus gracilior ..Podocarpus fern pine
Podocarpus macrophyllus .... Yew pine
Populus ....Popular
Potentilla fruticosa ....Potentilla
Prunus ....Japanese plum
Prunus caroliniana .... Cherry laurel
Prunus ilicifolia ....Hollyleaf cherry
Prunus laurocerasus ....Laurel cherry
Prunus lusitanica ....Portugal laurel
Pseudotsuga menziesii .... Douglas fir
Punica granatum ....Pomegranate
Pyracantha .... Pyracantha
Pyrus kawakamii .... Evergreen pear
Raphiolepis indica .... Indian hawthorn
Rhamnus alaternus ....Italian buckthorn
Rhamnus frangula 'Columnaris' ... Tallhedge buckthorn
Rosa banksiae ....Lady Bank's rose
Rosa bracteata 'Mermaid' ...... Mermaid rose
Rosa multiflora ....Japanese rose
Rosa rugosa .... Rugosa rose
Rosmarinus officinalis ....Rosemary
Spiraea ....Spiraea
Syringa x chinensis ....Chinese lilac
Syringa patula .... Dwarf Korean lilac
Syringa vulgaris .... Lilac
Tamarix aphylla ....Tamarisk
Tsuga canadensis ....Canadian hemlock
Tsuga heterophylla ....Western hemlock
Viburnum .... Viburnum
Xylosma congestum ....Shiny xylosma

Elaeagnus pungens, silverberry, tolerates wind and high heat. It is drought tolerant after it is established.

Raphiolepis indica, Indian hawthorn, is popular for low-maintenance situations. Here it is used as a buffer next to a highway.

PLANTS FOR POOR SOILS

Abelia x grandiflora ....Glossy abelia
Acacia longifolia ....Sydney golden wattle
Acer campestre .... Hedge maple
Acer ginnala ....Amur maple
Arbutus unedo ....Strawberry tree
Arctostaphylos densiflora
  'Howard McMinn' .... Manzanita
Atriplex lentiformis 'Breweri' ....Brewer
  saltbush
Baccharis pilularis .... Dwarf coyote brush
Berberis ....Barberry
Buxus microphylla var. *japonica* .. Japanese
  boxwood
Calocedrus decurrens .... California
  incense cedar
Caragana arborescens ..... Siberian pea tree
Carissa grandiflora ....Natal plum
Carpinus betulus ....Hornbeam
Ceratonia siliqua ....Carob
Chaenomeles speciosa .... Japanese quince
Cornus mas .... Cornelian cherry dogwood
Cornus stolinfera ....Red-osier and
  dogwood
Cotoneaster lucidus .... Hedge cotoneaster
Cupressus glabra ....Arizona cypress
Dodonea viscosa ....Hopbush
Elaeagnus angustifolia ....Russian olive

Elaeagnus pungens ....Silverberry
Eucalyptus ....Eucalyptus
Euonymus alata .... Winged burning bush
Euonymus japonica .... Evergreen euonymus
Euonymus kiautschovica
  'Manhattan' ....Euonymus
Feijoa sellowiana .... Pineapple guava
Ilex x altaclarensis 'Wilsonii' .... Wilson's
  holly
Ilex x aquipernyi .... Holly
Ilex cornuta 'Burfordii' ....Burford holly
Ilex crenata ....Japanese holly
Ilex x meserveae .... Blue holly
Ilex 'Nellie R. Stevens' .... Holly
Ilex pernyi ....Perny holly
Ilex vomitoria ....Yaupon
Ilex verticillata ....Winterberry
Juniperus .... Juniper species
Ligustrum ....Deciduous privets
Ligustrum lucidum .... Glossy privet
Lonicera tatarica .... Tatarian honeysuckle
Malus sargentii ....Sargent crabapple
Myrtus communis .... Myrtle
Nandina domestica ....Nandina
Nerium oleander ....Oleander
Osmanthus fragrans .... Sweet osmanthus
Osmanthus heterophyllus ....False holly
Physocarpus opulifolius ....Dwarf ninebark
Pinus eldarica ....Mondell pine

Pinus nigra ....Austrian pine
Pittosporum tobira .... Tobira mock orange
Plumbago auriculata ....Plumbago
Populus ....Poplar
Prunus ilicifolia ....Hollyleaf cherry
Prunus laurocerasus ....Laurel cherry
Prunus maritima ....Beach plum
Punica granatum ....Pomegranate
Pyrus kawakamii .... Evergreen pear
Raphiolepis indica ....Indian hawthorn
Rhamnus alaternus ....Italian buckthorn
Rhamnus cathartica ......Common buckthorn
Rosa rugosa .... Rugosa rose
Rosmarinus officinalis ....Rosemary
Spiraea ....Spiraea
Tamarix aphylla .... Tamarisk
Tilia cordata ....Littleleaf linden
Viburnum .... Viburnum

SEACOAST SITES

People who live near the ocean may be restricted by codes from building high walls and fences for privacy. A hedge or screen is the answer. *Myoporum laetum* will grow in pure beach sand, but its range is limited to Zone 10. These plants are almost as good, surviving in wet, salty winds and sandy soils characteristic of seacoast sites.

Ilex crenata, Japanese holly, for poor soils.

Rosmarinus officinalis, rosemary, for poor soils.

SEACOAST SITES, CONTINUED

Acacia longifolia ....Sydney golden wattle
Carissa grandiflora ....Natal plum
Cotoneaster lucidus .... Hedge cotoneaster
Dodonea viscosa ....Hopbush
Escallonia rubra .... Escallonia
Eucalyptus globulus 'Compacta' .... Dwarf
        blue gum
Eucalyptus lehmannii ....Bushy yate
Euonymus japonica .... Evergreen euonymus
Pittosporum crassifolium ....Karo
Pittosporum tenuifolium ....Black-
        stemmed pittosporum
Pittosporum tobira .... Tobira mock orange
Podocarpus gracilior ..Podocarpus fern pine
Populus alba 'Bolleana' ....Bolleana poplar
Prunus maritima ....Beach plum
Punica granatum ....Pomegranate
Rosa rugosa .... Rugosa rose
Rosa banksiae ....Lady Bank's rose
Tamarix aphylla .... Tamarisk

SHADY SITES

The shady environment is cool and moist. Shade is cast by trees and buildings. The north side of a building in the Northern Hemisphere is continually shaded. It is an ideal place for an outdoor living area in hot, dry climates. Many plants survive in heavy shade by developing an open, loose form with fewer but larger leaves that catch all available light. An open form is not desirable for hedges, but it may be acceptable for screens and espaliers. Few fruit develop in locations with less than six hours of natural or artificial light a day. These plants are adapted to shady sites.

Acer circinatum ....Vine maple
Arbutus unedo ....Strawberry tree
Camellia japonica ....Camellia
Camellia sasanqua ....Sasanqua camellia
Cocculus laurifolius ....Cocculus
Cotoneaster lucidus ....Hedge cotoneaster
Eriobotrya japonica .... Loquat
Euonymus alata 'Compacta' .... Winged
        burning bush
Euonymus fortunei ....Wintercreeper
Euonymus kiautschovica
  'Manhattan' ....Euonymus
Gardenia jasminoides ....Gardenia
Ilex x altaclarensis 'Wilsonii' .... Wilson's
        holly
Ilex glabra ....Inkberry
Ilex verticillata .... Winterberry
Laurus nobilis ....Grecian laurel
Mahonia aquifolium .... Oregon grape
Nandina domestica ....Nandina
Osmanthus heterophyllus ....False holly
Pittosporum .... Pittosporum species
Podocarpus gracilior ..Podocarpus fern pine
Podocarpus macrophyllus .... Yew pine
Prunus laurocerasus ....Laurel cherry
Prunus lusitanica ....Portugal laurel

Pseudotsuga menziesii .... Douglas fir
Pyracantha ....Pyracantha
Rhamnus cathartica ......Common buckthorn
Rhododendron .... Azalea and rhododendron
Ribes alpinum ....Alpine currant
Rosa bracteata 'Mermaid' ...... Mermaid rose
Sequoia sempervirens ....Coast redwood
Syzygium paniculatum ....Eugenia
Taxus ....Yew
Tsuga canadensis ....Canadian hemlock
Tsuga heterophylla ....Western hemlock
Vaccinium corymbosum .... Blueberry
Viburnum ....Viburnum species

PLANTS FOR WET SOILS

Baccharis pilularis .... Dwarf coyote brush
Bambusa ....Bamboo
Elaeagnus pungens ....Silverberry
Eucalyptus ....Eucalyptus
Ilex glabra ....Inkberry
Ilex verticillata .... Winterberry
Ilex vomitoria ....Yaupon
Malus sargentii ....Sargent crabapple
Populus ....Poplar
Rhamnus cathartica ......Common buckthorn
Salix purpurea ....Purple-osier willow
Sequoia sempervirens ....Coast redwood
Tamarix aphylla ....Tamarisk
Thuja occidentalis ....American arborvitae
Vaccinium corymbosum ....Blueberry
Viburnum dentatum ....Arrowwood
Viburnum opulus ....European
        highbush cranberry

Bambusa species, bamboo, for wet soils.

Rhododendron for shady sites.

FINE TEXTURE

These plants have small leaves. Use them for contrast with coarse and unusually textured foliage. They are excellent subjects for shearing.

Abelia x grandiflora ....Glossy abelia
Arctostaphylos densiflora
  'Howard McMinn' .... Manzanita
Artemisia abrotanum ....Southernwood
Baccharis pilularis .... Dwarf coyote brush
Berberis buxifolia .... Magellan barberry
Berberis darwinii .... Darwin barberry
Berberis thunbergii .... Japanese barberry
Buxus .... Boxwood cultivars
Caragana arborescens ..... Siberian pea tree
Cotoneaster lucidus .... Hedge cotoneaster
Cupressus glabra ....Arizona cypress
Cupressus sempervirens
  'Stricta' .... Italian cypress
Euonymus japonica ....Euonymus
                                        dwarf cultivars
Ilex vomitoria ....Yaupon
Myrsine africana .... African box
Myrtus communis .... Myrtle
Myrtus communis
  'Microphylla' .... Dwarf myrtle

Nandina domestica ....Nandina
Pinus mugo mugo .... Mugo pine
Pinus strobus ....White pine
Plumbago auriculata ....Plumbago
Podocarpus gracilior ..Podocarpus fern pine
Podocarpus macrophyllus .... Yew pine
Potentilla fruticosa ....Potentilla
Prunus ilicifolia ....Hollyleaf cherry
Punica granatum ....Pomegranate
Rhamnus alaternus ....Italian buckthorn
Rhododendron obtusum .... Kurume azalea
Ribes alpinum ....Alpine currant
Rosa 'Cecile Brunner' ....Sweetheart rose
Rosmarinus officinalis ....Rosemary
Salix purpurea ....Purple-osier willow
Santolina chamaecyparissus ....Lavender
                                        cotton
Sequoia sempervirens .... Coast redwood
Spiraea nipponica
  'Snowmound' ....Snowmound spiraea
Syzygium paniculatum ....Eugenia
Tamarix aphylla .... Tamarisk
Taxus ....Yew
Teucrium chamaedrys .... Germander
Thuja occidentalis ....American arborvitae
Tsuga canadensis ....Canadian hemlock
Tsuga heterophylla ....Western hemlock

COARSE AND UNUSUAL TEXTURE

This is a selected list of plants with large or striking leaves. Use them for special effects, for close-up viewing and for contrast with fine-textured foliage. Shearing makes leaves look ragged. Cut individual shoots back one by one to shape plants.

Bambusa .... Bamboo
Eriobotrya japonica .... Loquat
Fagus sylvatica 'Asplenifolia' .... Beech
Feijoa sellowiana .... Pineapple guava
Hibiscus syriacus ....Rose of Sharon
Magnolia grandiflora ...... Southern magnolia
Nandina domestica ....Nandina
Pittosporum crassifolium ....Karo
Pittosporum tobira .... Tobira mock orange
Prunus laurocerasus ....Laurel cherry
Raphiolepis indica
  'Majestic Beauty' .... Indian hawthorn
Rhododendron maximum ....Rosebay
                                        rhododendron
Viburnum dentatum ....Arrowwood
Viburnum lentago ....Nannyberry

Texture is a visual impression formed by appearance of leaves or needles, branches, new growth, pruning technique and color. Here, varying textures of clipped hedge, sheared passageway and feathery new growth make a unique garden entry.

Taxus baccata—English yew

Pinus strobus—white pine

Taxus x media 'Hatfieldii'—Hatfield's yew

Prunus laurocerasus—English laurel

Pinus mugo—Swiss mountain pine

Feijoa sellowiana—pineapple guava

Juniperus chinensis 'Heitzii'—Heitzii juniper

Thuja occidentalis—American arborvitae

Buxus sempervirens—English or common boxwood

Functional Forms **41**

LEAF COLOR

Plants with colored leaves create special effects. Green is a color too, but it is not as noticeable because it is so basic and pleasing. If green is not the primary color in a garden composition, the garden may seem imbalanced or disquieting. Medium greens, dark greens and blue-greens recede into the background to form the fundamental framework. For a list of the best of these plants, see *Framework and Backdrop,* page 45. Use other colors for accents.

DARK-GREEN LEAVES

Acer ginnala ....Amur maple
Arbutus unedo ....Strawberry tree
Berberis darwinii ....Darwin barberry
Berberis mentorensis ....Mentor barberry
Berberis thunbergii ....Japanese barberry
Camellia japonica ....Camellia
Camellia sasanqua .... Sasanqua camellia
Carissa grandiflora ....Natal plum
Carpinus betulus ....Hornbeam
Ceratonia siliqua ....Carob
Chaenomeles speciosa .... Flowering quince
Citrus ....Citrus
Coculus laurifolius ....Cocculus
Cornus mas .... Cornelian cherry dogwood
Cotoneaster lucidus .... Hedge cotoneaster
Crataegus grus-galli .... Cockspur thorn
Cupressus sempervirens
  'Stricta' .... Italian cypress

Eriobotrya japonica .... Loquat
Escallonia rubra ....Escallonia
Euonymus fortunei .....Bigleaf wintercreeper
Euonymus japonica .... Evergreen euonymus
Euonymus kiautschovicus
  'Manhattan' ....Euonymus
Fagus sylvatica ....Beech
Forsythia x intermedia
  'Arnold Dwarf' ....Forsythia
Gardenia jasminoides ....Gardenia
Hibiscus rosa-sinensis ..... Tropical hibiscus
Lagerstroemia indica ....Crape myrtle
Laurus nobilis ....Grecian laurel
Lonicera korolkowii 'Zabeli' ....Zabel's
  honeysuckle
Mahonia aquifolium .... Oregon grape
Myrtus communis .... Myrtle
Nerium oleander ....Oleander
Osmanthus heterophyllus ....False holly
Osmanthus fragrans .... Sweet osmanthus
Photinia x fraseri ....Photinia
Picea abies ....Norway spruce
Pinus eldarica ....Mondell pine
Pinus mugo mugo .... Mugo pine
Pinus nigra ....Austrian pine
Pittosporum tobira .... Tobira mock orange
Pittosporum undulatum ....Victorian box
Podocarpus macrophyllus .... Yew pine
Populus alba 'Bolleana' ....Bolleana poplar
Potentilla fruticosa ....Potentilla
Prunus caroliniana .... Cherry laurel
Prunus ilicifolia ....Hollyleaf cherry
Prunus laurocerasus ....Laurel cherry

Prunus lusitanica ....Portugal laurel
Pseudotsuga menziesii .... Douglas fir
Pyrus communis .... Pear
Pyrus hybrid ....Pear-apple
Pyrus kawakamii .... Evergreen pear
Raphiolepis indica ....Indian hawthorn
Rhamnus frangula 'Columnaris' ... Tallhedge
  buckthorn
Rhamnus alaternus ....Italian buckthorn
Rhamnus cathartica ......Common buckthorn
Rhododendron maximum ....Rosebay
  rhododendron
Rhododendron ..PJM hybrid rhododendrons
Ribes alpinum ....Alpine currant
Rosmarinus officinalis ....Rosemary
Sequoia sempervirens .... Coast redwood
Spiraea prunifolia plena .... Bridal-wreath
  spirea
Syringa chinensis ....Chinese lilac
Syringa vulgaris .... Lilac
Syzygium paniculatum .... Eugenia
Taxus baccata .... English yew
Taxus baccata 'Stricta' ....Irish yew
Taxus cuspidata .... Japanese yew
Taxus media .... Intermediate yew
Tsuga canadensis ....Canadian hemlock
Tsuga heterophylla ....Western hemlock
Viburnum dentatum ....Arrowwood
Viburnum japonicum .... Viburnum
Viburnum lantana ....Wayfaring tree
Viburnum opulus .... European highbush
  cranberry
Viburnum tinus .... Laurustinus

Ligustrum japonicum—Japanese privet

Tsuga canadensis—Canadian hemlock

Pittosporum tobira 'Variegata'— variegated pittosporum

YELLOW-GREEN LEAVES

Greens in the light or yellow range appear to advance and seem closer in perception, especially when lit from behind by the sun. These greens are also useful for lighting up dark corners.

Acacia longifolia .... Sydney golden wattle
Acer circinatum .... Vine maple
Arctostaphylos densiflora
   'Howard McMinn' .... Manzanita
Buxus microphylla
   var. *koreana* .... Korean littleleaf box
Calocedrus decurrens .... California incense cedar
Cupressocyparis leylandii
   'Castelwellian Gold' .... Cupressocyparis
Ligustrum x vicaryi .... Vicary golden privet
Physocarpus opulifolius
   'Dart's Gold' .... Golden ninebark
Pittosporum eugenioides .... Lemonwood
Populus nigra 'Italica' ....Lombardy poplar
Punica granatum .... Pomegranate
Xylosma congestum ....Shiny xylosma

RED AND PURPLE LEAVES

Reds and purples are the most striking leaf colors. A garden with more red or purple than green is rarely successful. It takes a great deal of skill and taste to create a pleasing picture when these colors are used for a mass hedge or screen planting. Try them as accent, single espalier, topiary or as a low hedge in front of a simple green backdrop.

RED LEAVES

Grown in full sun, these plants have bronze or red-tinted new leaves. Shearing or pruning repeatedly to stimulate new growth produces the most pronounced color effect. Tone color down to a rich green by placing plants in part or full shade.

Mahonia aquifolium .... Oregon grape
Nandina domestica ....Nandina
Photinia x fraseri ....Photinia
Syzygium paniculatum .... Eugenia

PURPLE LEAVES

Berberis thunbergii
   'Atropurpurea' .... Japanese barberry cultivars
Dodonea viscosa 'Purpurea' and
   'Saratoga' ....Purple hopbush
Fagus sylvatica 'Atropunicea' Copper beech
Fagus sylvatica 'Riversii' .... Purple beech

VARIEGATED LEAVES

Variegated plants have leaves with white or yellow markings. They are traditionally used to light up dark corners or for accent.

Elaeagnus pungens ....Silverberry
Euonymus fortunei ....Euonymus— variegated cultivars
Euonymus japonica ...... Variegated cultivars
Ilex aquifolium .... Many variegated cultivars
Ligustrum japonicum
   'Silver Star' .... Japanese privet
Osmanthus herterophyllus
   'Variegata' ....Variegated false holly
Pittosporum tobira
   'Variegata' .... Variegated tobira
Rhamnus alaternus
   'Variegata' ....Variegated Italian buckthorn

Crataegus phaenopyrum—Washington thorn

Berberis thunbergii 'Atropurpurea'— red-leaf Japanese barberry

Dodonaea viscosa 'Purpurea'—purple hopbush

Escallonia rubra—escallonia

Euonymus alata—winged burning bush

Mahonia aquifolium—Oregon grape

Elaeagnus angustifolia—Russian olive

FALL FOLIAGE COLOR

Plants with exceptional fall color produce a brilliant, temporary accent that emphasizes a sense of time and the passing of the seasons. This special effect may not be suited to subtropical climates unless the color harmonizes with the fall color of permanent, evergreen plants.

Euonymus alata 'Compacta', compact winged burning bush, in fall color.

Forsythia—forsythia

FRAMEWORK AND BACKDROP

Use a hedge or a screen with simple, fine texture and solid, green color to form a quiet framework for a garden. These plants have few distracting features. Choose evergreens for year-round permanence. Beech and hornbeam are the only deciduous plants that hold their leaves through winter.

Arbutus unedo .... Strawberry tree
Bambusa .... Bamboo species
Berberis x mentorensis .... Mentor barberry
Buxus .... Boxwood cultivars
Calocedrus decurrens .... California incense cedar
Camellia japonica .... Camellia
Camellia sasanqua .... Sasanqua camellia
Carissa grandiflora .... Natal plum
Carpinus betulus .... Hornbeam
Ceratonia siliqua .... Carob
Chamaecyparis lawsoniana .... Port Orford cedar
Citrus .... Citrus—see lists page 111
Cocculus laurifolius .... Cocculus
Cupressocyparis leylandii .... Cupressocyparis
Cupressus glabra .... Arizona cypress
Cupressus sempervirens 'Stricta' .... Italian cypress
Dodonea viscosa 'Green' ..... Green hopbush

Elaeagnus pungens .... Silverberry
Escallonia rubra .... Escallonia
Euonymus alata .... Winged burning bush
Euonymus fortunei .... Wintercreeper
Euonymus japonica .... Evergreen euonymus
Euonymus kiautschovica 'Manhattan' .... Euonymus
Fagus sylvatica .... Beech
Gardenia jasminoides .... Gardenia
Hibiscus rosa-sinensis ..... Tropical hibiscus
Ilex .... Holly
Juniperus .... Juniper species
Laurus nobilis .... Grecian laurel
Ligustrum ....Deciduous privet
Ligustrum japonicum .... Japanese privet
Ligustrum lucidum .... Glossy privet
Ligustrum texanum .... Waxleaf privet
Lonicera korolkowii 'Zabeli' .... Zabel's honeysuckle
Lonicera tatarica .... Tatarian honeysuckle
Mahonia aquifolium .... Oregon grape
Myrica californica .... Pacific wax myrtle
Mysine africana .... African box
Myrtus communis .... Myrtle
Nandina domestica ....Nandina
Nerium oleander .... Oleander
Osmanthus fragrans .... Sweet osmanthus
Osmanthus heterophyllus ....False holly
Picea abies .... Norway spruce
Picea glauca .... White spruce
Pinus eldarica ....Mondell pine
Pinus strobus ....White pine
Pittosporum crassifolium .... Karo

Pittosporum tenuifolium ......Black-stemmed pittosporum
Pittosporum tobira .... Tobira mock orange
Pittosporum undulatum .... Victorian box
Podocarpus gracilior ..Podocarpus fern pine
Podocarpus macrophyllus .... Yew pine
Prunus caroliniana .... Cherry laurel
Prunus laurocerasus ....Laurel cherry
Prunus lusitanica ....Portugal laurel
Pseudotsuga menziesii .... Douglas fir
Rhamnus alaternus ....Italian buckthorn
Rhamnus frangula 'Columnaris' ...Tallhedge buckthorn
Rhododendron maximum ....Rosebay rhododendron
Sequoia sempervirens ....Coast redwood
Syringa x chinensis ....Chinese lilac
Syzygium paniculatum .... Eugenia
Tamarix aphylla ....Tamarisk
Taxus baccata .... English yew
Taxus baccata 'Stricta' ....Irish yew
Taxus cuspidata .... Japanese yew
Taxus x media .... Intermediate yew
Teucrium chamaedrys .... Germander
Thuja occidentalis ....American arborvitae
Tilia cordata .... Littleleaf linden
Tsuga canadensis ....Canadian hemlock
Tsuga heterophylla ....Western hemlock
Viburnum dentatum ....Arrowwood
Viburnum japonicum .... Viburnum
Viburnum suspensum Sandankwa viburnum
Viburnum tinus .... Laurustinus
Xylosma congestum ....Shiny xylosma

Large-scale screen of Foster's holly increases sense of separation between building and courtyard, and serves as a backdrop for statuary.

Special Features

DECORATIVE FLOWERS AND FRUIT

For flowers or fruit on a hedge or screen, it is usually necessary to follow a special pruning schedule, or do no pruning at all. Most of these plants are worthy of show-off espalier treatment. Special pruning instructions are given on page 91.

Abelia x grandiflora ....Glossy abelia
Arctostaphylos densiflora
 'Howard McMinn' ....Manzanita
Berberis ....Barberry
Camellia japonica ....Camellia
Camellia sasanqua .... Sasanqua camellia
Caragana arborescens ..... Siberian pea tree
Carissa grandiflora ....Natal plum
Chaenomeles speciosa .... Flowering quince
Cornus mas .... Cornelian cherry dogwood
Cornus stolonifera .... Red-osier dogwood
Cotoneaster lucidus .... Hedge cotoneaster
Crataegus crus-galli .... Cockspur thorn
Crataegus .... Common hawthorn
Escallonia rubra ....Escallonia
Eucalyptus ....Eucalyptus species
Feijoa sellowiana .... Pineapple guava
Forsythia x intermedia ....Forsythia
Forsythia ovata 'Ottawa' .... Ottawa forsythia
Gardenia jasminoides ....Gardenia
Hisbiscus rosa-sinensis ... Tropical hibiscus
Hibiscus syriacus ....Rose of Sharon
Lagerstroemia indica ....Crape myrtle
Lavandula ....Lavender
Lonicera korolkowii 'Zabeli' ....Zabeli's honeysuckle
Lonicera tatarica .... Tatarian honeysuckle
Mahonia aquifolium .... Oregon grape
Malus baccata 'Columnaris' .... Columnar Siberian crabapple
Malus pumila .... Apple
Malus sargentii ....Sargent crabapple
Magnolia grandiflora ...... Southern magnolia
Myrtus communis .... Myrtle
Nerium oleander ....Oleander
Philadelphus x virginalis ....Mock orange
Photinia x fraseri .... Photinia
Physocarpus opulifolius 'Nanus', 'Dart's Gold' ....Dwarf ninebark
Pittosporum eugenioides .... Lemonwood
Pittosporum tobira .... Tobira mock orange
Pittosporum undulatum .... Victorian box
Plumbago auriculata ....Plumbago
Potentilla fruticosa ....Potentilla
Prunus lusitanica ....Portugal laurel
Prunus maritima ....Beach plum
Punica granatum ....Pomegranate
Pyracantha .... Pyracantha
Pyrus communis .... Pear
Pyrus hybrid ....Pear-apple
Pyrus kawakamii .... Evergreen pear
Raphiolepis indica .... Indian hawthorn
Rhododendron .... Azalea and rhododendron
Rosa .... Rose
Rosmarinus officinalis ....Rosemary
Santolina chamaecyparissus ....Lavender cotton
Spiraea .... Spiraea species
Syringa x chinensis ....Chinese lilac
Syringa patula .... Dwarf Korean lilac
Syringa vulgaris ....Lilac
Syzygium paniculatum ....Eugenia
Tilia cordata ....Littleleaf linden
Vaccinium ashei ....Rabbiteye blueberry
Vaccinium corymbosum ....Blueberry
Viburnum ....Viburnum species
Weigela florida .... Weigela

Eucalyptus erythrocorys—red-cap gum

Nandina domestica—nandina

Carissa grandiflora—natal plum

EDIBLES

Dual-purpose plants are great where space is limited. The hedge or screen that encloses your garden can also provide you with fruit or herbs. City dwellers can grow and harvest citrus, pears or apples as well-managed espaliers on a balcony. Prune carefully if a harvest is your objective. Screens, carefully shaped hedges and espaliers produce more edibles than sheared hedges. If your climate is too severe for citrus or other cold-tender fruit, try growing them in containers for temporary screens and move them indoors during winter.

Many of these edibles are delicious fresh. Some are too tart or bland for eating out of hand, but make fine preserves.

Temporary screens can provide privacy and produce in summer. Tomatoes, runner beans and cucumbers climb chain-link fences. Try sunflowers or raspberries in a hedgerow.

Arctostaphylos densiflora
'Howard McMinn' .... Manzanita

Carissa grandiflora ....Natal plum
Ceratonia siliqua ....Carob
Chaenomeles speciosa .... Flowering quince
Citrus ....Citrus
Cornus mas .... Cornelian cherry dogwood
Corylus avellana ....Filbert
Crataegus .... Hawthorn
Elaeagnus angustifolia ....Russian olive
Elaeagnus pungens ....Silverberry
Eriobotrya japonica .... Loquat
Fagus sylvatica .... Beech
Feijoa sellowiana .... Pineapple guava
Malus pumila .... Apple
Mahonia aquifolium .... Oregon grape
Prunus ....European plum
Prunus ....Japanese plum
Prunus ilicifolia ....Hollyleaf cherry
Prunus maritima ....Beach plum
Punica granatum ....Pomegranate
Pyrus communis .... Pear
Pyrus hybrid ....Pear-apple
Rosa .... Rose
Syzygium paniculatum .... Eugenia
Tilia cordata .... Littleleaf linden
Vaccinium ashei ....Rabbiteye blueberry
Vaccinium corymbosum .... Blueberry

Citrus are among the best ornamental edibles.

A fence that is attractive, encloses, provides privacy and fruit—what more could you ask for? These are 'Golden Delicious' apples, espaliered on post and wire.

These are the edible *hips*, or fruit, of *Rosa rugosa*, rugosa rose.

Flowers of *Abelia x grandiflora,* glossy abelia, attract bees.

FRAGRANCE

Use these plants to enclose patios or screen windows. Fragrance is particularly delightful on warm nights. Everyone has space for at least one espalier against the bedroom wall.

Acer ginnala ....Amur maple
Annona cherimola .... Cherimoya
Calocedrus decurrens .... California
 incense cedar
Citrus ....Citrus
Elaeagnus pungens .... Silverberry
Gardenia jasminoides .... Gardenia
Laurus nobilis .... Grecian laurel
Lavandula ....Lavender
Lonicera nitida .... Box honeysuckle
Magnolia grandifolia ...... Southern magnolia
Myrtus communis .... Myrtle
Osmanthus fragrans .... Sweet osmanthus
Osmanthus heterophyllus ....False holly
Philadelphus x virginalis ....Mock orange
Pinus strobus ....White pine
Pittosporum eugenioidea .... Lemonwood
Pittosporum tobira .... Tobira
 mock orange cultivars
Pittosporum undulatum .... Victorian box
Pseudotsuga menziesii .... Douglas fir
Raphiolepis indica
 'Majestic Beauty' .... Indian hawthorn
Rosa .... Rose
Syringa ....Lilac
Tilia cordata .... Littleleaf linden

HERBAL HEDGES AND BORDERS

Artemisia .... Southernwood and artemisia
Ilex paraguayensis ....Maté
Laurus nobilis .... Grecian laurel
Lavandula ....Lavender
Osmanthus fragrans .... Sweet osmanthus
Rosa rugosa .... Rugosa rose
Rosmarinus ....Rosemary
Santolina chamaecyparissus .... Lavender
 cotton
Teucrium chamaedrys .... Germander

WINTER SILHOUETTE

Deciduous screening plants are useful when a leafy effect is desired but where climate is too severe for broadleaf evergreens. These plants have a striking branch silhouette when out of leaf. Shearing ruins their form.

Acer circinatum .... Vine maple
Berberis thunbergii .... Japanese barberry
Chaenomeles speciosa .... Flowering quince
Cornus mas .... Cornelian cherry dogwood
Cornus stolonifera .... Red-osier dogwood
Elaeagnus angustifolia ....Russian olive
Euonymus alata .... Winged burning bush
Ilex verticillata .... Winterberry
Lagerstroemia indica ....Crape myrtle
Populus alba 'Bolleana' ....Bolleana poplar
Populus nigra 'Italica' ....Lombardy poplar
Populus simonii 'Fastigiata' ....Pyramidal
 Simon's poplar
Salix purpurea ....Purple-osier willow
Viburnum dentatum ....Arrowwood

Unclipped *Teucrium chamaedrys,* germander, edges path. It can also be sheared into neat, boxlike form.

Flowering screen of *Syringa* species, lilac, adds fragrance to a garden. Base of plant is sparse, so it is filled in with low planting.

HONEY AND BEES

These hedges serve as bee forage plants for nectar and pollen. A few bee boxes and a skilled beekeeper produce honey. If you are allergic to bee stings, avoid growing these plants.

Abelia x grandiflora ....Glossy abelia
Artemisia ....Artemisia
Caragana arborescens ....Peatree
Citrus ....Citrus
Crataegus ....Hawthorn species
Eriobotrya japonica ....Loquat
Escallonia ....Escallonia
Eucalyptus ....Eucalyptus
Euonymus kiautschovica .... Evergreen
euonymus
Feijoa sellowiana .... Pineapple guava
Lavandula ....Lavender
Ligustrum ....Privet
Mahonia aquifolium .... Oregon grape
Malus baccata ....Crabapple
Prunus laurocerasus ....Laurel cherry
Pyracantha ....Pyracantha
Rosmarinus officinalis ....Rosemary
Salix purpurea ....Blue arctic willow
Syzygium paniculatum ....Eugenia
Tilia cordata ....Littleleaf linden

ATTRACT BIRDS

Trees and shrubs are the only refuge for birds in cities and suburbs. Hedges or screens that produce berries, fruit or nuts attract birds and squirrels to your property. These plants provide them with an important source of food and nesting habitat. Do not plant bird attractors as screens near airports. Birds flocking to feed on berries are an aviation hazard.

Berberis ....Barberry
Cornus mas ....Cornelian cherry dogwood
Cotoneaster lucidus ....Hedge cotoneaster
Crataegus ....Hawthorn
Elaeagnus angustifolia ....Russian olive
Elaeagnus pungens ....Silverberry
Euonymus alata ....Winged burning bush
Fagus sylvatica ....Beach
Feijoa sellowiana ....Pineapple
Ilex ....Holly
Lonicera korolkowii 'Zabeli' ....Zabel's
honeysuckle
Lonicera tatarica ....Tatarian honeysuckle
Lonicera x xylosteum
'Clavey's Dwarf' ....Clavey's dwarf
honeysuckle
Malus baccata 'Columnaris' ... Columnar
Siberian crabapple
Malus sargentii ....Sargent crabapple
Myrica californica ....Pacific wax myrtle
Pyracantha ....Pyracantha
Rhamnus frangula 'Columnaris' ... Tallhedge
buckthorn
Rosa ....Rose
Rosmarinus officinalis ....Rosemary
Syzygium paniculatum ....Eugenia
Vaccinium ashei ....Rabbiteye blueberry
Vaccinium corymbosum ....Blueberry
Viburnum ....Viburnum

CLASSIC SHAPING

These plants have long been popular for formal shaping and spatial definition because they can be pruned severely. They are useful as hedges wherever space is limited. Those marked with an * asterisk are favorite topiary subjects. Some of these are more suited to pillar and poodle forms than to elaborate, animal-shaped topiary.

*Buxus .... Boxwood
Berberis thunbergii 'Erecta' .... Truehedge
columnberry
Camellia sasanqua .... Sasanqua camellia
Carpinus betulus .... Hornbeam
Citrus lemon ....True lemon
Euonymus japonica
'Grandifolia' ....Euonymus
Fagus sylvatica .... Beech
*Ilex .... Holly—evergreen species
*Juniperus .... Juniper species
*Laurus nobilis .... Grecian laurel
*Ligustrum japonicum .... Japanese privet
Ligustrum lucidum .... Glossy privet
*Myrtus communis .... Myrtle
*Myrsine africana .... African box
Osmanthus fragrans .... Sweet osmanthus
Podocarpus macrophyllus .... Yew pine
*Podocarpus gracilior Podocarpus fern pine
*Prunus-caroliniana .... Cherry laurel
*Pyracantha .... Pyracantha
Rhamnus alaternus ....Italian buckthorn
*Syzygium paniculatum .... Eugenia
*Taxus .... Yew
Thuja .... Arborvitae
*Tsuga canadensis ....Canadian hemlock
Tsuga heterophylla ....Western hemlock
*Viburnum tinus .... Laurustinus

Berries of *Ilex verticillata*, winterberry, bring in the birds.

Classically shaped plant forms require time, patience and experience, but allow you to create special effects.

Regional Favorites

Different systems can be used to determine plant adaptation. The United States Department of Agriculture (USDA) uses a zoning system based on average minimum temperatures. Most nurseries use the USDA zoning system, and it is used in this book.

In addition, other factors besides minimum temperatures affect plant growth. They include humidity, high temperatures, percentage of sunshine, proximity to large bodies of water, length of growing season, rainfall and soil type.

The following lists organize plants by regions, taking many of these factors into account. Use the lists as a guide, along with the USDA zone recommendations, to help make your plant selections. Detailed descriptions of the regions are given, along with USDA zone map, on page 95.

For the best recommendations, consult with local sources. Nursery personnel and state and county extension agents are knowledgeable in selecting and growing plants in your particular area.

PACIFIC NORTHWEST AND COASTAL BRITISH COLUMBIA

Abelia x grandiflora ....Glossy abelia
Acer campestre ....Hedge maple
Acer circinatum ....Vine maple
Acer ginnala ....Amur maple
Arbutus unedo ....Strawberry tree
Berberis ....Barberry species
Buxus microphylla
   var. *japonica* ....Japanese boxwood
Buxus sempervirens ....English boxwood
Calocedrus decurrens .... California incense cedar
Camellia japonica ....Camellia
Ceratonia siliqua ....Carob
Chamaecyparis lawsoniana ....Port Orford cedar
Cornus mas .... Cornelian cherry dogwood
Crataegus ....Hawthorn species
Cupressocyparis leylandii .... Leyland cypress
Escallonia rubra ....Escallonia
Euonymus ....Euonymus species
Forsythia x intermedia ....Forsythia
Hibiscus syriacus ....Rose of Sharon
Ilex .... Holly
Juniperus chinensis ....Chinese juniper
Juniperus virginiana ....Eastern red cedar
Laurus nobilis ....Grecian laurel
Ligustrum .... Privet
Mahonia aquifolium .... Oregon grape
Malus pumila .... Apple
Malus baccata 'Columnaris' .... Columnar Siberian crabapple
Malus sargentii ....Sargent crabapple
Myrica californica .... Pacific wax myrtle
Nandina domestica ....Nandina
Osmanthus heterophyllus ....False holly
Philadelphus x virginalis ....Mock orange
Photinia x fraseri ....Photinia
Picea abies ....Norway spruce
Picea glauca ....White spruce
Pinus mugo mugo .... Mugo pine
Pinus nigra ....Austrian pine
Pittosporum tobira .... Tobira mock orange
Potentilla fruticosa ....Potentilla
Prunus caroliniana ....Carolina cherry
Prunus laurocerasus .... English laurel
Prunus .... European and Japanese plum
Prunus lusitanica ....Portugal laurel
Pseudotsuga menziesii .... Douglas fir
Pyracantha coccinea .... Pyracantha
Rhamnus alaternus ....Italian buckthorn
Rhamnus cathartica ......Common buckthorn
Rhamnus frangula 'Columnaris' ... Tallhedge buckthorn
Rhododendron ....Rhododendron and azalea species
Rosmarinus officinalis ....Rosemary
Sequoia sempervirens ....Coast redwood
Spiraea ....Spiraea species
Syringa x chinensis ....Chinese lilac
Syringa persica ....Persian lilac
Syringa vulgaris ....Common lilac
Rosa .... Rose
Taxus .... Yew species
Thuja occidentalis ....American arborvitae
Thuja plicata ....Western red cedar
Tsuga canadensis ....Canadian hemlock
Tsuga hererophylla ....Western hemlock
Vaccinium corymbosum .... Blueberry
Viburnum ....Viburnum species
Weigela .... Weigela

CALIFORNIA

Abelia x grandiflora ....Glossy abelia
Acacia longifolia ....Sydney golden wattle
Acer circinatum ....Vine maple

Photinia x fraseri—photinia

Prunus laurocerasus—English laurel

Arbutus unedo .... Strawberry tree
Arctostaphylos densiflora
    'Howard McMinn' .... Manzanita
Atriplex lentiformis 'Breweri' ....Brewer
    saltbush
Baccharis pilularis .... Dwarf coyote brush
Bambusa ....Bamboo
Buxus microphylla
    var. japonica ....Japanese boxwood
Calocedrus decurrens .... California
    incense cedar
Camellia japonica ....Camellia
Camellia sasanqua .... Sasanqua camellia
Ceratonia siliqua ....Carob
Cupressocyparis leylandii . Leyland cypress
Cupressus sempervirens 'Stricta' ....
    Italian cypress
Eucalyptus species ....Eucalyptus
Feijoa sellowiana .... Pineapple guava
Hibiscus rosa-sinensis ..... Tropical hibiscus
Ilex ....Holly—see list page 124
Juniperus chinensis ....Chinese juniper
Ligustrum japonicum .... Japanese privet
Ligustrum lucidum .... Glossy privet
Ligustrum texanum .... Waxleaf privet
Magnolia grandiflora ..... Southern magnolia
Malus pumila .... Apple
Myrica california .... Pacific wax myrtle
Myrsine africana .... African box
Nandina domestica ....Nandina
Nerium oleander ....Oleander
Photinia x fraseri ....Photinia
Pinus eldarica ....Mondell pine
Pittosporum .... Pittosporum species
Podocarpus gracilior ..Podocarpus fern pine
Podocarpus macrophyllus .... Yew pine
Prunus caroliniana .... Cherry laurel
Prunus ilicifolia ....Hollyleaf cherry
Prunus laurocerasus ....Laurel cherry

Psidium .... Strawberry guava
Punica granatum ....Pomegranate
Pyrus communis 'Seckel' ....Pear
Pyrus ....Pear-apple or Asian pear
Pyrus kawakamii .... Evergreen pear
Raphiolepis indica .... Indian hawthorn
Rhamnus alaternus ....Italian buckthorn
Rosa .... Rose—see list page 160
Santolina chamaecyparissus ....Lavender
    cotton
Sequoia sempervirens .... Coast redwood
Tamarix aphylla ....Tamarisk
Tilia cordata .... Littleleaf linden
Teucrium chamaedrys .... Germander
Thuja plicata ....Western red cedar
Vaccinium ashei ....Rabbiteye blueberry
Viburnum suspensum ....Sandankwa
Viburnum tinus .... Laurustinus
Xylosma congestum ....Shiny xylosma

DESERT CLIMATES
Abelia x grandiflora ....Glossy abelia
Acacia longifolia .... Sydney golden wattle
Arbutus unedo .... Strawberry tree
Atriplex lentiformis 'Breweri' ....Brewer
    saltbush
Baccharis pilularis .... Dwarf coyote brush
Calocedrus decurrens .... California
    incense cedar
Ceratonia siliqua ....Carob
Cupressus glabra .... Arizona cypress
Dodonaea viscosa ....Hopbush
Eucalyptus ....Eucalyptus species
Euonymus kiautschovica
    'Manhattan' ....Euonymus
Feijoa sellowiana .... Pineapple guava
Gardenia jasminoides ....Gardenia
Hibiscus rosa-sinensis ..... Tropical hibiscus

Ilex x altaclarensis 'Wilsonii' .. Wilson's holly
Ilex cornuta 'Burfordii' ....Burford holly
Ilex vomitoria ....Yaupon
Juniperus chinensis ....Chinese juniper
Juniperus scopulorum .... Rocky
    Mountain juniper
Lagerstroemia indica ....Crape myrtle
Ligustrum .... Privet
Ligustrum lucidum .... Glossy privet
Lonicera korolkowii 'Zabeli' ....Zabel's
    honeysuckle
Myrtus communis ....Myrtle
Nandina domestica ....Nandina
Nerium oleander ....Oleander
Osmanthus fragrans .... Sweet osmanthus
Osmanthus heterophyllus ....False holly
Photinia x fraseri ....Photinia
Pinus eldarica ....Mondell pine
Pittosporum tobira .... Tobira mock orange
    cultivars
Plumbago auriculata ....Plumbago
Podocarpus macrophyllus .... Yew pine
Prunus caroliniana .... Cherry laurel
Prunus ilicifolia ....Hollyleaf cherry
Prunus laurocerasus ....Laurel cherry
Prunus lusitanica ....Portugal laurel
Punica granatum ....Pomegranate
Pyracantha koidzumii .... Pyracantha
Raphiolepis indica .... Indian hawthorn
Rhamnus alaternus ....Italian buckthorn
Santolina chamaecyparissus ....Lavender
    cotton
Syringa x chinensis ....Chinese lilac
Tamarix aphylla ....Tamarisk
Viburnum tinus .... Laurustinus
Xylosma congestum ....Shiny xylosma

Juniperus species—juniper

Syringa species—lilac

UPPER SOUTH

Acer campestre .... Hedge maple
Acer ginnala ....Amur maple
Cornus stolonifera .... Red-osier dogwood
Forsythia x intermedia ....Forsythia
Euonymus kiautschovica
  'Manhattan' ....Euonymus
Pinus mugo mugo .... Mugo pine
Pinus nigra .... Austrian pine
Pinus strobus ....White pine
Taxus .... Yew species
Thuja occidentalis .... American arborvitae
Syringa persica ....Persian lilac
Syringa vulgaris ....Common lilac

GULF COAST AND FLORIDA

Abelia x grandiflora ....Glossy abelia
Bambusa .... Bamboo
Berberis x mentorensis ....Mentor barberry
Berberis thunbergii .... Japanese barberry
Buxus microphylla
  var. japonica ....Japanese box
Buxus microphylla var. koreana ....Korean
                                        littleleaf box
Buxus sempervirens .... Common boxwood
Calocedrus decurrens .... California
                                        incense cedar
Camellia japonica .... Camellia
Carissa grandiflora ....Natal plum
Chaenomeles speciosa .... Flowering quince
Citrus ....Citrus
Cocculus laurifolius ....Cocculus
Cupressus sempervirens 'Stricta' ....Italian
                                        cypress
Dodonaea viscosa ....Hopbush
Elaeagnus angustifolia ....Russian olive
Elaeagnus pungens .... Silverberry
Eriobotrya japonica .... Loquat
Euonymus alatus .... Winged burning bush
Euonymus fortunei .... Wintercreeper
Euonymus japonica .... Evergreen euonymus
Feijoa sellowiana .... Pineapple guava
Gardenia jasminoides .... Gardenia
Hibiscus syriacus ....Rose of Sharon
Ilex x altaclarensis 'Wilsonii' .. Wilson's holly
Ilex x aquifolium .... Holly, English holly
Ilex x aquipernyi 'Brilliant' .... Holly
Ilex cassine ....Dahoon holly
Ilex cornuta ....Chinese holly
Ilex crenata ....Japanese holly
Ilex glabra ....Inkberry
Ilex latifolia ....Lusterleaf holly
Ilex opaca ....American holly
Ilex pernyi ....Perny holly
Ilex vomitoria ....Yaupon
Juniperus chinensis ....Chinese juniper
Juniperus virginiana ....Eastern red cedar
Lagerstroemia indica ....Crape myrtle
Laurus nobilis .... Grecian laurel
Ligustrum japonicum .... Japanese privet
Ligustrum lucidum .... Glossy privet
Ligustrum obtusifolium
  regalianum .... Regal privet
Ligustrum ovalifolium .... California privet
Ligustrum 'Suwanee River' .... Privet
Lonicera .... Honeysuckle
Magnolia grandiflora ...... Southern magnolia
Mahonia aquifolium .... Oregon grape
Murraya paniculata ....Orange jessamine—
                                        see Citrus
Myrsine africana .... African boxwood
Myrtus communis .... Myrtle
Nandina domestica ....Nandina
Osmanthus fragrans .... Sweet osmanthus
Osmanthus heterophyllus ....False holly
Philadelphus x virginalis ....Mock orange
Photinia x fraseri .... Photinia
Pinus eldarica ....Mondell pine
Pittosporum tobira .... Tobira mock orange
Podocarpus gracilior ..Podocarpus fern pine
Podocarpus macrophyllus .... Yew pine
Populus alba 'Bolleana' ....Bolleana poplar
Populus nigra 'Italica' ....Lombardy poplar
Potentilla fruticosa ....Potentilla
Prunus caroliniana .... Carolina cherry
Prunus laurocerasus .... English laurel
Punica granatum ....Pomegranate
Pyracantha coccinea .... Pyracantha
Raphiolepis indica .... Indian hawthorn
Rhododendron indicum .... Southern
                                        indica azalea
Rhododendron obtusum .... Kurume azalea
Rosmarinus officinalis ....Rosemary
Rosa .... Rose
Spiraea ....Spiraea
Tilia cordata .... Littleleaf linden
Vaccinum ashei ....Rabbiteye blueberry
Viburnum opulus .... European
                                        highbush cranberry
Viburnum suspensum ....Sandankwa

MIDWEST

Acer campestre .... Hedge maple
Acer ginnala ....Amur maple
Berberis koreana ....Korean barberry
Berberis x mentorensis ....Mentor barberry
Berberis thunbergii .... Japanese barberry
Buxus microphylla
  var. koreana .... Korean littleleaf box
Buxus sempervirens ....English box
Caragana arborescens ..... Siberian pea tree
Carpinus betulus .... Hornbeam
Cornus mas .... Cornelian cherry dogwood
Cornus stolonifera .... Red-osier dogwood
Cotoneaster lucidus .... Hedge cotoneaster

Nandina domestica—nandina

Buxus microphylla var. *japonica*—Japanese boxwood

Crataegus grus-galli .... Cockspur thorn
Crataegus phaenopyrum . Washington thorn
Elaeagnus angustifolia .... Russian olive
Euonymus alatus .... Winged burning bush
Forsythia x intermedia .... Forsythia
Ilex meserveae .... Blue holly
Ilex verticillata .... Winterberry
Juniperus chinensis .... Chinese juniper
Juniperus scopulorum .... Rocky
Mountain juniper
Juniperus virginiana .... Eastern red cedar
Ligustrum amurense .... Amur privet
Ligustrum vulgare 'Cheyenne' ..... Cheyenne
privet
Lonicera korolkowii 'Zabeli' .... Zabel's
honeysuckle
Lonicera x xylosteum
'Clavey's Dwarf' .... Lonicera
Malus baccata 'Columnaris' .... Columnar
Siberian crabapple
Malus pumila .... Apple
Malus sargentii .... Sargent crabapple
Philadelphus x virginalis .... Mock orange
Physocarpus opulifolius 'Nanus' .... Dwarf
ninebark
Picea abies .... Norway spruce
Picea glauca .... White spruce
Pinus mugo mugo .... Mugo pine
Pinus nigra .... Austrian pine
Pinus strobus .... White pine
Potentilla fruticosa .... Potentilla
Pseudotsuga menziesii .... Douglas fir
Rhamnus cathartica ...... Common buckthorn
Rhamnus frangula 'Columnaris' ... Tallhedge
buckthorn
Salix purpurea .... Purple-osier willow
Spiraea .... Spiraea
Syringa x chinensis .... Chinese lilac
Syringa persica .... Persian lilac

Syringa vulgaris .... Common lilac and
French lilac cultivars
Thuja occidentalis .... American arborvitae
Tsuga canadensis .... Canadian hemlock
Viburnum dentatum .... Arrowwood
Viburnum lantana .... Wayfaring tree
Viburnum lentago .... Nannyberry
Viburnum opulus .... European
highbush cranberry

EAST

Abelia x grandiflora .... Glossy abelia
Acer campestre .... Hedge maple
Acer ginnala .... Amur maple
Berberis koreana .... Korean barberry
Berberis x mentorensis .... Mentor barberry
Berberis thunbergii .... Japanese barberry
Buxus microphylla
var. koreana .... Korean littleleaf box
Carpinus betulus .... Hornbeam
Cornus mas .... Cornelian cherry dogwood
Cornus stolonifera .... Red-osier dogwood
Crataegus .... Hawthorn species
Elaeagnus angustifolia .... Russian olive
Euonymus alatus .... Winged burning bush
Euonymus kiautschovica
'Manhattan' .... Euonymus
Fagus sylvatica .... Beech
Forsythia x intermedia .... Forsythia
Hibiscus syriacus .... Rose of Sharon
Ilex crenata .... Japanese holly
Ilex x meserveae .... Blue holly
Ilex opaca .... American holly
Ilex verticillata .... Winterberry
Juniperus chinensis .... Chinese juniper
Juniperus virginiana .... Eastern red cedar
Ligustrum .... Deciduous privets
Malus pumila .... Apple

Malus baccata 'Columnaris' .... Columnar
Siberian crabapple
Malus sargentii .... Sargent crabapple
Nandina domestica .... Nandina
Philadelphus x virginalis .... Mock orange
Physocarpus opulifolius .... Ninebark
Picea abies .... Norway spruce
Picea glauca .... White spruce
Pinus mugo mugo .... Mugo pine
Pinus nigra .... Austrian pine
Pinus strobus .... White pine
Potentilla fruticosa .... Potentilla
Prunus maritima .... Beach plum
Pseudotsuga menziesii .... Douglas fir
Pyracantha coccinea .... Pyracantha
Rhamnus cathartica ...... Common buckthorn
Rhamnus frangula 'Columnaris' ... Tallhedge
buckthorn
Rhododendron obtusum .... Kurume azalea
Rosa .... Rose
Salix purpurea .... Purple-osier willow
Spiraea .... Spiraea species
Syringa x chinensis .... Chinese lilac
Syringa persica .... Persian lilac
Syringa vulgaris .... Common lilac
Taxus cuspidata .... Japanese yew
Taxus x media .... Intermediate yew
Thuja occidentalis .... American arborvitae
Tsuga canadensis .... Canadian hemlock
Vaccinium corymbosum .... Blueberry
Viburnum dentatum .... Arrowwood
Viburnum lantana .... Wayfaring tree
Viburnum lentago .... Nannyberry
Viburnum opulus .... European
highbush cranberry
Weigela .... Weigela

Rosa rugosa—rugosa rose

Taxus x media—intermediate yew

ESPALIERS

Most pliable trees and shrubs make fine espaliers, but edible espaliers have obvious advantages. Training fruit against walls is a practice that began in Western culture with the Romans, and reached a state of high art in medieval castle and monastery gardens. Apples and pears benefited from the heat that radiated from the garden walls. Herbs laid out nearby in intricate beds flourished in full sun—free from the shade of trees. In warm, Mediterranean climates, rosemary and grapes were the favored espalier subjects.

Espalier methods range in complexity from planting pre-trained forms available from nurseries to complicated techniques that are more like botanic architecture. Low-maintenance espaliers in simple, free-form patterns are composed of relatively slow-growing plants that do not require constant pruning.

Every espalier needs some support and attention for at least three growing seasons. Shapes are attained gradually. After the desired pattern is formed, maintenance consists of checking and retying supports, snipping out unwanted growth and rubbing off buds before they develop into unwanted branches. Some espaliers mature into large plants with stout trunks and branches. Supports may be removed when plants reach this size.

PATTERNS
Informal patterns are attractive arrangements of branches that do not conform to a traditional shape. Minimum training is necessary. You simply follow your imagination and the plant's natural branching character.

Formal patterns conform to traditional designs. Branches are trained to follow defined lines. Because the requirements are strict, few plants can be manipulated into formal patterns. Those that are adapted to formal training are the most versatile plants to espalier. A list of these plants appears on page 61. Apples and pears are included in this group. These can take on any shape, from horizontal, French-style, garden borders only one foot high to elaborate, lattice patterns known as the *Belgian fence*.

PLACEMENT GUIDELINES
Many fruit and flower espaliers benefit from the protection of windbreaks. But espaliers placed too close to windbreak plants will be forced to compete with them for nutrients and light. This may slow plant growth, which is an advantage in some cases. Consider the particulars of your situation before you plant.

Be aware of the sun's exposure when selecting a wall support for an espalier. Some plants thrive in cool shade; others prefer sunny heat. Fruit trees need about six hours of sunlight daily. South-facing walls receive the most sun and heat. East-facing walls receive morning sun and afternoon

Left: Container espaliers take up little space, can be positioned wherever growing conditions are most favorable and move when you do. Pruning is easy during the deciduous dormant period, when the form is clearly visible. Above: 'Golden Delicious' apple, trained on post-and-wire supports, is a heavy producer of fruit.

shade. West-facing walls get morning shade and intense afternoon sun. Shade from nearby trees or buildings may alter amounts of sunshine available to espaliers.

Heat from the sun is radiated off exposed walls and paving. This is an advantage or a liability. In mild-climate regions, heat-loving plants thrive when placed directly against south- or west-facing walls. A site out of the wind with an overhang usually provides protection from frost. This permits you to grow varieties slightly out of their normal range.

In hot-summer climates, heat from south- and west-facing walls may cook fruit and scorch espaliers. To avoid this, train on a wire or wood frame positioned about 6 inches from the wall. In cold-winter climates, place cold-tender plants subject to frost damage out of the wind in a shady or partly shady location.

Fruit-producing espaliers trained on post-and-wire fences will be exposed to the greatest amount of sunlight if fences run north to south.

CHOOSING THE PATTERN AND THE PLANT

Pay close attention to shaping and pruning espaliers started from scratch during the first several seasons. Single cordons and informal fan patterns are the easiest. Complicated forms in three dimensions are for dedicated, experienced gardeners only.

Pick a plant variety to suit the pattern, or vice versa. Many species are not suited to formal, symmetrical shapes. Generally, slow-growing plants make good espaliers. It is also necessary to know the mature size of plants. Plan spacing and supports when you select a pattern to determine the number of plants to buy. A single cordon hedge effect requires spacing plants 1 to 3 feet apart. Dwarf fruit are spaced about 6 to 8 feet apart. Full-size trees and shrubs spread 10 to 20 feet or more.

Plants with arching branches, notably *Pyracantha* and *Forsythia* species, can be trained to spread much greater than their branches normally grow.

If you are planting more than one espalier, choose one variety for a uniform appearance, or several varieties for a mosaic effect. A selection of varieties with different fruit maturity dates—early, midseason and late—will extend the harvest season.

ROOTSTOCKS

Dwarfs are recommended for apple and pear espaliers. They begin to bear fruit at a young age, and their growth is more restrained than full-size trees.

A wide variety of apple rootstocks are available. Many are labeled simply as "dwarf" or "semidwarf" with no further explanation. However, some labels give more specific details. For example, you might see the initials M

Espalier Supports for Cold Locations

At night, cold air flows down hillsides and slopes. It can be trapped by solid plantings or walls, freezing espaliers and nearby plants. Espaliers trained against open fences or on post-and-wire supports allow air to pass through.

and M.M. M stands for *Malling*. M.M. stands for *Merton-Malling*. These names designate the origin of the rootstock. M.7 and M.M.106 are both semidwarf. M.M.106 is slightly larger. M.9 and M.4 are more dwarf. These trees will always require support, and are excellent if 6 feet is the maximum desired height. They produce more fruit than non-dwarfs for the space occupied. M.26 is a dwarf with a faster growth rate than most other dwarfs. M.2 and M.M.111 produce large, vigorous trees adapted to poor soil conditions.

ERECTING SUPPORTS

Materials for the espalier frame should be sturdy and built to last. Nails, screws, angle irons, pipe, bars, nipples, turnbuckles and wires should be galvanized to resist rust. Use 8- to 16-gage wire, depending on the ultimate size of the plant variety selected. The smaller the gage number, the thicker the wire. Vinyl-clad wire is rust resistant. Black wire is practically invisible on free-standing supports. Choose colors to blend with wall surfaces.

Bamboo poles or lightweight wood stakes are often used for additional support between wires. It is not necessary to treat them with a preservative to resist rotting, but other wood, especially fence posts, should be treated. Or, use pressure-treated lumber. See page 58.

Fasten espalier branches loosely with plastic plant ties or plain cord. If fasteners are tied too tight, they girdle and kill branches. Check ties regularly—at least once a year.

Take advantage of existing surfaces when you build the support. Espaliers can be tied directly to chain-link fences. Wood fences do not absorb and release as much heat as block walls, and are easy to nail. Trace patterns directly on the support with wire. The method of wall support that you choose depends on whether plants can grow directly against walls in your climate.

Nail or drill into walls or into the mortar joints between bricks or blocks. Insert expansion bolts to hold hardware securely. For more securely structured frames, attach wooden posts or angle irons with holes to accept screws and support wires. Space supports to allow plants to spread.

Chain-link fence provides support for many kinds of espaliers. 'Comice' pear greatly improves the appearance of the fence and creates privacy.

Post-and-wire framework supports apple espalier. It is important to build supports to last: They will be in use for many years.

Substantial frames placed 6 inches or more from the wall surface should be held in place with threaded pipe. Drill into walls, force in a lead collar and screw in threaded pipe. Attach a wire, welded rebar or wood frame. If desired, finish off threaded pipe ends with flanges.

It is possible to train branches directly around pipes, as long as they are placed at predetermined distances for formal patterns, and training is done in gradual stages.

POST CONSTRUCTION FOR FREE-STANDING SUPPORTS

Most free-standing supports utilize post-construction techniques used in fencing. After posts are set, a wire or wood trellis is installed. Posts may be positioned close to walls or included in the landscape like a fence.

Use wooden 2x4 or 4x4 posts or 1-1/2-inch-diameter metal pipe fence posts. Posts must be buried *at least* 2 feet deep in the ground. A poured concrete collar will hold posts more securely than tamped earth.

Space posts according to espalier pattern and plant size. Place one plant between posts set 6 to 10 feet apart, or position two plants 6 feet apart between 4x4 posts set 12 feet apart.

String wire at regular, 12- to 36-inch intervals, depending on espalier pattern. Some people position plants first to determine the height of the lowest wire. No matter what interval is chosen, wire courses should be parallel. Choose a wire gage that can support the plant's mature weight and the distance spanned. Eight gage is best for posts spaced farther than 6 feet apart.

Position screw eyes on end posts. Drill holes through middle posts in alignment with screw eyes. String wire between posts, and place a turnbuckle at one end of each wire to hold them taut. Variation: Use 4x4 end posts with screw eyes and turnbuckles. String wires and pull taut. Attach wire to 2x4 middle posts with staples.

You can build wooden trellises or buy them prefabricated. Install trellises against walls or on free-standing supports. It is helpful to devise a way to remove the trellis if painting or other maintenance is necessary. You can also nail trellises to fence posts. Do not force the trellis to span large distances that will produce sagging. Eight feet is the recommended maximum span for a 2x4. Consult the HPBook, *Fences, Gates and Walls,* for more information on trellis construction.

Espaliers in containers can be supported by small poles or posts inserted directly into the soil, or nail them onto the sides of the container. String wire at intervals on this framework. Frames of welded *rebar,* steel construction rod, are also useful. The simplest framework consists of a few stakes nailed to the back of the container or poked into the soil.

LUMBER PRESERVATIVES

Wooden posts placed in direct contact with the ground are susceptible to rot. Decay can be delayed by using *pressure-treated wood.* This is lumber treated with preservatives forced deep into the cells of the wood. Pressure-treated lumber may have a greenish or brownish color. Many types are safe to use around plants. Use wood designated as *LP-22* for ground-contact applications. Use *LP-2* for above-ground use.

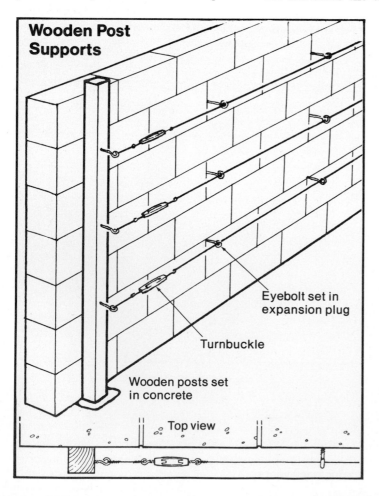

Wooden Post Supports

Eyebolt set in expansion plug

Turnbuckle

Wooden posts set in concrete

Top view

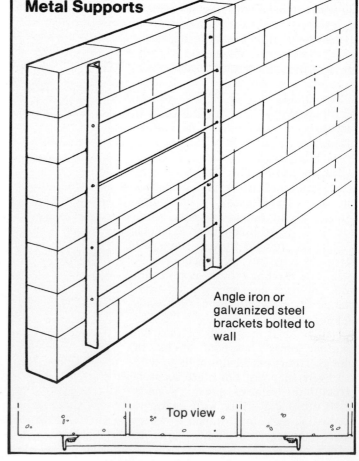

Metal Supports

Angle iron or galvanized steel brackets bolted to wall

Top view

Apple espaliers on a small balcony are located high above a city street. Plants are exposed to strong winds, so they require heavy-duty supports.

Metal bracing is bolted to wooden framework and railing to support espaliers in winds.

Espalier pattern is a formal Verrier palmette. Wooden framework and plant produces a light, screening effect.

Post-and-Wire Supports

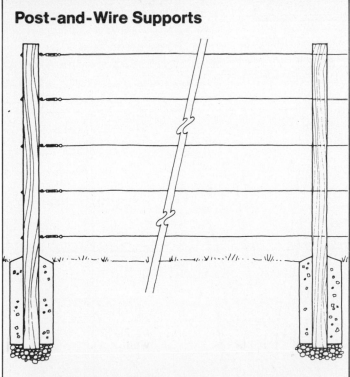

Use 8- to 16-gage wire, depending on mature size of plant. Turnbuckle keeps wire taut. Poured concrete holds better than tamped earth.

Training Formal Patterns

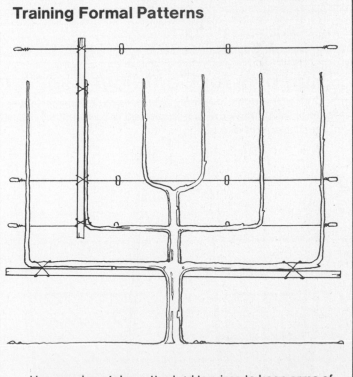

Use wooden stakes attached to wires to keep arms of espaliers straight.

You can apply a preservative yourself. Use copper or zinc naphthenate, trade name Cuprinol. It is not toxic to plants, but it turns wood greenish. This is rarely a problem because espalier limbs usually cover their framework. If green wood is objectionable, paint it, or treat only the portion that will be in contact with the soil.

Preservatives can be brushed or rolled on. But for best penetration, soak lumber in a large container or trough full of preservative. Make a trough of concrete blocks or 4x4's, and line it with plastic.

Whenever you saw through treated lumber, including pressure-treated lumber, paint preservative on the freshly cut ends. Do not burn wood scraps of treated lumber: Toxic fumes can be released.

Avoid using creosote and *penta,* pentachlorophenol, as preservatives. They are toxic to plants and humans.

BUYING PLANTS

Before planting, take a sketch of your espalier pattern to the nursery and ask a knowledgeable clerk for help. If you do not buy pre-trained espaliers, choose young, vigorous plants. They respond well to training. Deciduous varieties purchased bare root are inexpensive and ready to prune. Deciduous fruit trees should be one- or two-year-old *whips*—straight stems.

If you are planting fruit-producing plants, ask about pollination requirements. Some require a pollinator nearby to produce fruit. Ask about the rootstock if the plant is not labeled. Keep in mind that apple and pear dwarfs or semidwarfs bear fruit earlier than full-size trees.

PLANTING

Review pages 73 to 81 for basic information on soil preparation, heeling in and other planting procedures. In addition, here are some special pointers for planting espaliers.

If you are planting fruit trees, be sure the graft union, if present, is at least 2 inches above the ground *after* the soil has been watered and tamped down. The union is a bulge just above the roots where the *scion*—the trunk of the tree—was grafted.

Cordons are often grown at a 30° to 45° angle to increase the number of fruiting spurs. These trained forms are called *oblique* cordons. They grow more slowly so they are easy to control, and require less height than the same-size vertical cordon. This means they are more productive. For the most effective results, plant oblique cordons at an angle or lower them gradually later on. Position the scion so it will be on the top side of oblique cordons.

Place plants at least 6 inches from walls or fences to permit trunks to expand. Space plants according to their ultimate size or the size you plan to prune them. Space single upright or oblique cordons 1 foot or more apart. Space dwarf fruit trees 6 to 8 feet apart. Apples on M.27 rootstock should be planted 4 feet apart; M.9 rootstock 10 feet apart; M.26 rootstock 10 to 12 feet apart; M.106 rootstock 12 to 15 feet apart; M.2, M.7

Supports for Container Espaliers

For plants with heavy limbs, attach espalier supports directly to container. If limb growth is expected to be relatively lightweight, insert supports into soil.

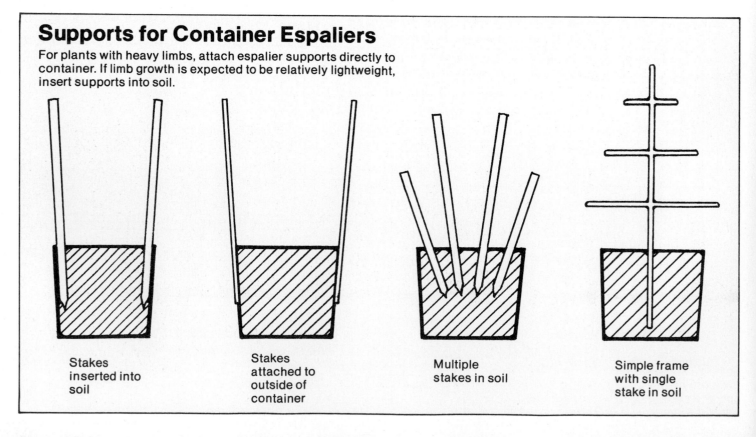

Stakes inserted into soil

Stakes attached to outside of container

Multiple stakes in soil

Simple frame with single stake in soil

and M.111 rootstock 15 to 18 feet apart.

Wall footings often extend below ground into the area where you might want to place your espalier rootball. If this is the case, bend the roots carefully to get as close to the wall as possible. Or, place the plant at an angle, pointing the trunk toward the wall. You can gradually train the trunk back and up against the wall.

Espaliers trained against a wall often blossom earlier than free-standing trees. This can create a problem if another tree is needed to bloom at the same time as a pollinator. Plant an additional espalier on the same wall, or graft on a pollinator branch.

Organic or inorganic fertilizers supply necessary plant nutrients. High-nitrogen fertilizers stimulate fruit trees to produce fast, undesirable, woody growth. Be conservative in applying fertilizer to fruit trees. Too little is better than too much. Wait for the second growing season before fertilizing and then apply a conservative amount of a slow-release type.

Both productive and functional, edible espalier of sweet oranges requires infrequent but careful pruning.

INFORMAL ESPALIERS

Acer circinatum .... Vine maple
Berberis .... Barberry
Camellia japonica .... Camellia
Camellia sasanqua .... Sasanqua camellia
Caragana arborescens lorbergi .... Ferny caragana
Carissa grandiflora .... Natal plum
Chaenomeles speciosa .... Flowering quince
Citrus .... Citrus—all varieties
Cocculus laurifolius .... Cocculus
Cornus mas .... Cornelian cherry dogwood
Cotoneaster .... Cotoneaster
Crataegus .... Hawthorn
Cydonia oblonga .... Fruiting quince
Dodonaea viscosa 'Green' .. Green hopbush
Dodonaea viscosa 'Purpurea' and 'Saratoga' .... Purple hopbush
Elaeagnus pungens .... Silverberry
Eriobotrya japonica .... Loquat
Escallonia 'Balfouri' .... Escallonia
Eucalyptus caesia .... Eucalyptus
Eucalyptus erythrocorys .... Red-cap gum
Eucalyptus orbifolia .... Round-leafed mallee
Euonymus alata .... Winged burning bush
Euonymus fortunei .... Wintercreeper
Euonymus japonica .... Evergreen euonymus
Euonymus kiautschovica 'Manhattan' .... Euonymus
Feijoa sellowiana .... Pineapple guava
Forsythia x intermedia .... Forsythia
Gardenia jasminoides .... Gardenia
Hibiscus syriacus .... Rose of Sharon
Ilex .... Holly
Juniperus .... Juniper
Lagerstroemia indica .... Crape myrtle
Ligustrum japonicum .... Japanese privet
Ligustrum texanum .... Waxleaf privet
Magnolia grandiflora ...... Southern magnolia
Malus pumila .... Apple
Malus sargentii .... Sargent crabapple
Nerium oleander .... Oleander
Osmanthus fragrans .... Sweet osmanthus
Osmanthus heterophyllus .... False holly
Philadelphus x virginalis .... Mock orange

Photinia x fraseri .... Photinia
Plumbago auriculata .... Plumbago
Podocarpus gracilior .. Podocarpus fern pine
Podocarpus macrophyllus .... Yew pine
Prunus ..... European and Japanese varieties
Prunus caroliniana .... Cherry laurel
Prunus laurocerasus 'Zabeliana' ...... English laurel
Prunus serrulata 'Amanogawa' ..... Japanese flowering cherry
Punica granatum .... Pomegranate
Pyracantha fortuneana 'Graberi' Pyracantha
Pyracantha coccinea 'Government Red' .... Pyracantha
Pyrus communis .... Pear
Pyrus hybrid .... Pear-apple
Pyrus kawakamii .... Evergreen pear
Raphiolepis indica 'Majestic Beauty' .... Indian hawthorn
Rhododendron .... Some rhododendron varieties
Rosa .... Rose
Rosmarinus officinalis .... Rosemary
Taxus .... Yew species
Viburnum tinus .... Viburnum
Weigela florida .... Weigela
Xylosma congestum .... Shiny xylosma

FORMAL ESPALIERS

Camellia japonica .... Camellia
Camellia sasanqua .... Sasanqua camellia
Forsythia x intermedia .... Forsythia
Ilex cornuta 'Burfordii' .... Burford holly
Ilex crenata .... Japanese holly
Citrus limon .... Lemon—see Citrus
Magnolia grandiflora ...... Southern magnolia
Malus pumila .... Apple
Prunus serrulata 'Amanogawa' ..... Columnar Japanese flowering cherry
Pyracantha 'Graberi' .... Pyracantha
Pyrus communis .... Pear
Pyrus hybrid .... Pear-apple
Pyrus kawakamii .... Evergreen pear
Taxus cuspidata .... Japanese yew
Taxus x media .... Intermediate yew

Pyrus kawakamii, evergreen pear, as informal espalier.

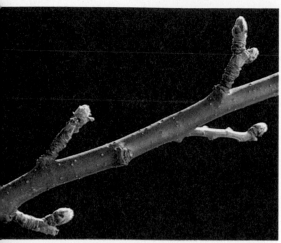

Long-lived spur common to apples, above, and pears is a type of branch that lives for years, producing the flowering buds that develop into the fruit.

Short-lived spur found on apricots, above, also produces flower buds. Spur dies within two to five years and must be pruned periodically so that it will be replaced with new growth.

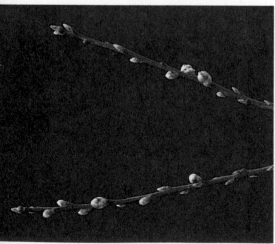

Peaches and nectarines bear fruit on shoots that must be replaced yearly. For this reason, a continual supply of new, young wood is essential. Severe pruning each year helps ensure optimum fruiting.

CLASSIC PATTERNS

Forcing plants into patterns goes against their nature, but is a challenge that produces lovely, lacy structures. Classic, time-honored espalier patterns were not devised simply to make use of small spaces or to be purely ornamental. They evolved as early horticulturists learned to control the vigor of major branches, referred to as *limbs* or *arms,* to avoid excess woody growth. This in turn increased the yield of fruit.

Apples and pears are traditional espalier subjects. They form *spurs*—short, stubby, modified branches—that bear the flower buds that produce flowers and fruit. Because fruit tree branches are generally more vigorous when allowed to grow upright, training them to grow at a more horizontal angle forces energy into the spurs, accelerating their development. Branches can be trained to the desired angle from the start, or gradually lowered. Begin lowering branches in the dormant season after one season of fast, vertical growth. The latter approach produces the pattern in less time.

Slow, diligent training is the key to success with formal espaliers. The word "formal" in garden history has come to mean *symmetrical, ordered, somewhat geometric and neat.* Espalier specialist Dr. Robert Stebbins of Oregon State University has this comment on formal espaliers: "The formal patterns were designed to achieve an equilibrium between growth and fruiting throughout the tree without excessive amounts of pruning. Informal patterns are easier than formal types, but production and fruit quality may be less."

Most classic patterns have retained their French names. There are many variations of the patterns and their names. The word "espalier" has been applied to at least one specific pattern. The French use it to describe a tree that has branches attached directly to a wall. In this book, any plant trained to a flat plane is an espalier.

In the past, skilled gardeners used espaliers of various plants to form the walls of three-dimensional garden structures, grafting branches together where they crossed. You can use versatile, single cordons to form arches or pattern edges. Try to cover your support framework with espalier limbs and single cordons.

PRUNING ESPALIERS

Prune espaliers as often as necessary during the growing and dormant seasons to maintain the pattern. Pinching out buds you know you do not want to develop is an effective control method. Remove watersprouts and suckers whenever they appear.

Summer pruning of apples and pears is recommended to promote greater spur formation. Spurs that form may be much longer than their slow-growing counterparts on deciduous fruit trees pruned during the dormant season.

Start pruning in late spring or early summer after the first flush of growth. Cut back side shoots to three buds 4 to 6 inches long from the main limb. New shoots will sprout from the cuts. Whenever new shoot growth is longer than 10 or 12 inches, cut back to one or two buds from the last cut.

Usually a minimum of two summer prunings are necessary. One pruning each month in summer is better.

In cold climates, avoid pruning in late summer. Early fall frosts can damage the new, cold-tender growth stimulated by pruning. Wait until the dormant season to remove unwanted growth.

Avoid pruning the *main leader,* the central trunk or stem, until it has reached the desired length. Pruning this limb stimulates a new, vigorous extension leader to form. This new leader is often bare of spurs and is usually not as easy to hold to a pattern as other branches.

Tying vigorous shoots so their tips face down may force them to form flower buds. Shoots that never attain a length greater than 9 inches often have fruiting buds at their tips. Do not cut these back. Some experts recommend pinching out flower buds in the first spring after planting to prevent fruit formation. If you do this, be very careful not to damage spurs. Thin excess fruit from spurs when they are thumbnail size. Again, be careful not to damage spurs. As trees mature, their spurs can become crowded with buds. Thin spurs of weak and excess buds, leaving about two or three buds per spur.

The classic patterns shown on the following pages are for people who like to clip and prune. Others should not avoid espaliers, but they should let the plant determine its own informal pattern.

Espalier, Tier or Horizontal T

This popular pattern is called *espalier* in Europe. It is known in the United States as a *tier espalier* or *horizontal T* to distinguish it from other espalier patterns. Use plants from the *formal* list, page 61. Prune them to force branches to form at desired locations.

Cut back a leader to just above three buds. This stimulates buds to produce several new shoots. Train new shoots to the pattern. These beginning steps are the same steps that are necessary to start the *palmette oblique, Belgian fence, Verrier palmette* and *U-shaped* espaliers, described in the following pages. You can also start a horizontal T using a young, branched tree. To do this, make the cut, and lower the best remaining one or two branches gradually, using stakes tied to the wires.

This pattern with a first level approximately 12 inches above the soil makes a classic garden border. It is often called a *single horizontal cordon*. A double tier maintained at the second-wire level produces a low-hedge effect. Several tiers create a full-hedge effect.

The disadvantage of the horizontal T is sporadic limb vigor. Watersprouts tend to form on vigorous, low limbs close to the central leader. The ends of these lower limbs tend to lose vigor. Cut out watersprouts, but don't prune excessively or it can disrupt the balance between shoot growth and fruiting. Train limbs straight to avoid excessive watersprout formation. Tie or tape as much as necessary.

Develop only three tiers on dwarf fruit. Develop more tiers on full-size trees.

Ancient apple in a horizontal T covers a lathhouse wall. This is the formal pattern that most people associate with the word *espalier*.

Tier or Horizontal T

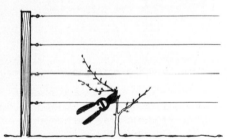

1. Head bare-root whip or young branched tree at or near first wire. Leave at least three buds or branches below cut. Tie branches to wire below cut.

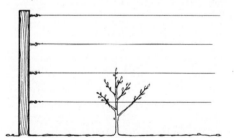

2. During first growing season, permit buds to develop into shoots.

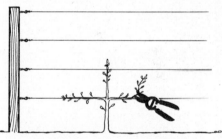

3. Choose three best shoots and remove others. Train two horizontally along wires and one vertically. Shorten long branches so all are approximately equal in length.

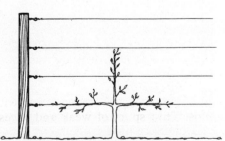

4. During the growing season, prune or pinch plant regularly to maintain the pattern. Shorten side shoots and subshoots to spurs.

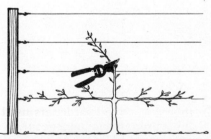

5. In second dormant season, head plant at or near second wire. Repeat process of training new shoots and central leader from buds that develop next season.

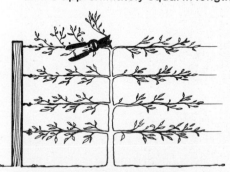

6. A minimum of four years is required to obtain an espalier this height. Each dormant season, repeat steps 1 through 4 as necessary to hold pattern and develop spurs.

Single Cordons

The name *cordon* means *rope, ribbon* or *cord*. Single cordons are the simplest espalier form. They are straight stems with severely shortened branches. On fruit trees, these shortened branches are loaded with fruit buds, making the cordon one of the most efficient fruit-producing forms. Many varieties can be grown in a space no taller or wider than most fences. Choose plants from the *formal* list only.

Vertical cordons are versatile. They are often combined with other espalier patterns to form edges at the end of a row. They are easy to train up end posts to conceal framework. For a hedge effect, space 1 to 3 feet apart and train on post-and-wire frames.

Or, stake plants individually without a framework. The farther apart cordons are spaced, the more open their screening effect. Use them as fences or as dividers to separate different sections of the garden. Vertical cordons can also be trained like vines into arches or over pergolas.

Oblique cordons are trained at a 30° to 60° angle from the ground. Plant at the desired angle or lower plants gradually as they grow. Training at an angle permits the cordon to grow longer yet still be within arm's reach. It also encourages increased fruit production.

Oblique cordons grow more slowly than vertical cordons so more energy is forced into *fruiting* buds instead of into *leaf* and *shoot* buds. For rows run-

ning north to south, point tops toward the north. For rows running east to west, point tops toward the east. Oblique cordons also make an attractive screen.

Horizontal cordons are the classic French kitchen-garden border. Apple or pear whips are bent down gradually and trained horizontally 12 to 18 inches above the soil. It is actually easier to achieve the look of a horizontal cordon by pruning in the horizontal-T espalier manner described on page 63.

The *Braided* and *Arcure* variations shown on page 65 produce lovely, light screening effects. Both begin as single cordons, then one branch is trained to a pattern. Maintaining them requires constant pinching.

Vertical Cordon

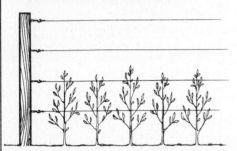

1. Select high-headed or unpruned trees. Stake individual plants or train on wire framework. Cut back side shoots to spurs. Do not cut back leader.

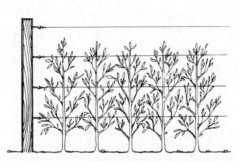

2. Maintain dominant central leader. Prune new side shoots to spurs. Prune old side shoots, permitting subshoots to develop, then cut back to spurs.

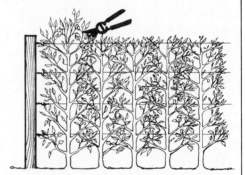

3. Continue to shorten side shoots and subshoots. Prune leader only when it reaches desired height.

Oblique Cordon

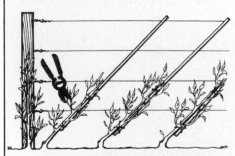

1. Select high-headed or unpruned trees. Space 2 to 3 feet apart at a 60° to 45° angle with bud union on top. Tie to stakes that are attached to wires. Cut back side shoots to spurs. Keep them at this length. Do not cut back leader. Plant a single, vertical cordon at end of row.

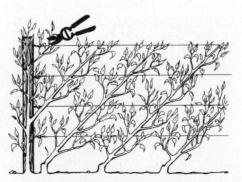

2. Do not prune leader until desired height is reached. Prune new side shoots to spurs. Keep old side shoots shortened to spurs, permitting spurs to form. Remove stakes when trunks are stout enough to stand alone. Tie trunks to wires.

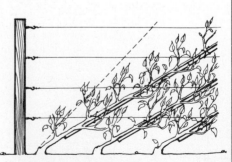

3. Optional: Lower cordons gradually to 30° angle. This allows branches to grow longer, controls vigorous growth and forces more fruit. Do not cut back leaders if you plan to lower cordons.

Single, vertical cordons of apples planted approximately 1-1/2 feet apart look like a hedge and produce an abundant crop.

Horizontal and Braided Variations

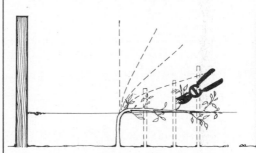

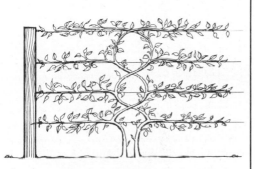

1. Horizontal: Plant whips and bend trunk gradually down, using stakes as necessary. Shorten all side shoots to spurs. Train leader as long as desired along wire.

1. Braided: Plant two whips and bend trunks gradually down. Allow two side shoots to develop. Shorten all other shoots.

2. Braided: Train original two shoots to braided pattern over the seasons. Train single side shoots as horizontals along wires. Shorten all others to spurs.

Arcure Variation

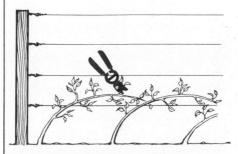

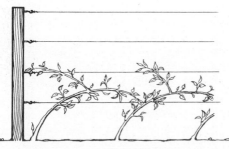

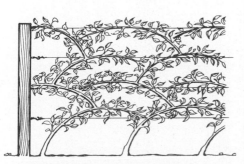

1. Arcure: Select whips that are 3 to 4 feet tall. Plant at a slight angle. Allow new growth to begin, then bend and tie whips to form arches. Leave only one new shoot for each plant at top center of arch.

2. At end of first growing season, bend top center shoot down in opposite direction of arch and tie in place. Remove all but one of its top center shoots.

3. Repeat process to develop successive arched branches. Shorten all side shoots to spurs. Prune regularly to maintain pattern. There will be little increase in length of oldest shoots growing at an angle.

Palmette Oblique

Traditionally, this pattern has all tiers of branches trained at the same angle—narrow, broad or 45°, depending on available space. The pattern is formed much like the horizontal T, so choose plants from the *formal* list only.

The training technique illustrated here does not produce as stylized a palmette as the traditional method. Branch angles are chosen to regulate fruiting. The bottom tier is trained at 45°, the middle tiers spread more obliquely and the top tier is horizontal. Permit the branches to grow as far as possible for greatest fruit yield. You can regulate the angle of each individual branch to control branch vigor. Gradually lower over-vigorous branches by training to almost-horizontal. This forces energy into the fruit buds. Train weak branches at an upright angle until the desired length is obtained. Gradually lower them to the chosen angle.

Arms—limbs or branches—of palmette oblique can be raised or lowered to control fruiting.

Palmette Oblique

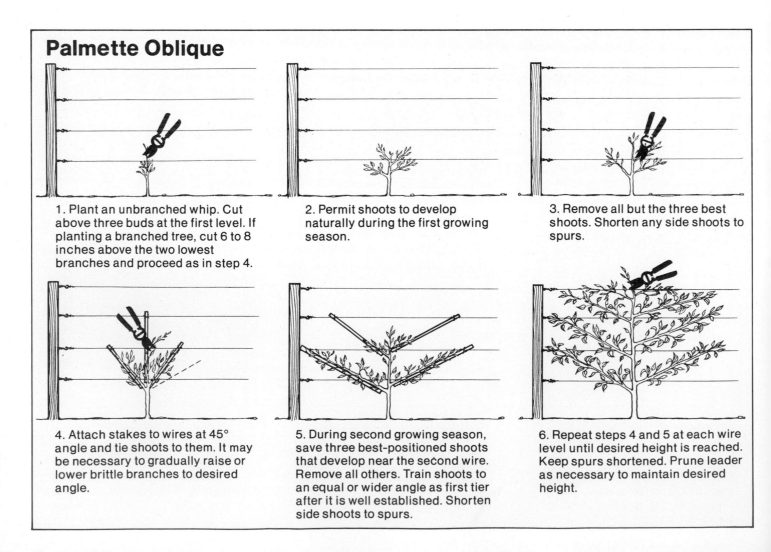

1. Plant an unbranched whip. Cut above three buds at the first level. If planting a branched tree, cut 6 to 8 inches above the two lowest branches and proceed as in step 4.

2. Permit shoots to develop naturally during the first growing season.

3. Remove all but the three best shoots. Shorten any side shoots to spurs.

4. Attach stakes to wires at 45° angle and tie shoots to them. It may be necessary to gradually raise or lower brittle branches to desired angle.

5. During second growing season, save three best-positioned shoots that develop near the second wire. Remove all others. Train shoots to an equal or wider angle as first tier after it is well established. Shorten side shoots to spurs.

6. Repeat steps 4 and 5 at each wire level until desired height is reached. Keep spurs shortened. Prune leader as necessary to maintain desired height.

Belgian Fence

The charm of this pattern is due to its elegant, open, lattice effect that is especially apparent when deciduous trees are out of leaf. A dramatic, finished appearance requires exact spacing in a straight line, training all arms to the same angle and positioning all crotches, or Y's, at the same level. At least three trees plus two single cordons at the ends are necessary to complete the pattern edges.

The longer a Belgian fence is extended, the greater its visual impact. Five feet is the recommended minimum height. An angle of 45° is traditional for the Y's. The illustrations on this page have 60° angles.

This is a formal pattern, devised specifically for apples or pears. It is possible to use mixed varieties of apples and pears within the same fence. Advanced horticulturists can also train lemons, apricots, plums, cherries, peaches or nectarines to this pattern if trees are spaced farther apart. Other trees with large leaves from the formal list, page 61, require greater spacing to display the pattern. Spacing farther than 2 feet produces a more oblique diamond shape.

Oblique cordons planted alternately left and right in a row at 45° also produce a Belgian fence effect.

The *losange variation,* illustrated below, also requires wider spacing to display the finished pattern. This method permits side branches to develop, which quickly produces a dense effect. For these reasons, the losange is well suited to large-scale uses where space is not a limitation.

Beautiful lattice pattern of Belgian fence is most noticeable on deciduous plants when they drop their leaves.

Belgian Fence

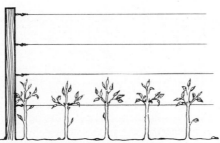

1. Space whips evenly. Cut above two buds at first desired level, 1 to 2 feet above soil. It may be necessary to adjust wire level to whip height.

2. Permit shoots to develop naturally through first growing season.

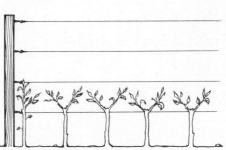

3. Remove all but the two best shoots. Leave one inward-facing shoot on the end cordon to form pattern edge.

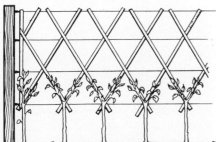

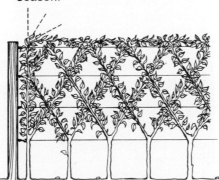

4. Attach stakes to wires at a 45° or 60° angle. Tie shoots to stakes. It may be necessary to decrease angle and gradually lower stakes to chosen angle. Train end cordons vertically. Select branches and train at chosen angle to complete pattern. Shorten side shoots that develop spurs.

5. Do not prune leaders in the following years. When desired height is reached, gradually bend leaders horizontally and train along to wire for a finished edge. Keep side shoots shortened to spurs.

Losange variation: Space whips at least 2 feet apart. Follow steps 1 through 3 for Belgian fence. As two shoots grow, allow two side shoots to develop at second wire level. Train them at a 45° angle to pattern on stakes.

Verrier Palmette

This popular, formal palmette pattern was named for Louis Verrier, a French horticulturist who taught the art of espalier in the middle part of the 19th century. Choose plants from the *formal* list only for this pattern.

There are many ways to train plants to the Verrier palmette. Use a post-and-wire framework and strong stakes tied securely to the wires to support the vertical arms. They require a rigid frame to keep them straight. Henry Leuthardt Nursery in New York state recommends that eyebolts be set into the wall behind the arms at the exact position where they will be bent. Arms are then tied to horizontal or vertical wires strung between the eyebolts. Stakes are used to supplement the framework. See illustration, page 59.

The pattern starts in the same way as a tiered espalier. When branches have reached a length of at least 12 inches they are gradually bent up in 5° to 10° increments. Space tiers about 12 inches apart. Keep the distance equal between vertical arms.

If the branches are too stiff to turn up at a sharp angle, make fine saw cuts halfway through the limbs 1 to 2 inches apart on the outer sides of the bend. This permits a sharp bend to be made. Cuts usually heal in a season.

Old pear in a six-arm Verrier palmette pattern is sturdy enough to stand with no support. Few espaliers hold their pattern when supports are removed.

Verrier Palmette

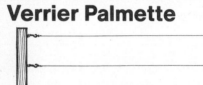
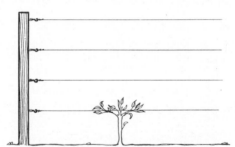
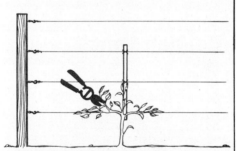

1. Plant an unbranched whip. Cut above three buds at first desired level, often only 6 inches above soil. Leave three buds below this first cut.

2. Permit new shoots to develop naturally through first growing season.

3. Select three best shoots and remove others. Shorten any side shoots to spurs. Tie stake to wires and train leader vertically up stake. Train branches horizontally along wire.

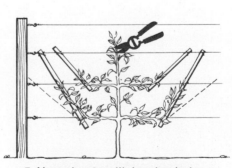
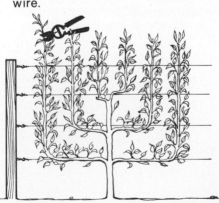
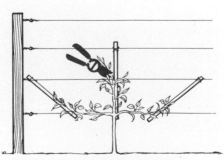

4. During dormant season, tie stakes to wires. If branches are the desired length, gradually bend branches up first tier. Cut leader at height of second wire.

5. New shoots will develop below cut, as in step 2. Select three best shoots as in step 3. Continue bending first branches as necessary to upright position. Bend second tier when branches reach desired length. Cut leader at height of third wire in dormant season.

6. Repeat previous steps to develop third tier. Finish bending second tier to pattern. Train arms as high as desired, then maintain at that level. Some plants will hold pattern without support when they are mature. Remove frames if desired.

U-Shapes

Most of the general remarks about Verrier palmette espaliers apply to formal U-shapes, including the necessity of choosing plants from the *formal* list only. The single U and U with a center vertical limb are also called *multiple vertical cordons*. They may be grown obliquely like cordons, but they are formed in a manner similar to a Verrier palmette. The distance between each vertical arm should be equal. Some people train short horizontal branches off the U's at even distances along the wires to increase the amount of fruiting wood.

Verrier palmette is easier to train than double and triple U-shapes, and is more productive. The triple U is sometimes called a *candelabra*. It is difficult to form and the training takes a lot of time. The double and triple U prevents excess vigor of limbs close to the trunk. All limbs are equally balanced in vigor.

Four-armed Verrier palmette pears add visual relief to a blank wall.

U-Shapes

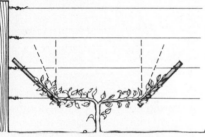

1. Single U: Begin with steps 1 and 2 of Verrier palmette on page 68. Cut out all but two best shoots. Train these horizontally along wires until desired length is obtained. Bend tips up gradually, using stakes tied to wires.

2. Permit branches to grow as high as desired and maintain them at that length.

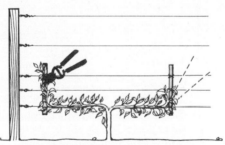

1. Double U: Follow steps 1 and 2 of Verrier palmette. Save two shoots and train horizontally along wires. Bend up as shown for Single U. In dormant season, cut branches at height of second wire above two buds.

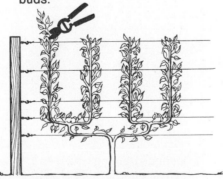

2. Permit shoots to develop below cut. Save two best shoots and remove all others. Train shoots horizontally along wires, bending them up, using stakes tied to wires. Maintain at desired height.

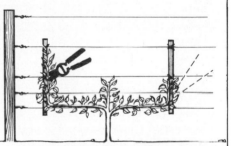

1. Triple U: Begin with steps 1 and 2 of Verrier palmette, but save *three* shoots. Train one up and two horizontally along wires. Bend up two outer branch tips like single U. Then cut all three at height of second wire above two buds.

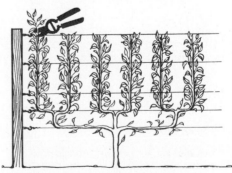

2. Allow new shoots to develop at second cut. Select best two and remove all others. Train these shoots horizontally along wires and bend up, using stakes. Maintain at desired height.

Drapeau Marchand

Early fruit production is the benefit of this training method originating in Anjou, France. Drapeau Marchand is an informal pattern, but maximum fruiting on apples, pears and figs is still possible. Other fruit to try with this method include peach, nectarine, plum, citrus and apricot.

Some people train the bottom branch on the downward side of the trunk up to the lowest wire. This creates a fuller appearance.

To make the pruning and training steps for this pattern easy to follow, the plants in the illustrations appear more formal than they actually are. In the garden, the effect is more loose and casual. Many commercial orchards use this method and it is well suited to windy sites.

Drapeau Marchand is an informal pattern that is usually easy to maintain. Maximum fruiting on many kinds of plants, including apples, pears and figs is possible when grown in this form.

Drapeau Marchand

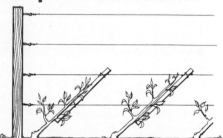

1. Plant whips or branched trees at 40° to 60° angle. Tie plant to first wire, or tie to stakes attached to wires if length exceeds wire. Space trees by size, approximately 8 to 12 feet apart for many dwarfs. Do not prune leader.

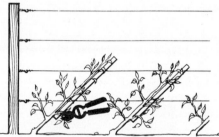

2. At planting time, tie any existing branches to wires at 45° angle at opposite direction. Do not prune except to shorten branches growing outward and on downward side of trunk to spurs.

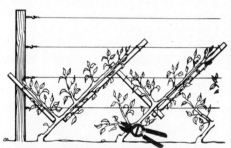

3. During growing season, continue training leader at chosen angle. Train branches at 45° in opposite direction. Tie to wires or use supplemental stakes. Shorten branches growing outward and downward. In summer, shorten side shoots on major branches to spurs.

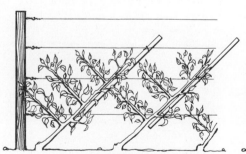

4. Avoid major pruning the following dormant season. Remove dead or poorly spaced spurs and branches.

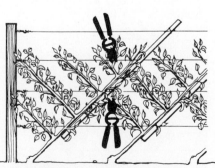

5. Continue training leader and branches. Shorten side shoots through the growing season. Cut back branches that cross adjacent trees.

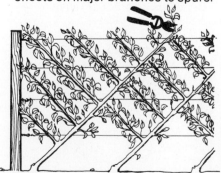

6. Each dormant season, follow process in step 4. Train major limbs in summer and shorten other shoots to spurs as in step 3. Maintain branches at desired length and leader at desired height. Remove stakes and hold pattern by tying loosely to wires.

Fan

This informal pattern was designed for fruit trees. It is suited to peaches and nectarines that are pruned heavily each year to renew fruit-bearing wood. The fan is popular for figs, plums, apricots, cherries and other trees that are difficult to train formally. It is also a favorite pattern for apples and pears because it is easy and it looks natural. Fans are traditionally trained against walls to take advantage of heat that is radiated back toward the plant. A post-and-wire framework is shown, but a variety of framing systems may be used. Training a fan on a wooden trellis is particularly popular.

The basic objective with this pattern is to create a permanent structure of major limbs that fan over an allotted space. Spurs or shoots along the major limbs produce fruit. Short spurs may grow in any direction. Remove outward-growing shoots or those that point toward the wall.

Peaches and nectarines that need a continual supply of new wood are pruned every year just after new spring growth, when shoots are about 12 inches long. Prune each new shoot back to two buds. Two new shoots will develop from these buds. The following spring, permit one of these shoots to bloom and prune the other shoot back to two buds.

Every year the shoot permitted to bloom will produce fruit. The shoot that was pruned back will produce the new shoots needed the following year. This ensures a continual supply of new wood. Allow new shoots to grow about 15 inches long before tying them to the flat surface support.

Fan

1. Plant an unbranched whip and cut above three buds. Or plant a branched tree and shorten side shoots to spurs.

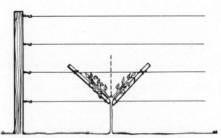

2. Several shoots will appear in spring. Save two of the best. Tie these shoots to stakes attached to wires. Train at 45° angle. Remove backup shoots (dotted lines), when major shoots are established.

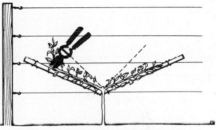

3. Shorten two major branches to about half their length. Lower to a 30° angle. Do this gradually to prevent breakage. Remove any side shoots.

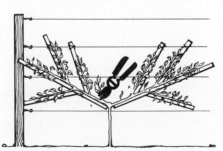

4. Permit shoots to develop naturally through the second growing season. Choose two shoots on the upper side of each major branch—one on its end to extend its length, and one on the downward side. Tie these shoots to stakes and remove all others.

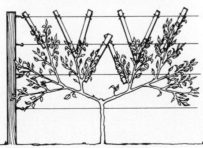

5. During the dormant season, cut back each of the major and secondary branches by one-third. In the third growing season, permit shoots to develop on secondary branches. Choose four best as in step 4, removing others. Use stakes as necessary. During fourth growing season, shorten framework arms by one-fourth.

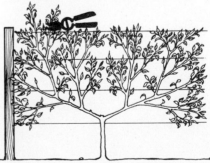

6. Permit new shoots to develop every 4 inches along framework arms. Pinch their tips in late summer. Do not remove them in the dormant season. They will bear fruit the following year. Remove first shoots after harvest for varieties requiring annual removal of wood. Permit framework arms to grow to desired length. Prune them in dormant season by one-fourth if they are not growing vigorously.

PLANTING AND CARE

4

A uniform hedge or screen consists of many plants of the same variety. If you plan to plant a hedge of substantial size, it is a good idea to contact a nursery or landscape contractor in advance of your planting date. Find out if the quantity and cultivar of the species you want are available. Wholesale nurseries occasionally sell large numbers of plants to individuals who provide their own delivery. The variety you choose should be suited to your climate and site conditions.

Plants are available bare root, balled and burlapped or in containers. These three kinds of stock are described in step-by-step planting procedures on pages 79 to 81. No matter what kind of stock you choose, always buy from a reputable supplier. Check labels to be sure you have been given the correct species or cultivar.

Home propagation is much more economical than buying nursery stock, but hedges and screens started from seeds, cuttings or by replanting suckers take one to four years longer to reach maturity. In addition, a seed source or existing planting must be located before home propagation can begin.

Methods for starting plants at home are illustrated on page 75. Anyone undertaking a large-scale installation of hedges or screens should consider propagating their own plants. Check encyclopedia listings on pages 96 to 172 to see if the species is an easy subject to propagate. Cultivars must be propagated vegetatively, usually from cuttings. However, many are illegal to propagate this way because they are patented.

PLANT PLACEMENT
Plants should be carefully placed at correct distances from sidewalks or property lines and from each other in a row. The most important thing to consider is the ultimate width of the plants or the mature trimmed form. Calculate the size of screen or hedge at maturity. Be realistic. All plants look tiny in the nursery, but most plants grow rapidly.

Position the *planting line* at half the mature width from the outside edge of your hedge or screen. For example, a 3-foot-wide hedge should be placed at least 1-1/2 feet from a path. An 8-foot-wide screen should be placed at least 4 feet from a path.

Spacing between plants is based on growth rate, pattern, density, ultimate size and whether plants will be shaped into hedges or left untrimmed as screens. Screens are spaced slightly less than the mature width of the plant, or closer for dense, quick coverage. Sheared hedge plants are spaced closer still to compensate for pruning and to create a solid base. The narrower or lower the hedge, the closer the spacing. Check the encyclopedia descriptions for specifics on spacing.

Left: Gardener does a final touch-up with hand shears on this finely trimmed hedge. Above: Balled-and-burlapped rhododendrons are ready to plant. Planting zone has been cleared of turf and weeds.

Spacing plants closer together is more costly but a pleasing appearance is obtained more quickly. If plants are spaced two feet apart or less, it is easier to mass-plant them in a trench. Dig individual holes when plants are spaced three feet or more apart.

Two staggered rows of plants provide a dense cover, but they are difficult to weed. This procedure is recommended only for large-scale, informal installations of shelterbelts, tree windbreaks, boundary barriers or screens and snowcatches.

PLANTING PREPARATIONS

Proper preparation of the planting site gets plants off to a good start and helps ensure rapid growth.

Basic soil preparation should be done before you bring plants home from the nursery. This way plants can go into the ground as soon as possible. Keep roots cool and moist if you are unable to plant immediately. Cluster container plants and balled and burlapped stock closely together in a shaded spot. Water plants and keep them watered until they are planted. "Heel-in" bare-root stock as shown in the illustration on page 76.

Lay Out the Planting Line—Basic preparation begins with laying out the length of the planting line. Position the line by eye or by precise measure. The more tailored, architectural or formal the effect you want, the more care you should take to align plant stems and trunks in one, unwavering, uniformly spaced row. Lay out the planting line with stakes and string. Use stakes and string to designate a weed-free and turf-free area on both sides of the planting line. This is the *planting zone*. Make the zone about three feet wide for hedges, slightly narrower for borders and slightly wider for screens.

Eliminate Weeds and Turf—Remove stakes and string marking the planting line and clear the planting zone of weeds and turf. There are two ways to eliminate weeds: Apply a chemical weed killer, an *herbicide,* or regularly remove weeds by manual means over one or two growing seasons.

If you choose to remove weeds by hand, strip sod or till weeds with a power tiller by hand, in the fall. Till or hand-pull weeds that reappear in spring or summer.

If you choose to use the easier, weedkiller approach, consider using

Position plant in planting hole at the same level as it was in the container. Some gardeners position plants slightly higher than ground level to allow for settling of the soil.

It is important to know the correct spacing for various plants if you want a solid hedge or screen. These *Thuja* species plants are spaced too far apart, creating a "rippled" effect. Spacing guidelines for plants are provided on pages 93 to 172.

Propagation

Seeds

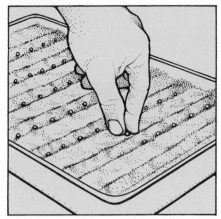

1. Plant large seeds about 1/4 inch deep with 1 to 2 inches between seeds. Firm soil. Scatter tiny seeds over soil, then press into soil with flat of your hand.

2. Cover with sheet of plastic or glass to retain humidity and to keep seeds from drying out. Some seeds germinate best in darkness. Cover with newspaper or board.

3. Transfer seedlings to pots. Or, plant where needed if they have reached sufficient size and weather permits.

Cuttings

1. Make 3- to 5-inch-long cuttings of existing plants. Make cut just below a leaf node. Cut off oldest leaves.

2. Make a fresh cut on stem. Hormone rooting powder speeds root formation on some cuttings. Moisten the base of cutting and lightly coat tip with powder.

3. Place cuttings in soil mix. Mix should be porous. Use perlite alone, or a mixture of perlite, vermiculite or peat moss.

Layering

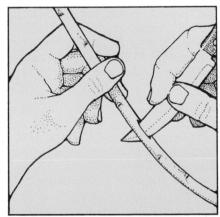

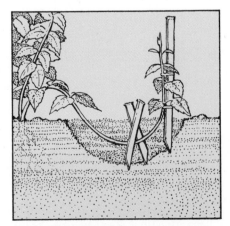

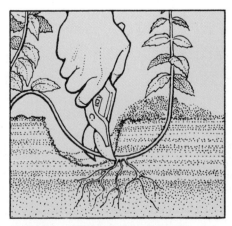

1. Allow a long, flexible stem to grow near base of plant. Notch or wound with knife to help speed root formation.

2. Cover stem with 3 to 4 inches of soil and hold in place with wooden stakes or rocks. Bend the growing tip upward and support with a stake.

3. Keep soil moist. Allow 4 to 6 weeks for roots to form. After this time, cut off and transplant where desired.

When You Bring Plants Home

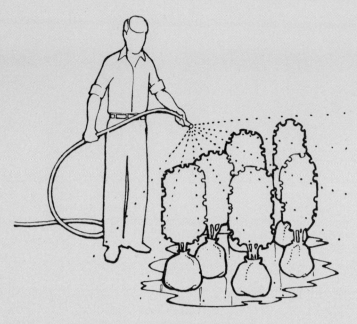

It is best to get plants in the ground as soon as you bring them home from the nursery, but this is not always possible. Group balled and burlapped plants or plants in containers together in a shaded location. Plants shade and support each other, and are easier to water. Keep rootball or container soil moist until planting time.

Bare-root plants should be *heeled-in* if you are unable to plant right away. Plants are heeled in by placing roots in a shallow hole, and covering them with peat moss, sawdust or soil. Heel-in plants in a shaded location, and keep roots moist until planting time. Plant as soon as possible, before root growth begins.

the herbicide *glyphosate,* sold under the trade names Roundup and Kleenup. Vegetation can be removed and planting can begin 7 days after application. Always read and follow label directions before applying any chemical.

Plant in fall, winter or spring, depending on your climate and the nursery stock to be planted—container, bare root or balled and burlapped.

Dig Holes or Trench—After vegetation is eliminated from the planting zone, dig the planting holes or trench. Water deeply one or two days prior to make this job easier. Pile soil on one side of the trench or holes. This becomes the *backfill.* Power augers, available from rental outlets, make excavation jobs fast and easy, but they often glaze the soil surface. Be sure to roughen sides of the planting holes so roots are able to penetrate the soil.

If planting seeds, cuttings or small plants, simply turn over soil in the planting zone.

Amend The Soil—Amending the backfill with organic matter is an optional step. Organic matter added to sandy soil helps retain moisture and nutrients. Organic matter added to clay soil increases drainage and air circulation, while helping to prevent compaction.

Some horticulturists recommend mixing 50% soil mix into the backfill soil. The mix should be as similar as possible to the original soil around the plant rootball. Another way to get plants off to a good start is to add *at least* 30% organic matter to the backfill.

Plants may require a certain acid or alkaline soil pH. If you are planting blueberries, for example, soil pH must be acid. A soil test is essential whenever large quantities of plants are being installed. Test for pH with an inexpensive home testing kit, or have your soil checked by a professional lab.

PLANTING

Follow step-by-step planting procedures as shown on pages 80 and 81 according to the type of nursery stock and spacing. Plants that are not symmetrically branched can be turned so the underdeveloped side faces the sun. This favors growth on that side.

A notched board or marked stick laid across the planting zone at regularly spaced intervals is handy to check spacing.

Individual planting holes were dug for this row of yews. Note the even spacing between plants.

After placing plants, add backfill soil and water to settle. Do not allow plants to settle below the level at which they were originally grown. Raise by gently inserting shovel beneath rootball and lifting up. Raise plant, firm soil and water again. The bud union on grafted plants should be approximately 2 inches above the soil level.

Form a watering basin around plants. Mound a small rim of soil around individual plants or along the length of the trench with backfill soil. If you live in an area subject to heavy rainfall, do not form a watering basin. Plants may receive too much water.

Staking plants is sometimes necessary. In locations where the wind blows consistently from one direction, lean plants about 3 inches toward the wind. Grafted plants have a bud union where the rootstock is joined with the top part of the plant. The union should be faced away from prevailing winds. If plants cannot stand alone, you have obtained poor plant stock. Stake as a last resort. Stakes are a crutch that prevent trunks from developing their own strength. Use loose ties so trunks can move in the wind. Reduce the wind's force by pruning foliage. Cut back bare-root, deciduous stock to 18 inches or a few buds above ground level. Remove stakes the following year or as soon as they are no longer necessary.

PRUNING AFTER PLANTING

An essential part of the planting process forgotten by many gardeners is pruning. It may seem wasteful to cut back small, new plants, but pruning stimulates growth. Pruning also helps balance the top growth with the microscopic root hairs that feed the plant. Many were damaged in the planting process.

The basic pruning strategy for newly planted hedges is to clip off top growth until sides and base are dense. Clipping off top growth is called *topping,* which stimulates lower buds to produce leaf growth. Screens and many coniferous, needled evergreen hedges should not be topped. Instead, thin plants by about one-third to compensate for root damage and to encourage branching. Thin according to the pruning method that best fits the plants you have selected. See pages 89 to 91.

Fast-growing, deciduous and broad-leaf evergreen species are pruned more severely than moderate and slow-growing species. Coniferous needled evergreens have special pruning requirements. Mounding border forms or low, unsheared, informal hedges are usually shaped by pinching out errant growth. Pinch back frequently the first few years. This stimulates dense foliage growth.

After you have planted, watered, checked plant position and pruned, apply a *mulch,* a layer of material over the root zones of plants. An organic mulch of rotted manure or compost helps reduce moisture lost through evaporation, and modifies soil temperatures. A mulch is also an effective way to prevent weeds. To avoid crown rot, keep mulch away from stems or trunks.

Keep the soil moist for several weeks after planting. After plants are established, gradually reduce watering frequency.

Planting Basics

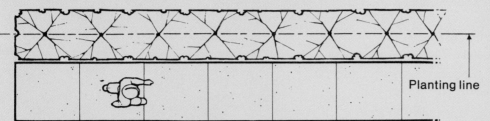

Planting Near Walks

Be careful when placing plants near walkways, or you will always battle the plant's natural growth habit. Place plants in a planting line at a distance equal to half the plant's mature width. For example, if a plant grows to 4 feet wide, the planting line should be located 2 feet away from walk.

Planting line

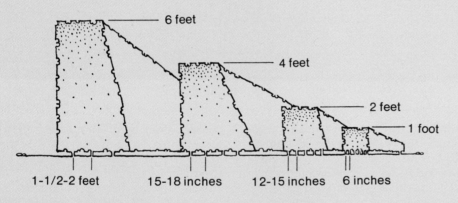

Allow for Access

Leave sufficient access space between hedge and adjacent property line to ease clipping chores.

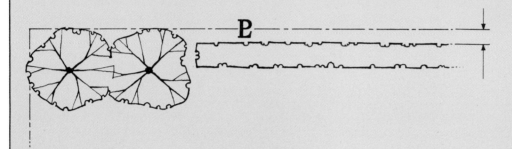

6 feet

4 feet

2 feet

1 foot

1-1/2-2 feet   15-18 inches   12-15 inches   6 inches

Spacing Guidelines

The space allowed between plants varies according to height of hedge. Follow these general guides. Space plants 1-1/2 to 2 feet apart for 6-foot-high hedge. Space 15 to 18 inches for 4-foot-high hedge. Space 12 to 15 inches apart for 2-foot-high hedge. Space 6 inches apart for 1-foot-high hedge.

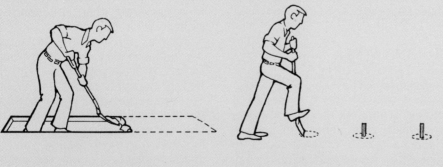

Planting Trench or Holes?

If plants are to be spaced less than 3 feet apart, dig a trench for planting. For plants spaced 3 feet or more apart, it is best to dig individual holes.

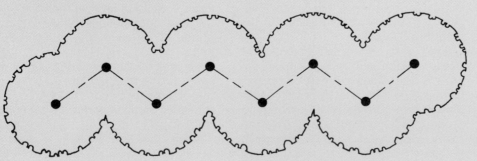

Stagger Plantings for Windbreaks

For the most effective windbreak, boundary barrier or snowcatch, arrange plants in a staggered, double-row pattern.

Buying Plants

Young plant

Old plant showing rootbound roots at soil surface

Avoid buying plants with circled roots showing at surface.

Good

Bad

Look for a balanced root system.

In Containers

Most broadleaf evergreens are grown in containers. Deciduous stock past the bare-root season (dormant season), and needled or broadleaf evergreens that were not sold balled and burlapped are also planted in containers. Look for plants in 1-gallon-size containers. Plants in larger containers provide more coverage when planted, but younger, less-expensive plants often grow more quickly and catch up within a few years. Young plants are vigorous and inexpensive, and respond well to training and pruning.

Have nursery personnel cut metal cans if you will be planting immediately. Plants grown in plastic containers can be slipped out easily when the rootball soil is moistened. Paper-pulp pots eventually rot away in the ground. They can be cut down the sides to speed the process. Some border plants are available in 4-inch pots or flats.

The example illustrated on pages 80 and 81 is for plants spaced 2 feet apart in a trench. For wider spacing, dig individual holes.

Balled and Burlapped

Most needled evergreens and many broadleaf evergreens are available with their roots bound in a ball shape in burlap or a synthetic material. Plant is grown in the ground for three or four years. The rootball is dug up, wrapped in the material and sold.

The rootball should be in proportion to the *caliper*—the distance around the stem near roots of the plant. A 1/2-inch caliper should have a minimum 12-inch-diameter rootball. A 2-inch caliper should have a minimum 24-inch-diameter rootball.

Balled and burlapped plants are usually planted in spring. Poke around in the top inch of soil to check for circled or kinked roots.

The example illustrated on pages 80 and 81 is for plants spaced approximately 3 feet apart in individual holes. For closer spacing, dig a trench.

Bare Root

Most deciduous plants are available bare root when in a *dormant* stage. The roots are bound in plastic without soil, which reduces the cost. Plants are usually one to three years old. The nursery often prunes lower branches from bare-root stock. If possible, buy plants before the branches are pruned if you plan to plant screens or windbreaks.

Plant bare-root plants near the end of the dormant season—late winter or when ground thaws.

The example illustrated on pages 80 and 81 is for plants spaced approximately 3 feet apart in individual holes. For closer spacing, dig a trench.

Planting from Containers

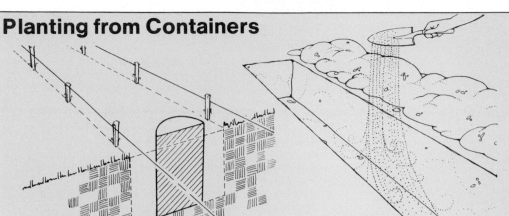

1. Lay out trench with stakes and string. Remove weeds or turf. Trench width should be twice container width. Trench depth should be 1 or 2 inches less than rootball.

2. Dig the trench. Soil from the trench will be the *backfill.* Sprinkle general-purpose fertlizer in bottom of trench and mix into soil.

3. Remove plants from containers. Handle rootball gently. If roots are severely matted and circled, use a knife to slice through rootball.

Planting Balled and Burlapped

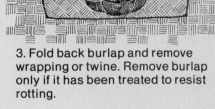

1. Lay out trench the same as containers, step 1 above. Use stakes to mark locations of planting holes. Dig hole, making width equal to twice rootball. Depth should be 1 or 2 inches less than rootball.

2. Gently place plant in hole. Position at same level as its original soil line. There is often a lighter or darker color on the trunk to indicate this.

3. Fold back burlap and remove wrapping or twine. Remove burlap only if it has been treated to resist rotting.

Planting Bare Root

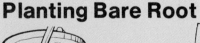

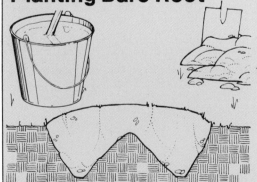

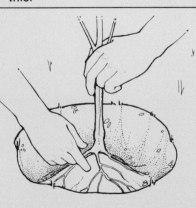

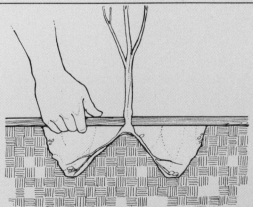

1. Dig hole just wide and deep enough to accommodate roots without crowding. Make a cone-shaped mound of soil in center of hole.

2. Prune away dead or broken roots. Spread roots evenly over cone.

3. Using a shovel or stake as a guide, check height of plant. Position at same level as the original soil line. There is often a lighter or darker color on the trunk to indicate this.

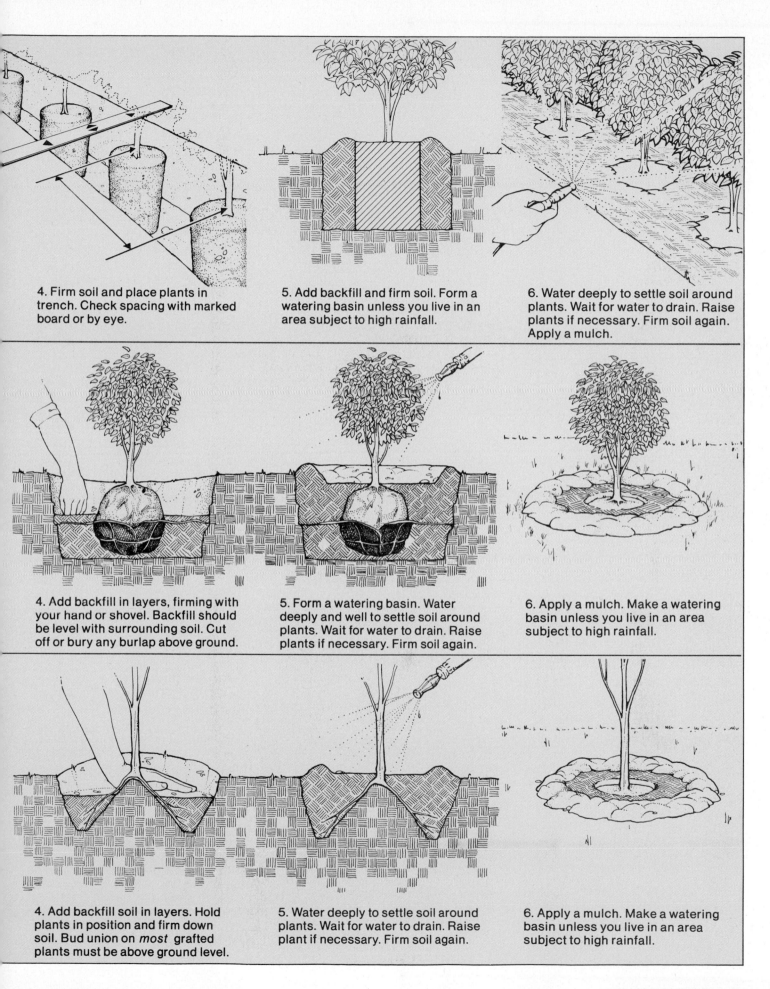

4. Firm soil and place plants in trench. Check spacing with marked board or by eye.

5. Add backfill and firm soil. Form a watering basin unless you live in an area subject to high rainfall.

6. Water deeply to settle soil around plants. Wait for water to drain. Raise plants if necessary. Firm soil again. Apply a mulch.

4. Add backfill in layers, firming with your hand or shovel. Backfill should be level with surrounding soil. Cut off or bury any burlap above ground.

5. Form a watering basin. Water deeply and well to settle soil around plants. Wait for water to drain. Raise plants if necessary. Firm soil again.

6. Apply a mulch. Make a watering basin unless you live in an area subject to high rainfall.

4. Add backfill soil in layers. Hold plants in position and firm down soil. Bud union on *most* grafted plants must be above ground level.

5. Water deeply to settle soil around plants. Wait for water to drain. Raise plant if necessary. Firm soil again.

6. Apply a mulch. Make a watering basin unless you live in an area subject to high rainfall.

Planting and Care **81**

Pruning After Planting

Fast-Growing Deciduous or Broadleaf Evergreen Plants

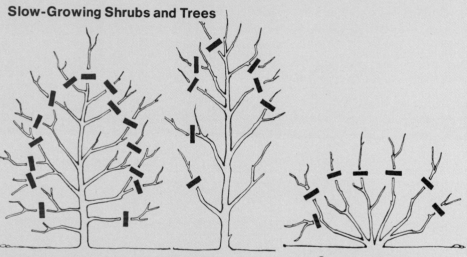

Deciduous hedge or screen: Cut back to approximately 6 inches from the soil. Leave several side shoots.

Broadleaf evergreen hedge: Shear tops and sides back about one-third.

Hedge only: Within six months after planting, trim tops and sides often to encourage dense branching.

Slow-Growing Shrubs and Trees

Hedge: Head back the main stem leader and side shoots by about one-third.

Screen: Prune by thinning the main stem leader and side shoots approximately one-third.

Screen variation: For multiple-stem, deciduous shrubs or broadleaf evergreens thin all branches by one-third.

Needled Evergreens

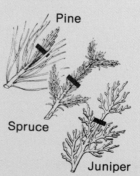

Pine

Spruce

Juniper

Hedge or screen: Prune branch tips lightly. Do not cut back leader unless topping is advised for variety.

Hedge only: Needled evergreens respond to pruning in different ways. See page 91.

Prune candles of pines halfway to make foliage more bushy. Prune junipers early in the season so spring growth covers wound. Prune new growth of spruce back by half.

FIRST-YEAR MAINTENANCE

Both hedges and screens require deep, regular watering during their first year. Watering deeply encourages deep rooting. Fertilizing speeds growth, but if slow-release fertilizer is applied at planting, further applications are not necessary.

Hedges and screens require some pruning the day they are planted, but pruning requirements are different after plants become more established. Screens require little if any pruning after their first pruning. If you have planted a screen or a hedge that will be lightly shaped or "informal," turn to page 83.

Hedges require careful shaping the first year or two following planting to develop dense branching and strong form. The most important part of shaping is keeping the top of the hedge narrower than the base. This allows for more even growth and exposure to the sun. Start pruning from the bottom and work up. Keep cutting the top back until the sides and base are dense, gradually permitting the hedge to reach the desired height.

In most cases, do not cut back the tops of needled evergreen conifer hedges. Note special requirements and limitations in the encyclopedia descriptions.

Fine-textured, broadleaf evergreens and deciduous plants with small leaves should be sheared. Shoots on plants with large leaves should be cut back one by one to prevent a ragged look. Another method for pruning plants with large leaves is to shear just before the spring burst of new growth. The ragged cut leaves are quickly covered with fresh new foliage.

Hedge and border plants are planted closely together. This crowding forces roots to compete for moisture and nutrients. Regular clipping stimulates the plants to produce new leaves. Root competition and continually stimulated growth means that these forms should receive at *least* one annual application of slow-release fertilizer. Remove weeds as soon as they are noticed to eliminate competition. After hedges have grown to become dense, weeds are usually eliminated naturally by the shade created under the hedge plants.

Pruning Hedges the Second and Third Year

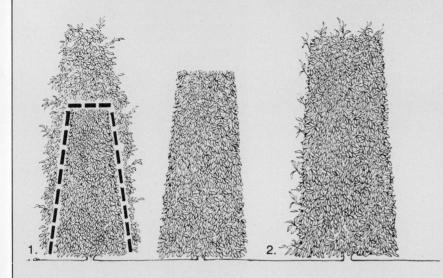

Fast-Growing, Deciduous or Broadleaf Evergreen Plants

1. Second year: In the spring, cut back severely, removing about half of the new growth. Every month or so, shear sides and top to maintain the desired form. In cold-winter climates, do not prune at the end of summer—it will promote new, cold-tender growth. Shape deciduous hedges during their dormant season. In mild-winter climates, shear sides and top as necessary to maintain desired form.

2. Third year: Every month or so, shear sides and top to maintain the desired form. In cold-winter climates, do not prune at the end of summer—it will promote new, cold-tender growth. Shape deciduous hedges during their dormant season. In mild-winter climates, shear as necessary to maintain desired form. Follow these pruning techniques each year.

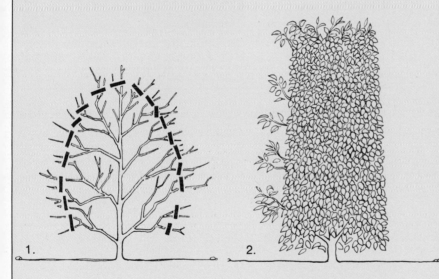

Slow-Growing Shrubs and Trees

1. Second year: With slow-growing plants, pruning is necessary only once or twice a year. Remove about one-third of new growth, keeping base of plant wider than the top. Shape deciduous hedges—except *Fagus* and *Carpinus* species—during their dormant season.

2. Third year: Pruning is necessary only once or twice a year. Plants are now large enough to be given their shaped form. Cut to the outline desired. Do not cut back the top until hedge reaches its ultimate height. Follow these pruning techniques each year.

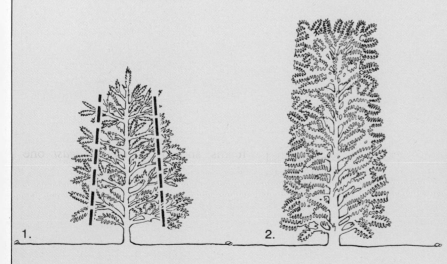

Needled Evergreens

1. Second year: Trim and top at the appropriate time for particular conifer species. Shape to the desired form. Do not let conifers get out of bounds, or it may be difficult to reclaim plantings. Pruning back below young, green needles usually leaves stubby, unattractive growth.

2. Third year: Follow second-year pruning techniques the third year, and each subsequent year.

SHEARING

There are many methods for attaining crisp, sheared, hedge lines. Some of these are illustrated on page 86. No matter what method you choose to follow, it is important to shear sides of the hedge first, then the top. Start at the bottom and work up, maintaining a slight, inward taper. This taper keeps the base foliage dense because sunlight penetrates all the way down to the bottom of the plant. This taper is often referred to as *batter,* a word that evolved from the connection between architecture and hedges. Tall hedgewalls sometimes have steep batter to accentuate their image of stability.

Choosing a hedge form is basically a matter of personal taste. Slightly tapering sides prevent sparse bottoms. Triangular tops shed snow more readily and help prevent branch breakage in severe winters. Some people give their hedge tops graceful curves or create decorative accents. Some shear one side and prune the foliage on the other to expose the trunks.

TOPIARY

Topiary means to shape a plant into a dense, unnatural form, usually an animal or geometric shape. Topiary has been popular through the centuries. Many plants listed in the encyclopedia may be sheared into topiary forms. Traditional species for this treatment include *Taxus, Buxus, Laurus, Myrtus, Ligustrum japonicum, Syzygium* and *Tsuga.* Consider planting topiary in containers. They can move when you do.

MAINTENANCE OF SCREENS AND SHAPED HEDGES

Taking care of screens or lightly shaped hedges is simple during the years after planting. Maintenance normally consists of one annual pruning and fertilizing with slow-release commercial fertilizer. Cut out diseased or dead wood and remove branches that detract from beauty or form. Suckers may be removed, left to contribute to the density of the hedge or screen or replanted to extend the line.

Lightly shaped or informal hedges

Topiary is the art of sculpting plants with pruning shears. Animal shapes and geometric forms are popular.

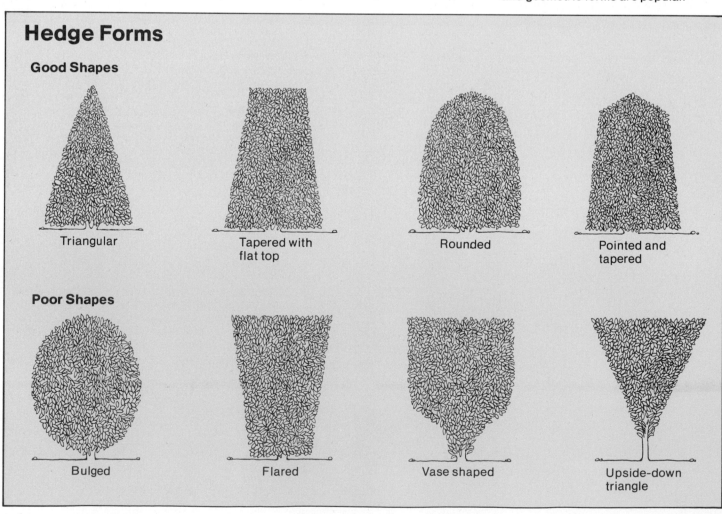

Hedge Forms

Good Shapes

Triangular

Tapered with flat top

Rounded

Pointed and tapered

Poor Shapes

Bulged

Flared

Vase shaped

Upside-down triangle

Crisply sheared edges are essential for an elegant, formal hedge. This professional gardener clips the sides first, then the top. He does it all by eye—experience is his guideline. Some professional techniques are shown on page 86.

Many gardeners shear one section of hedge at a time. Platform on sturdy sawhorses makes a safe support for each section of work.

Electric hedge shears speed up trimming, but a steady hand is needed to avoid overclipping.

and screens can be pruned in various ways to control size or stimulate new growth or flowers. Shoots are usually cut back one by one. The timing depends on several factors. Most deciduous species are lightly shaped in their dormant season—winter—by thinning. Plants that bloom in spring on shoots developed during the previous year should be pruned right after their flowers fade. Plants that bloom in summer or fall on shoots that develop the same year should be pruned in early spring.

In general, prune plants that produce berries or fruit after the berries or fruit have disappeared or after they have been harvested. Specific pruning times for most species are listed in the encyclopedia. Detailed pruning descriptions for apples and pears are shown in the espalier chapter.

Many people prune shrubby screens every three or five years to revitalize them or to control their size. The same method is used for deciduous and broadleaf evergreen plants. Remove weak, dead or diseased growth. Cut about one-third of the oldest shoots to ground level. Prune deciduous species during the dormant season. Prune broadleaf evergreens in mild-winter climates during winter. In cold-winter climates, prune broadleafs in spring.

PROTECTING AGAINST COLD
Elaborate coverings to protect plants against cold are expensive, time consuming and unattractive. The best protection is to plant species adapted to your climate conditions.

Broadleaf evergreen species need the most care to make it through snowy weather in cold-winter climates. Certain site conditions favor their survival. A windbreak sometimes make it possible to grow broadleafs where they are not adapted. They need shelter from harsh winter winds that dry and damage their foliage. A partially shady or fully shaded site also favors their survival.

Never prune late in the summer in cold-winter climates. Pruning stimulates new growth. Young, cold-tender leaves are quickly killed by frosts.

Water deeply and well in late fall before the soil freezes. An *antidesiccant* is a protective film that can be sprayed on leaves at this time. It reduces moisture loss by inhibiting the natural process of *evapotranspiration* that continues through winter.

Broadleaf evergreens adapted to mild-winter climates have different requirements to protect them from cold. A plant growing in Zone 9 that is not reliable out of Zone 10 needs a special approach. Pruning, watering or fertilizing toward the end of summer encourages undesirable, new, cold-tender growth that is easily damaged by frost. Taper off watering as the end of summer nears to harden new tissue and make it woody.

Do not remove plants that have been killed to the ground by severe winter weather. Wait until all danger of frost has past, then cut out dead wood, water deeply, fertilize and mulch. New shoots usually appear in spring. Follow the correct pruning procedures for newly planted hedge or screen forms as given on page 82.

How Experts Maintain Crisp Hedge Lines

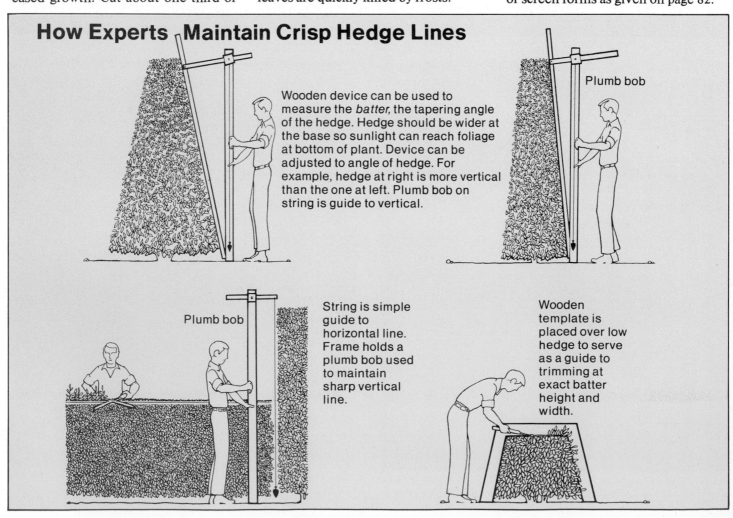

Wooden device can be used to measure the *batter,* the tapering angle of the hedge. Hedge should be wider at the base so sunlight can reach foliage at bottom of plant. Device can be adjusted to angle of hedge. For example, hedge at right is more vertical than the one at left. Plumb bob on string is guide to vertical.

Plumb bob

Plumb bob

String is simple guide to horizontal line. Frame holds a plumb bob used to maintain sharp vertical line.

Wooden template is placed over low hedge to serve as a guide to trimming at exact batter height and width.

RENOVATION

Most overgrown and neglected hedges and screens may be revitalized and restored by forcing new growth. Bare spots can be filled in by replacing dead plants. Cut out poorly placed, dead or diseased branches. Try renovation before taking the drastic step of replacing an entire hedge or screen.

Broadleaf evergreens should be renovated in early spring. Deciduous species should be renovated during the dormant season.

Few coniferous needled evergreens respond to severe pruning. Once they become overgrown, they are often replaced. Cutting back below current growth leaves stubs that will not resprout.

When you renovate, give your plants a healthy dose of the basics—*remove weeds, water deeply, fertilize and add a mulch.* For slow-growing screens, follow basic pruning techniques. Remove poorly placed, dead or diseased branches, thin overly long or weak branches. Lightly thin to stimulate new growth.

Cutting an overgrown screen down to size usually stimulates new growth. New height will be maintained slightly above ladder top.

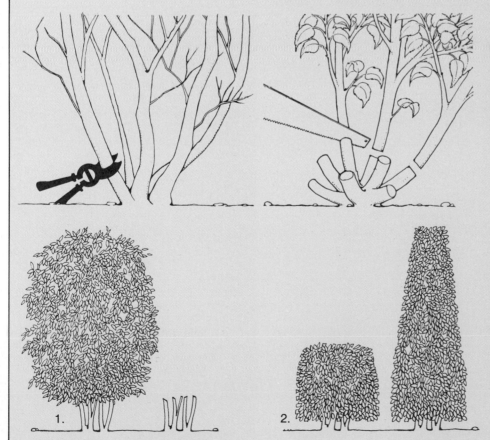

Renovation

Cut and Come Again Method

Twiggy Shrubs with Basal Shoots
Cut back to within a few inches of ground level in the appropriate season.

Shrubs with Stout Stems on a Basal Clump
Cut back to within 1 foot of the ground in the appropriate season. Remove poorly placed branches and stems entirely.

Fast-Growing Hedges that Tolerate Heavy Pruning
1. Cut deciduous plants back to a few inches. Cut evergreens back to within 1 foot of ground level.
2. Within the next six months, trim tops and sides of new growth often to encourage dense branching. Allow hedge to reach desired height gradually. Keep base wider than top. Resume regular pruning schedule after form is attained.

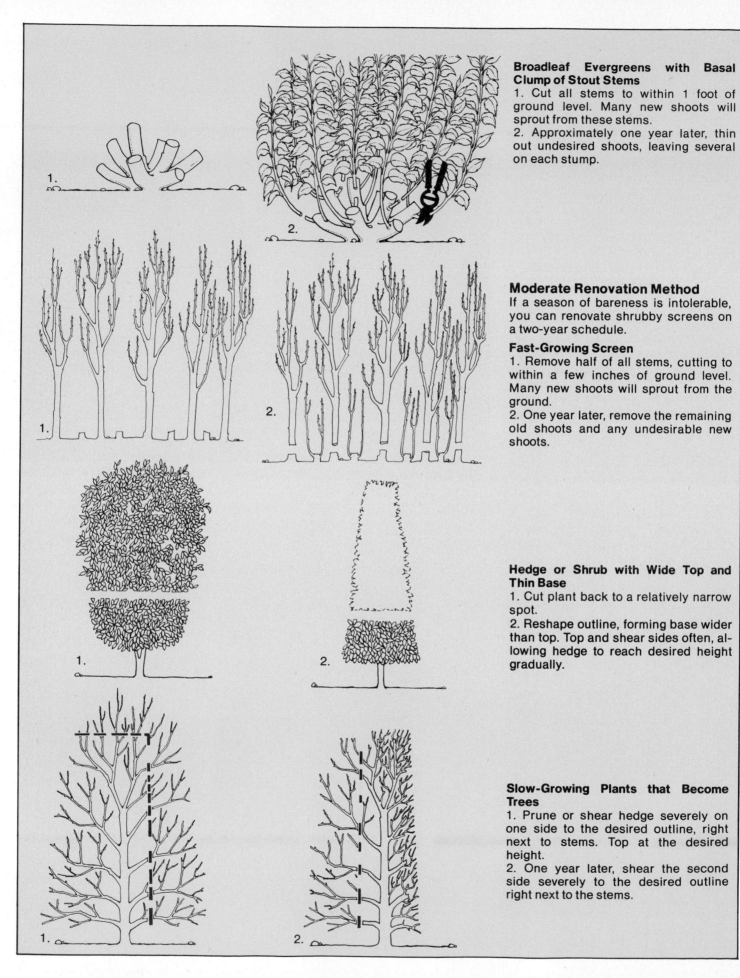

Broadleaf Evergreens with Basal Clump of Stout Stems
1. Cut all stems to within 1 foot of ground level. Many new shoots will sprout from these stems.
2. Approximately one year later, thin out undesired shoots, leaving several on each stump.

Moderate Renovation Method
If a season of bareness is intolerable, you can renovate shrubby screens on a two-year schedule.

Fast-Growing Screen
1. Remove half of all stems, cutting to within a few inches of ground level. Many new shoots will sprout from the ground.
2. One year later, remove the remaining old shoots and any undesirable new shoots.

Hedge or Shrub with Wide Top and Thin Base
1. Cut plant back to a relatively narrow spot.
2. Reshape outline, forming base wider than top. Top and shear sides often, allowing hedge to reach desired height gradually.

Slow-Growing Plants that Become Trees
1. Prune or shear hedge severely on one side to the desired outline, right next to stems. Top at the desired height.
2. One year later, shear the second side severely to the desired outline right next to the stems.

Principles of Pruning

Pruning stimulates and directs growth. Removing selected buds and branches controls and rejuvenates plants. It encourages them to fill in densely, take a certain form and produce bigger fruit and flowers.

WHY PRUNE?

Pruning stimulates and directs growth. Removing selected buds and branches controls and rejuvenates plants, encourages them to fill in densely, take a certain form and produce bigger fruit and flowers.

Hedges are shaped as a unit by shearing or by cutting individual shoots back, one by one. The goal is to maintain a certain form with crisply or softly defined edges. Screens and "informal" hedges are treated as a row of individual plants allowed to attain their natural form with only occasional pruning.

Strong winds have a great impact on plant growth. Thinning about one-third of the leaf surface in young windbreak plantings allows the wind to blow through more easily. This permits firm root establishment and vigorous growth.

Branches that are crowded and crossing each other and those that point in the wrong direction are also unattractive. Removing this growth produces a more pleasing, sculptural effect in unsheared screens and canopies.

Crowded hedge branches are desirable. Hedges are pruned to stimulate crowding and foliage density. Balance the form of a lopsided hedge or screen by removing excessive branches and foliage.

Coniferous needled evergreens have their own special pruning requirements. Not all may be headed back. Light thinning is recommended after planting. See encyclopedia listings for the best pruning times for individual species.

Suckers are vigorous, upright stems that grow from roots. They are usually pruned because they are unattractive. There is no need to remove suckers that contribute density to hedges, barriers and screens. Remove suckers that arise from grafted rootstock. They are worthless and drain plant vigor.

Watersprouts are vigorously growing, upright shoots that sap plant energy and detract from the beauty of unsheared screens and hedges. Remove watersprouts as soon as they are noticed.

PLANT FORMS AND PRUNING

When pruning plants, it helps to keep the natural form in mind. Not all plants grow in the same manner. Most are basically upright or rounded, but there are many variations on these forms.

Plants with a strong *leader,* main, uppermost stem or branch, usually develop an upright, pyramidal form. When a leader is cut back or removed, one of the lower buds or branches will assert dominance to grow upright, become the new leader and maintain the pyramidal form.

The other common shrub or tree form consists of multiple stems or branches of more or less equal dominance. Shape is more widely spreading and rounded.

Hedges are pruned to fit certain spaces or functions. Screens and informal hedges can be pruned to manipulate their shape, but it is easier to choose a plant with a natural form suited to the space it will fill.

To encourage more upright growth,

Trees are pruned up to create a high canopy. Tree branches have spread to make an overhead screen, providing filtered shade.

To maintain a *shaped* hedge, branches should be pruned back one by one. Branches of plants with large leaves should not be sheared or plants will have a ragged appearance.

thin branches that spread widely. To encourage more broad growth, thin or head back overly tall shoots. Try weighting down young branches to train them to grow horizontally.

DIRECTING AND SUPPRESSING GROWTH

A *terminal* bud is a bud positioned at the end of a branch or shoot. It is dominant and grows vigorously. Cut it off to stimulate a dormant, lower bud to *break*—sprout and form a side shoot. Side shoots grow in the direction their buds point. The one below the dominant bud or branch that is cut usually assumes dominance unless it is a *flower bud.* If this is the case, the next lower branch bud takes over dominance. Cut shoots of branches at an angle that points in the direction new growth will take. Don't cut too close, but don't leave a stub.

Another way to stimulate bud growth is to *nick* or *notch* the bark above the bud. A nick is a slit or incision in the bark. To notch, carefully remove a small piece of bark. The notch effect is more pronounced than a nick because the cut takes longer to heal. Either simulates the condition created by removing the terminal bud as described previously. Nick or notch techniques are particularly useful in formal espalier training where branches are needed at carefully selected locations along the trunk.

REMOVING GROWTH

Remove young shoots or buds that will grow into branches in undesirable locations as soon as they are noticed. Allowed to form as branches, you have two ways to remove them, depending on the size of the branch. For small branches, place blade of shears against trunk and cut branches. Never leave a stub, and do not paint with a sealant.

Large branches are cut in three steps to prevent the bark from ripping open a wound. Cut 1: Saw up from the bottom of the branch near actual cut location. Cut 2: Saw down from the top slightly farther from actual cut location. Branch will often break off before this cut is complete. Cut 3: Saw off stub flush with the bark at top slightly away from bark at bottom. This creates less wound tissue than a straight, flush cut.

Treating large pruning wounds with a sealant is a subject that creates disagreement among experts. Many believe sealants do more harm than good. If you decide to use a sealant, allow wound to dry before painting it on. Black-colored sealants are not recommended because they absorb too much heat.

Heading is one of the two basic pruning cuts. To *head* or *head back* means to cut the end of a branch or shoot to encourage a burst of growth in the buds below the cut. Most hedges are pruned by heading back shoots one by one. Or they are headed with clippers or shears. The burst of new growth that follows after makes it necessary to prune or shear again soon.

Power trimmers are a boon to busy gardeners because they make shearing quick and easy. But resist the temptation to shear every plant in sight. Many people shear indiscriminately and ruin the natural form of screens and informal hedges. These plants should be *thinned* to maintain a natural appearance.

Pinching is a heading cut that you do with your fingers instead of clippers. Pinching removes the growing tip

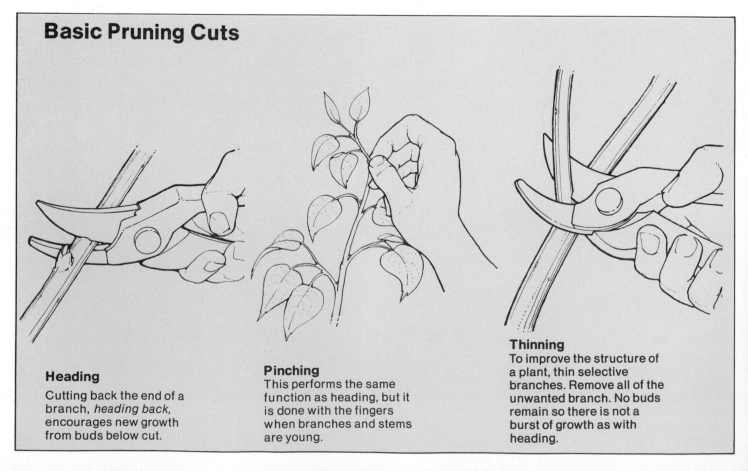

Basic Pruning Cuts

Heading
Cutting back the end of a branch, *heading back,* encourages new growth from buds below cut.

Pinching
This performs the same function as heading, but it is done with the fingers when branches and stems are young.

Thinning
To improve the structure of a plant, thin selective branches. Remove all of the unwanted branch. No buds remain so there is not a burst of growth as with heading.

when it is young and tender. It also stimulates dense foliage growth.

Thinning is the second basic pruning cut. To *thin,* remove wood by cutting out selected branches, stems or shoots. Few or no buds are left below a branch or shoot that has been removed from the plant, so there is no great burst of growth. Thinning takes more care but produces more controlled results. Some new growth will be stimulated. Energy is channeled to these and the remaining branches.

PRUNING CONIFEROUS NEEDLED EVERGREENS
Many plants are evergreen and many plants have needlelike leaves. But only those plants that bear cones are *coniferous.* They have special pruning and shearing requirements. Conifers should be watered well some hours before pruning to avoid needle or shear burn. *Taxus, Tsuga* and *Podocarpus* may be sheared severely whenever necessary. They are popular for topiary work. These and selected juniper cultivars are the only conifers that quickly sprout new growth. They are also easily renovated if they get out of bounds or decline in vigor. *Pinus*

strobus may also be renovated by severe pruning, but it takes several years for success and recovery.

As a rule, prune coniferous needled evergreens before, during or just after new growth. Never cut, shear or pinch below soft new needles or candles. Never remove branches unless you are absolutely sure you do not want foliage in that location. Do not top older trees. Do not let sheared hedges get out of bounds.

Conifers pruned too severely often produce dead twigs because most do not have latent buds below the needle area. Heavy pruning cannot stimulate buds to break, and the entire branch may die if it is cut back below the needle area.

PRUNING TO INCREASE FLOWER AND FRUIT SIZE
Reducing the number of fruit on a branch or spur increases the size of those remaining. When fruit are small, carefully thin out the excess. Leave space between remaining fruit roughly proportional to twice the mature fruit size. For example, thin plums to about 5 inches between

small fruit. Thin apples to about 8 inches between small fruit.

The same principle works to increase flower size except excess buds are *disbudded*—removed. You may wish to disbud small plantings in certain, close-up areas, such as an entryway. However, disbudding a large stretch of flowering hedge or screen is rarely worth the effort.

PRUNING DURING DROUGHT
When irrigation is necessary to keep plants alive but drought has reduced the available water supply, pruning techniques can help save plants. Thin foliage and branches from screens and informal hedges. Remove about one-third of plant. This reduces leaf surface and less water is lost from the soil reserve through natural plant processes.

Shearing hedges stimulates new growth that is less able to withstand water stress, so reduce shearing during drought. Thin espaliers or sacrifice less-valuable garden plants to give the espaliers water.

Hedges, screens and mature trees form the garden framework. Try to save them at all costs.

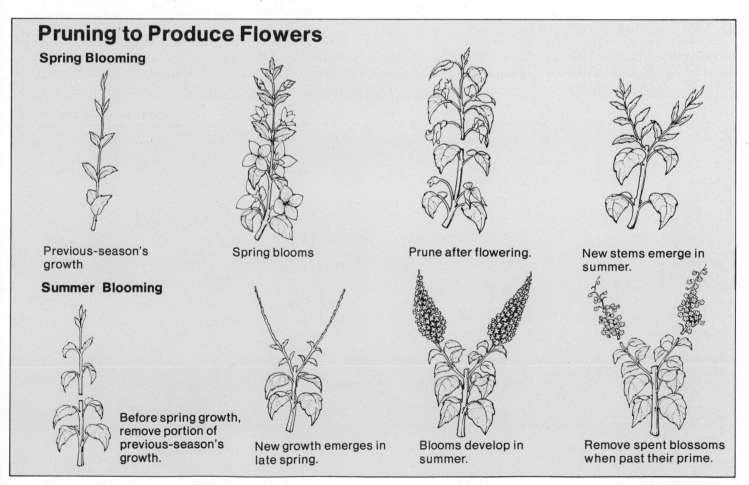

Pruning to Produce Flowers

Spring Blooming

Previous-season's growth

Spring blooms

Prune after flowering.

New stems emerge in summer.

Summer Blooming

Before spring growth, remove portion of previous-season's growth.

New growth emerges in late spring.

Blooms develop in summer.

Remove spent blossoms when past their prime.

5

ENCYCLOPEDIA

Almost all landscape plants can be grouped together in the garden to form hedges or screens, and any pliable tree or shrub can be trained as an espalier. This encyclopedia of plants adapted for use as hedges, screens and espaliers includes a range of plants for a variety of situations. Many worthy subjects were omitted because of space limitations.

Plants that are traditionally used as hedges, screens and espaliers are described in detail. Also included is a representative sample of the best plants for basic landscaping and for special situations. If you are searching for a plant to perform a particular landscape function, refer to the plant lists in Chapter 2.

SPECIAL EDIBLES
Plants that bear fruit and nuts are often overlooked for use as a hedge, screen or espalier. Anyone who is interested in dual-purpose landscaping should consider these plants. Many are included in the following pages.

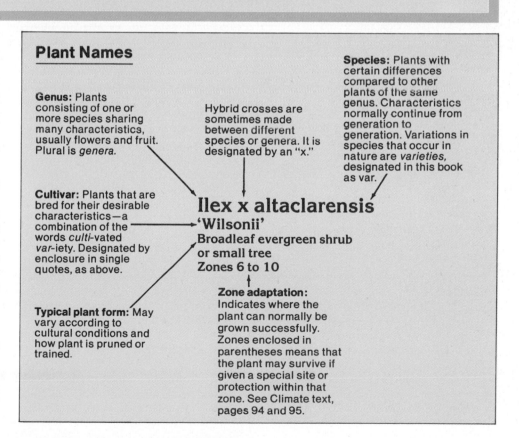

Plant Names

Genus: Plants consisting of one or more species sharing many characteristics, usually flowers and fruit. Plural is *genera.*

Cultivar: Plants that are bred for their desirable characteristics—a combination of the words *culti-*vated *var-*iety. Designated by enclosure in single quotes, as above.

Typical plant form: May vary according to cultural conditions and how plant is pruned or trained.

Hybrid crosses are sometimes made between different species or genera. It is designated by an "x."

Species: Plants with certain differences compared to other plants of the same genus. Characteristics normally continue from generation to generation. Variations in species that occur in nature are *varieties,* designated in this book as var.

Ilex x altaclarensis
'Wilsonii'
Broadleaf evergreen shrub or small tree
Zones 6 to 10

Zone adaptation: Indicates where the plant can normally be grown successfully. Zones enclosed in parentheses means that the plant may survive if given a special site or protection within that zone. See Climate text, pages 94 and 95.

Left: A close look at hedge, screen and espalier plants reveals a striking array of colors and textures. Above: An elevated view of a well-planned landscape demonstrates the beauty and utility of hedges and screens.

Climate

Not all plants are adapted to grow successfully in all areas. Temperature extremes, available sunshine, rainfall, humidity and other factors combine to determine if a plant will thrive, or even survive in a given location. Easiest to grow are those that are native to your climate and region, or from a similar climate. Shrubs from England thrive in the Pacific Northwest and British Columbia. Most plants native to tropical regions thrive in Florida. Those from South Africa, Australia and the Mediterranean flourish in many regions in California.

Many shrubs and trees are adapted to a range of growing conditions. They can be grown successfully in climates considerably different from their native homes. Some require special attention, such as careful site selection, or particular cultural practices. Gardeners who like to experiment will try—and often succeed—where conditions are far from being the best.

Planting and care techniques are given for each plant in the encyclopedia. Following these cultural recommendations will help ensure that plants get a good start and thrive. Some important cultural terms used in plant descriptions are explained below.

SUN
Sun—Exposure to full sunlight for most or all of the day.
Part Shade—Either dappled sunlight or sunlight for part of the day.
Shade—No direct sunlight. Full-shade areas are found under trees, overhangs, or on the north side of buildings, hedges or screens.
Reflected Heat and Sun—Intensely warm situations near walls or paving, which reflect sunlight and collect heat.

IRRIGATION
Drought Tolerant—Means that after a period of time, plants become established and can survive on rainfall without supplemental irrigation. Keep in mind that all plants require irrigation for about one year after they are planted.
Occasional Deep Irrigation—Drought-tolerant plants look best with water applied several times during dry periods. Apply water slowly so it soaks deeply into root zone.
Average Water—Irrigation applied when the top few inches of soil become dry.
Ample Water—Frequent irrigation so the soil is damp to the touch at all times.

SOIL
Well-Drained Soil—Sandy or loamy soil that drains quickly, so that soil is moist but not wet.
Poor Soil—Soil lacking in nutrients and usually alkaline.
Clay Soil—Soil that has large quantities of clay, which causes drainage to be poor.

USDA ZONES AND CLIMATE REGIONS
The minimum temperature that a plant is able to withstand is a common measure of its adaptability. This is termed *cold-hardiness*. Hardiness zones developed by the United States Department of Agriculture (USDA) are shown on the facing page. On this map, North America is divided into 10 zones based on *average* minimum temperatures.

Choosing plants because they are cold-hardy to your area is an oversimplified approach to plant selection. Other aspects such as climate, geography and soil type significantly affect adaptability. A plant that is adapted in terms of minimum temperature may fail to thrive or die due to other factors. This problem is particularly evident in Zones 8, 9 and 10. For example, the humid, high-rainfall summers in southern Florida, Zone 10, are quite different from those in southern California, also Zone 10.

On pages 50 to 53 are lists of plants labeled as Regional Favorites. These plants are generally adapted to certain, broad climate regions in the United States and Canada. Use these lists along with the USDA hardiness zones to determine if a plant can be grown successfully in your area.

CLIMATE REGIONS
Pacific Northwest and Coastal British Columbia—Conditions are cool and humid. Soil is acid. Most rainfall occurs in winter, with a yearly average of 30 to 45 inches.
California—Summers are hot and dry and winters are mild and rainy. Rainfall occurs mainly in winter with amounts ranging between 12 and 40 inches per year. Coastal areas have a more moderate climate and are often foggy in summer.
Desert Regions—This area includes primarily the Mojave, Colorado and Sonoran deserts. Summers are long and hot. Winters are moderate but subject to occasional frosts. Winter rains are widespread and usually gentle, but thunderstorms are common in summer.
Gulf Coast and Florida—Climate is hot and humid. The annual average temperature is 60F to 70F (15C to 21C). Rainfall is abundant, averaging 40 to 60 inches annually, and is distributed evenly throughout the year.
Upper South—Climate is warm and humid, with rainfall ranging between 40 and 70 inches per year. Rainfall is distributed evenly throughout the year, but peaks slightly in midsummer or early spring, when thunderstorms are most common. Summer drought occurs occassionally. Winters are colder than the lower South.
Midwest and Northeast—Winters are moderately long and severe, usually with snow cover. Rainfall is moderate, 24 to 45 inches per year, and occurs primarily in summer.

THE MANY MICROCLIMATES OF YOUR GARDEN
In addition to general climate zones, you need to be aware of the small climate variations in your garden. These variations are called *microclimates*. They are created by the same factors that make up your general climate, but on a smaller scale. A large microclimate is an oasis in a desert. A small microclimate is created by the cooling shade beneath a tree, or the reflected heat from a west-facing wall.

You can use microclimates to your advantage by placing plants in locations favorable to their growth. First, identify the microclimates in your garden. South- and west-facing exposures are warmer than those that face east or north. Low areas are usually cooler. Cold-tender plants such as citrus can be placed against west- or south-facing walls to take advantage of the warmer temperatures. An overhang also moderates temperatures to reduce the chance of frost damage.

Be aware that microclimates change with the seasons, influenced by the sun as it changes position in the sky. For more information on climate, see page 30.

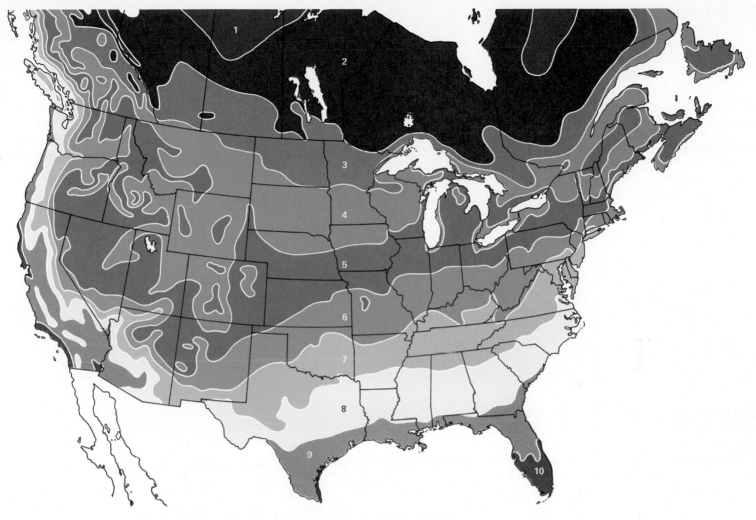

Hardiness Zones
of the United States and Canada

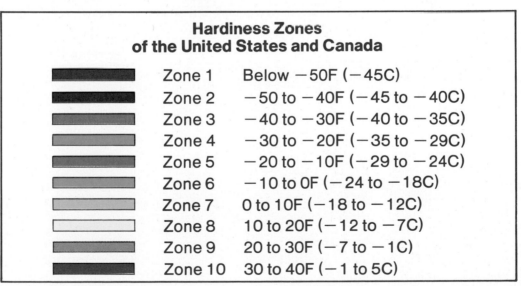

	Zone 1	Below −50F (−45C)
	Zone 2	−50 to −40F (−45 to −40C)
	Zone 3	−40 to −30F (−40 to −35C)
	Zone 4	−30 to −20F (−35 to −29C)
	Zone 5	−20 to −10F (−29 to −24C)
	Zone 6	−10 to 0F (−24 to −18C)
	Zone 7	0 to 10F (−18 to −12C)
	Zone 8	10 to 20F (−12 to −7C)
	Zone 9	20 to 30F (−7 to −1C)
	Zone 10	30 to 40F (−1 to 5C)

Each of the plants in the following pages shows recommended zone adaptations based on the hardiness zone map shown above, developed by the United States Department of Agriculture. To find out whether a plant will grow in your area, note which climate zone you live in, then refer to the plant description for the zone recommendation. A zone enclosed in parentheses indicates that the plant requires use of microclimates and frost-protection techniques to survive the cold temperatures in the zone. Note too, that climate zones and maps are based on average temperatures, and many small climates exist within a general climate zone. Because of these variables, it is possible that you can grow plants not rated for your zone. For the best, most reliable information on climate adaptation, consult your local county extension agent or nurseryman.

Abelia x grandiflora
Glossy abelia
Broadleaf evergreen shrub
Zones (5) to 10
A hybrid of species originally from China

Glossy abelia has glossy, pointed, dark-green leaves with bronze tints. Leaves are 1-1/2 inches long, sometimes smaller. Fine texture. Flowers are showy, tubular clusters, white or tinted pink, appearing summer to fall. Shearing destroys the graceful, natural form and lessens flower production. Semideciduous at 15F ($-9C$).

Height and spread: 8 to 10 feet by 5 to 6 feet. Can be maintained at 3 feet. Moderate growth rate.

Uses: Plant 2 to 3 feet apart for sheared or shaped hedge. Plant 3 to 5 feet apart for screen.

Valued for: Graceful, arching branches and abundant flowers. Looks lush with little maintenance.

Cultivars: 'Edward Goucher' is popular and widely available. Has same general characteristics as the species, except flowers are light pink, tinged with lavender. Mature height and spread of plant are less than the species—3 to 5 feet by 4 feet. Plant 1-1/2 to 2-1/2 feet apart.

Planting and care: Plant from containers after danger of frost is past, or in fall in mild-winter areas. Sun to part shade. Average soil. Average water requirement. Freezes to the ground at 0F ($-18C$), but usually recovers the following spring.

Acacia longifolia
(A. latifolia)
Sydney golden wattle
Broadleaf evergreen shrub
or small tree
Zones 9 and 10
Native to Australia

Plant appears to glow when backlit by the sun. Accepts shearing well. May be grown right to beach shoreline, where form is more prostrate. Tolerates poor soil and drought. Does not spread invasively. Relatively short-lived. Leaves are bright yellow-green, willowy, 3 to 5 inches long. Medium texture. Yellow flowers are not showy, but plant appears golden when they bloom.

Height and spread: 25 by 25 feet. Can be maintained at 6 feet. Fast growth rate.

Uses: Plant 3 to 8 feet apart for sheared or shaped hedge. Plant 15 feet apart for screen. Good for beach or highway planting.

Valued for: Luminous green foliage, billowy form, fast growth and low maintenance.

Planting and care: Plant from containers in any well-drained soil. Full sun or part shade. Does not require irrigation after it is established. Practically maintenance-free. Shear anytime.

Acer campestre
Hedge maple, Field maple
Deciduous tree or large shrub
Zones 5 to 8
Native to Europe and western Asia

This is one of the classic, British hedgerow plants. Leaves are dull, medium green, 2 to 4 inches long and lobed. Coarse texture. Shrubby, densely branched to the base. Seeds are winged. Yellow fall color, but not an outstanding feature.

Height and spread: 25 to 50 feet by 20 to 25 feet. Can reach 80 feet with age. Can be maintained at 4 feet. Slow to medium growth rate.

Uses: Plant 3 to 6 feet apart for sheared or shaped hedge. Plant 5 to 6 feet apart for screen.

Valued for: Exceptionally long-lived. Little pruning is required. Tolerant of city conditions.

Planting and care: Plant bare root, balled and burlapped, or from containers. Adapted to almost any well-drained soil, including poor, dry or sandy soils. Full sun or part shade. Average water requirement; will tolerate drought. Recovers from cold-temperature damage in one season.

Abelia x grandiflora—glossy abelia

Acer ginnala—amur maple

Acer ginnala
Amur maple
Deciduous shrub or small tree
Zones 2 to 8
Native to Siberia, Manchuria,
northern China and Japan

Amur maple is broad, globe shaped and bushy, with multiple stems. Useful, low-maintenance screen and colorful shrub year-round with few pests. Leaves drop in early fall. Leaves are dark green, 2 to 3-1/2 inches long with 3 lobes. Coarse texture. White or yellowish flowers are tiny and fragrant, preceding leaves in early spring. Bright-red seeds are borne in masses. Fall leaves are beautiful crimson, but may turn orange or yellow, depending on exposure. Leaves turn reddest in the sun.

Height and spread: 20 by 20 feet, more often 10 feet by 5 feet. Can be maintained at 6 feet. Rapid growth rate.

Uses: Plant 1 to 2 feet apart for sheared hedge. Plant 2 to 4 feet apart for shaped hedge. Plant 4 to 10 feet apart for screen.

Valued for: Low maintenance, cold resistance, early fall color and novel, fragrant flowers.

Planting and care: Plant balled and burlapped or from containers in almost any soil, moist or dry. Full sun or part shade. Appreciates ample water but tolerates less. Tolerant to cold.

Arbutus unedo
Strawberry tree
Broadleaf evergreen shrub
or small tree
Zones 7 to 10
Native to Ireland and the
Mediterranean

Strawberry tree has a wonderful multi-stem character and shaggy red bark. It makes an excellent screen in poor soils. Attractive when combined with Western natives. Resistant to oak-root fungus. Long-lived plant. Leaves are dark green, 2 inches long. Medium to coarse texture. Flowers are small, white and bell shaped. Fruit is like a small strawberry hanging from red stems. Edible as well as ornamental, but the taste and texture are bland. Fruit color changes from green to yellow to bright orange then red. All fruit colors are present at the same time on the plant, adding to its interest.

Height and spread: 10 to 25 feet by 10 to 25 feet. Occasionally reaches 35 feet high. Dwarf cultivars are available.

Uses: Plant 2 to 5 feet apart for a sheared or shaped hedge. Plant 4 to 8 feet apart for screen. Background. Canopy when pruned up.

Valued for: Exceptional performance in poor conditions, including drought tolerance and attractive fruit and flowers.

Cultivars: 'Compacta', 5 feet by 5 feet, has all the advantages of the species. Plant it in containers for a movable screen. 'Elfin King' is slightly smaller.

Planting and care: Plant from containers in any soil that has good drainage. Full sun to part shade. In desert areas, plant where it will receive some shade. Ample water is necessary the first growing season, thereafter plant thrives with little irrigation. Accepts pruning well. Few flowers when sheared.

Arctostaphylos densiflora 'Howard McMinn'
Manzanita
Broadleaf-evergreen shrub
Zones 9 and 10
Hybrid of California species

'Howard McMinn' manzanita makes a handsome, dense screen or sheared hedge. Excels on dry slopes. Combine with Western natives. Luminous, elegant appearance when backlit by the sun. Red branches. Leaves are shiny, pointed, less than 1 inch long. New leaves are bright yellow-green, darkening with age. Fine texture. Pinkish-white, bell-shaped flowers are borne in showy clusters, covering the plant in early spring. Fruit look similar to tiny apples, attractive to birds. Tart and edible—best as a jelly.

Arctostaphylos densiflora 'Harmony' is slightly larger. Considered superior, but is difficult to find.

Height and spread: 5 by 12 feet, usually 4 by 7 feet. Moderate growth rate.

Uses: Plant 3 to 4 feet apart for sheared or shaped hedge. Plant 6 feet apart for screen.

Valued for: Fine appearance with minimum maintenance and drought tolerance.

Planting and care: Plant from containers in any well-drained soil. Full sun, no shade. Minimal irrigation required after plant is established. Will thrive on summer irrigation with excellent drainage. Hardy to 15F (−9C). Tip-prune or shear to shape.

Arbutus unedo—strawberry tree

Artemisia

Southernwood
Deciduous shrub
Zones 5 to 10
Native to Eurasia

Southernwood makes a compact mound, popular for herb-garden borders or wherever gray foliage is desired. Sprigs hung in a closet are said to discourage moths. Leaves are greenish gray, tiny and fragrant. Fine texture. Flowers are yellowish white.

Height and spread: 3 to 5 feet by 3 to 5 feet.

Uses: Plant 12 to 15 inches apart for border.

Valued for: Lemon-scented, feathery gray foliage, mounding form and drought tolerance.

Cultivars: Many superior cultivars are available. Most make excellent borders. 'Silver King' is highly recommended.

Planting and care: Plant from containers or divisions in well-drained soil. Full sun or light shade. Requires little water after plant is established. Pinch to shape. Divide in spring or fall.

Atriplex lentiformis 'Breweri'

Brewer saltbush
Semievergreen broadleaf shrub
Zones 9 and 10
Native to the West Coast

This is an exceptionally tough plant, growing where most plants fail. Useful as a dry slope, fire buffer between rugged country and developed land. Excellent as a sheared hedge. Does best near the coast. Leaves are gray-green or gray, fleshy and triangular, to 2 inches long. Medium to coarse texture. Flowers are inconspicuous. Decorative, golden fruit are borne in clusters.

Height and spread: 3 to 8 feet by 6 to 8 feet. Can be maintained at 3 feet. Slow to moderate growth.

Uses: Plant 2 to 4 feet apart for sheared hedge or screen.

Valued for: Ability to survive in dry, alkaline and salty soils, and resistance to fire.

Planting and care: Plant from containers or cuttings in any soil. Best in full sun. Little water is necessary after first year, but plant looks more lush with occasional, deep irrigation. Hardy to 18F (−8C).

Baccharis pilularis

Dwarf coyote brush
Broadleaf evergreen shrub
Zones 8 to 10
Native to California

Compact, billowing form looks lush in drought, high desert, coastal or swampy situations. Excellent border or edging plant where water is limited. Give it room to spread. Most often grown as a low-maintenance ground cover. Leaves are bright green, less than 1/2 inch long, finely toothed. Ultra-fine texture. Inconspicuous flowers. Grow cultivars only, such as those listed on the next page.

Height and spread: 1/2 to 2 feet by 4 to 9 feet. Can be maintained much lower. Moderate to fast growth rate.

Uses: Plant 18 to 30 inches apart for border.

Valued for: Exceptional drought tolerance, fine leaf texture, low maintenance and fire-retardant properties.

Artemisia species—southernwood

Baccharis pilularis 'Twin Peaks'—dwarf coyote brush

Cultivars: 'Pigeon Point' retains its medium-green color all year. 'Twin Peaks' is yellow-green in spring, gray-green in summer.

Planting and care: Do not plant unnamed species. Plant cultivars from cuttings, flats or containers in any soil, in full sun. Plant needs little water after it is established, but tolerates frequent irrigation. Tip-prune any time to control spread. Cut out old wood and errant branches yearly before new spring growth begins.

Bambusa
Bamboo
Evergreen grass forms
Zones (8) to 10
Native to Asia

All bamboos recommended in this book are *clumping* varieties. Unlike *running* varieties, they will not spread invasively to become pests. Clumps expand in diameter gradually with age. A young clump sends up short canes. A mature clump sends up tall canes at a fast rate. Leaf drop produces a natural, weed-free mulch, which some gardeners find objectionable.

Uses: Bamboos make excellent screens and shaped hedges because of their fast, dense growth and their ability to grow in narrow spaces. Most can be planted in containers for movable screens. Airy appearance and dramatic texture lend a special mood to the garden. Effective as a background. Leaves produce a pleasing, rustling sound.

Valued for: Graceful appearance, exceptionally fast growth and tolerance of waterside conditions.

Planting and care: Plant from containers, divisions or rhizome cuttings after all danger of frost is past. Plants that are rootbound in containers grow fast. Tolerates most soils, but not alkaline conditions. Full sun or part shade. Water frequently and deeply. Fertilize monthly for fastest growth. Plantings look best with regular maintenance. To groom a clump, cut out unwanted canes, and nip out shoots as they emerge. Strip canes of low, sideshoots for graceful, stem silhouette.

Bambusa glaucescens 'Alphonse Karr'

Leaves are yellow-green to 4 inches long. Canes are yellow with green stripes. Mature clumps can be divided in spring and replanted. Each new clump should have several roots to get it off to a good start. Hardy to 15F (−7C).

Height and spread: Grows 10 to 15 feet high in a clump when pruned. Grows to 35 feet high if left alone.

Uses: Large-scale shaped hedge when planted 2 to 3 feet apart. Feature planting. Containers. Background.

Bambusa glaucescens riviereorum
Chinese goddess bamboo

Leaves are small and lacy on arching stems. They may turn straw color in winter. Fernlike texture. Hardy to 15F (−10C).

Height and spread: 4 to 6 feet high in clumps when pruned, to 8 feet high without control.

Uses: Plant 2 feet apart for shaped hedge or screen. Containers. Background planting.

Bambusa oldhamii
Timber bamboo, Oldham bamboo

Leaves are yellow-green as they age, deep green when young. Canes up to 3 inches in diameter grow at a fast rate when clumps are mature. Hardy to 20F (−7C). Makes a dense screen.

Height and spread: 15- to 25-foot-high clumps with control, to 40 feet without control.

Uses: Large-scale screen if planted 2 to 3 feet apart. Feature planting. Background. Windbreak.

Bambusa species, bamboo, with *Nandina domestica*, heavenly bamboo, at base.

Berberis buxifolia

Magellan barberry
Broadleaf evergreen shrub
Zones 6 to 10
Native to Chile

Magellan barberry has stiff, erect branches, making it a natural barrier plant. Leaves are green, spiny and leathery, 1 inch long or less. Fine texture. Flowers are orange-yellow. Berries are dark purple.

Height and spread: 6 feet by 6 feet. Can be maintained at 3 feet.

Uses: Plant 'Nana' 6 to 12 inches apart for border. Plant 9 to 18 inches apart for shaped hedge. Plant 1-1/2 to 3 feet apart for screen. Barrier.

Valued for: Low barrier and low maintenance.

Cultivars: 'Nana' grows 1-1/2 to 2 feet high, with a mounding growth habit. Yellow flowers.

Planting and care: Plant from containers in any soil. Sun or part shade. Average water requirement. Hardy to 0F (−18C).

Berberis darwinii

Darwin barberry
Broadleaf evergreen shrub
Zones 9 and 10
Native to Chile

This is the showiest *Berberis* species, but limited cold-hardiness reduces its range. Graceful, arching form. Leaves are dark green, 1 inch long, spiny and hollylike. Fine texture. Flowers are orange-yellow, showy and abundant. Berries are dark blue, attractive to birds.

Height and spread: 5 to 10 feet by 4 to 7 feet. Can be maintained at 4 by 3 feet.

Uses: Plant 1 to 2-1/2 feet apart for sheared or shaped hedge. Plant 1 to 4 feet apart for screen.

Valued for: Barrier planting, showy flowers and low maintenance.

Planting and care: Plant from containers, cuttings or by dividing runners. Spreads by underground runners. Tolerates any soil. Full sun or part shade. Average water requirement. Cut back to renew growth.

Berberis koreana

Korean barberry
Deciduous shrub
Zones 4 to 10
Native to Korea

This plant adds interest to the landscape the entire year. Leaves are medium green, medium texture. Small, yellow flowers appear in early spring. Berries are bright red, borne in small clusters. Red fall color. Snow settles attractively on the thorns. It suckers freely, an advantage for renewing hedge plantings and for improving its dense, barrier quality. Makes a coarse-textured hedge.

Height and spread: 6 to 8 feet by 4 feet. Fast growth rate.

Uses: Plant 9 to 24 inches apart for sheared or shaped hedge. Plant 2 feet apart for screen.

Valued for: Barrier planting, upright growth that requires little pruning, tolerance of difficult growing conditions and resistance to rust disease.

Planting and care: Plant bare root, balled and burlapped, from cuttings or containers. Adapts to any soil. Full sun or light shade. Average water requirement. To renew, cut back to the ground. Propagate by removing and planting suckers.

Berberis x mentorensis

Mentor barberry
Broadleaf semideciduous to evergreen shrub
Zones 5 to 8
Hybrid of Berberis julianae and Berberis thunbergii

A valuable hedge plant or small-space screen. Leaves are dark green, clean in appearance, 1 inch or longer. Medium texture. Flowers are small

Berberis darwinii—Darwin barberry

Berberis darwinii—Darwin barberry

and yellow. Berries are dull, dark red. Attractive, red fall color in cold-winter areas only. Elsewhere, leaves may turn bronze in fall. Often evergreen in Zones 7 and 8.

Height and spread: 5 to 7 feet by 5 to 7 feet. Can be maintained at almost any size.

Uses: Plant 15 to 18 inches apart for sheared or shaped hedge. Plant 1-1/2 to 2-1/2 feet apart for screen. Plant 6 to 18 inches apart for barrier, or plant two rows 6 inches apart. Background.

Valued for: Erect, neat habit with little or no pruning, thorny, impenetrable branches, low maintenance, and tolerance of city conditions.

Planting and care: Plant bare root, from cuttings or from containers in almost any soil. Full sun or light shade. Drought tolerant after plant is established. To renew plant, cut back to the ground just prior to new spring growth.

Berberis thunbergii
Japanese barberry
Deciduous shrub
Zones 3 to 10
Native to Japan

Because of its graceful, arching form, Japanese barberry is one of the most popular hedge plants since its introduction in 1875. There are many cultivars. The species is interesting all year. Leaves are deep green, small, up to 1 inch long. Fine texture. Flowers are small and yellow. Berries are small, bright red, decorating the plant into winter. They attract birds. Fall color is brilliant red.

Height and spread: 4 to 6 feet by 4 to 6 feet. Usually low and compact. Can be maintained at 3 feet. Fast growth rate. Dwarf cultivars are available.

Uses: Plant dwarf cultivars 6 to 12 inches apart for border. Plant 15 inches to 2 feet apart for sheared or shaped hedge. Plant 2 to 3 feet apart for screen.

Valued for: Thorny, impenetrable barrier planting, ease of growth in almost any situation.

Cultivars: 'Atropurpurea', red-leafed Japanese barberry, has bronzy red or purplish foliage. Develops best color in full sun. Leaves may be greenish in shade. Same general characteristics as the species, except it is slightly less cold tolerant. 'Erecta', truehedge columnberry, grows 7 feet high and spreads 3 feet wide. It can be maintained at 3 feet high. Similar to species except for upright branching habit. Little side shearing is necessary, but heading back the top makes new growth fuller. Plant 'Atropurpurea' or 'Erecta' 6 to 24 inches apart for a sheared or shaped hedge. Plant 18 to 24 inches apart for a screen.

Red-leafed dwarfs for borders: 'Atropurpurea Nana', 'Crimson Pygmy' and 'Rose Glow' have marbled, pinkish foliage darkening to bronze with age. All have dense, compact form—1-1/2 feet high by 2 feet wide. Slow to moderate growth rate. Require full sun to develop best foliage color.

Green-leafed dwarfs for borders: 'Nana' and 'Kobold' are bright-green, extra-dwarf, rounded forms.

For low hedges: 'Aurea' is a yellow-leafed dwarf. Low growth rate, 1-1/2 to 2 feet high by 1-1/2 to 2 feet wide. Full sun is required for foliage color.

Berberis thunbergii minor, box barberry, grows slowly to 3-1/2 feet high. Fine texture. Best as clipped hedge.

Planting and care: Plant bare-root plants, cuttings or from containers in any soil. Full sun or part shade. Average water, tolerates some drought. To renew plant, cut back to the ground. Any of the low forms are easily pruned to smaller dimensions.

Berberis thunbergii 'Atropurpurea Nana'—dwarf Japanese barberry

Berberis thunbergii—Japanese barberry

Berberis thunbergii 'Atropurpurea'—red-leafed Japanese barberry

Buxus

Box, boxwood
Broadleaf evergreen shrubs
or small trees
Zones 4 to 10 as indicated

Fine texture and slow growth rate are the greatest assets of boxwood. Plants live for hundreds of years, forming a permanent, garden framework. Shearing is usually not necessary. Some cultivars grow more rapidly than the species, but the ultimate height of most is unknown. Cuttings of exceptional varieties not available from nurseries may be obtained from boxwood societies.

Uses: There is a *Buxus* for almost any garden situation. Years of hybridizing have produced cultivars able to withstand extremely cold temperatures. *Buxus* is most often sheared into precise, geometric hedges, borders or fanciful topiary shapes. Plants are easy to maintain at almost any size. Natural, billowing form of plants make an exceptional screen. Unsheared, compact, dwarf varieties are unsurpassed for a border, edging or low hedge. Planted in containers, *Buxus* make movable screens or enclosures for roof gardens.

Valued for: Long life. Fine-textured, evergreen elegance. Slow growth rate. Ability to be sheared, or left as handsome, natural form. Easy to propagate. Minimal pruning requirements.

Planting and care: Plant balled and burlapped or from cuttings or containers in average, well-drained, garden soil. Full sun or part shade; part shade is best in hot-summer areas. Average water requirement. Prune after new spring growth. Late summer is traditional pruning time for mild-winter climates. Shearing in late summer in cold-climate regions stimulates tender growth that can be damaged by cold.

Boxwood are easy to grow where adapted. Choosing plants adapted to your area is the secret to success. A moist, well-drained site, regular applications of fertilizer and control of spider mites produces most attractive growth. A light mulch over root area conserves soil moisture. Heavy mulches, cultivating and ground covers that make a dense mat may damage roots, which grow close to the surface.

Buxus microphylla var. *japonica* is the only variety that will survive in hot, dry sites. *Buxus* in cold-climate areas need protection from wind and reflected heat. Prune frost-damaged growth back to green growth in early spring. If plants are killed to the ground, prune back to 3 inches above soil. Plants recover slowly but usually survive. To rejuvenate a neglected box hedge, prune out about one-third of the plant, then feed and water regularly.

Buxus microphylla var. japonica

Japanese boxwood
Zones (6) to 10
Native to Japan

Japanese boxwood makes an attractive, informal screen. Usually grown as a sheared hedge from 1 to 4 feet high. Popular for shaping into topiaries. Recovers quickly from late-spring frost damage. Round-tipped leaves are yellow-green, 1/2 to 1 inch long. Fine texture. Foliage takes on deep-bronze tint in cold-winter areas. Flowers are inconspicuous.

Buxus microphylla var. *japonica*—Japanese boxwood

Height and spread: 4 to 8 feet by 4 to 8 feet. Can be maintained at 6 inches. Slow to moderate growth rate is relatively fast for *Buxus*.

Uses: Border. Plant 1 to 2 feet apart for sheared hedge. Plant 1-1/2 to 2 feet apart for screen. Background. Topiary. Containers.

Valued for: Lush, bright foliage, and ability to withstand dry heat, extreme cold and slightly alkaline soil.

Cultivars: 'Green Beauty' grows dense and upright to 6 feet high or more. Leaves are dark green. Retains lush, green color in cold weather and summer heat. 'Richardii' also grows to 6 feet high or more. Upright form, faster growth rate than 'Green Beauty'. Leaves are shiny, medium green, larger, with notched tips.

Buxus microphylla var. koreana
Korean littleleaf box
Zones (4) to 10
Native to Korea

Korean littleleaf box is the most cold-tolerant *Buxus* species. It will survive in Zone 4 only in the most protected sites. Leaves are pointed, yellow-green, 1/4 to 1/2 inch long. Bronzy winter color. Shear once a year.

Height and spread: 3 by 7 feet. Usually grows to 1-1/2 feet high. Can be maintained at 1 foot high. Slow growth rate.

Uses: Border. Plant 8 to 12 inches apart for sheared hedge and 2 feet apart for shaped hedge. Containers. Topiary.

Valued for: Exceptional hardiness and fine texture.

Cultivars: 'Wintergreen' has foliage that bronzes slightly at 18F (−8C), but is one of the most cold-tolerant *Buxus*. Grows 1-1/2 feet high, spreading 4 feet wide. Grows less than 2 inches a year. Unsheared form is loose and not as attractive as species. 'Green Velvet' is a Canadian hybrid between Korean and English box. Grows to 3 feet high and 3 feet wide, but can be maintained much lower. Handsome, densely branching, rounded mound. Leaves are dark green. Retains lush, green color in cold winters. 'Compacta' is a hardy, ultra-fine textured, compact, rounded shrub. Round-tipped leaves are yellow-green, less than 1/2 inch long. Turns deep bronze color in full sun. Ex-tremely dwarf and dense. Best in partial shade as an unsheared border. Plant 8 to 15 inches apart or less. Grows to 6 by 8 inches, up to 15 by 15 inches with age. Slow growth rate. 'Green Pillow' has stiff branches that form a compact, irregular mound. Round-tipped leaves are dark green, less than 1/2 inch long. Ultra-fine texture. Slight bronze tint in cold-winter areas. No flowers. Grows to 8 by 12 inches. Old, well-cared-for specimens may grow to 2 by 4 feet. Extremely slow growth rate.

Buxus sempervirens
Common boxwood,
English box
Zones (5) to 10
Native to western Asia, southeastern Europe and North Africa

This is the classic boxwood grown by the Romans. Foliage is dense, billow-ing and mounded. With great age, it assumes a spreading, gnarled tree form. Does best in moist, mild-winter areas. Survives in protected locations in Zone 5. Best grown along the coast in the East. It will not survive in alka-

Bright-green hedge in foreground is *Buxus microphylla* var. *koreana*—Korean littleleaf box. In background at left is *Buxus sempervirens* 'Pullman'.

Buxus sempervirens—common boxwood

line soils or dry heat such as desert areas. Bees are attracted to the flowers. Warm, humid weather brings out leaf fragrance that is objectionable to some. Round leaves are dark bluish green, 1-1/4 to 1-1/2 inches long. Fine texture. Flowers are inconspicuous but fragrant.

Height and spread: 20 by 20 feet with age, usually a sheared hedge maintained at 4 to 8 feet. Slow growth rate.

Uses: Plant 1 to 2 feet apart for sheared hedge to 2 feet or more apart for screen. Background. Containers. Topiary.

Valued for: Long life, dark color and for defining garden spaces in a formal style.

Cultivars: 'Inglis' grows to 6 or 7 feet high. Slow growth rate. Pointed leaves are medium green, less than 1 inch long. Fine texture. Makes a handsome, informal mound, but some nursery catalogs describe its form as pyramidal or cone shaped. Highly rated for hardiness and appearance. 'Suffruticosa' edging boxwood, or suffruticosa edging box, is adapted to Zone 5 with care. Slow growth rate to 5 feet high in 150 years. Often grows 1-1/2 feet high, spreading 1 foot wide. Grows only 1/2 inch in two years. Leaves are light green, 3/4-inch long, shiny, with rounded tips. Slightly upright, dense and compact. Best as a low, billowing border planted 2 feet or less apart. Slow recovery from winter damage. Best in mild climates. Outstanding, ancient specimens can be seen in the South. 'Vardar Valley' grows 2 feet high, spreading 4 feet wide. May reach 3 feet by 7 feet with age. Grows more than 2 inches a year—fast for *Buxus.* Exceptional vitality and hardiness. Leaves are dark bluish green, less than 1 inch long, with pointed or round tips. Broad, compact, flattened mound, best as an unsheared low hedge planted 3 to 5 feet apart. Retains dark-green color through cold winters.

Calocedrus decurrens
(Libocedrus decurrens)
Incense cedar
Needled evergreen tree
Zones 7 to 10
Native to West Coast to Baja California

Mature form is dense and tight, rather formal in appearance. Stays shrublike for years, then quickly grows into a symmetrical pyramid. Branches sweep the ground. Flat, scalelike needles are yellow-green to medium green. Coarse texture. Cones are small, yellowish to reddish brown. Shaggy, reddish-brown bark.

Height and spread: 70 to 100 feet by 40 feet. Spread depends on location. Plants grown out of mountains are more narrow.

Uses: Plant 2 to 3 feet apart for sheared hedge. Plant 6 to 10 feet apart for screen. Windbreak. Noise buffer. Background. Excellent substitute for *Thuja* because of its greater resistance to pests and diseases, and superior appearance in winter.

Valued for: Fragrant foliage, symmetry and drought tolerance.

Planting and care: Plant from containers in average to poor soil in full sun. Irrigate deeply and infrequently to establish plant. Heat and drought tolerant after established.

Camellia japonica and Camellia sasanqua
Camellia
Broadleaf evergreen shrubs or small trees
Zones 7 to 10
Native to southern and eastern Asia

Camellias make wonderful, permanent hedges and screens. Centuries-old, sheared and sculpted sasanqua hedges are features in great Japanese gardens, where they are valued for their glossy, dark foliage rather than their flowers. Shearing eliminates or stimulates flowering, depending on timing.

Few hedge or screen specimens have the beauty of camellias in flower. They are also among the finest espalier plants. Most species and cultivars are slow growing. Plants are treelike with the best growing conditions. They eventually become low-maintenance screen plants after they are established. Excellent in containers.

Camellias have dark-green, leathery, glossy leaves that grow 1 to 4 inches long. Sasanquas are similar but have a smaller, narrower leaf. Medium texture. Flowers are single, or have numerous petals in double, semidouble, anemone, peony and other forms. Rarely fragrant. Many colors are available. *C. japonica* blooms fall or spring. *C. sasanqua* blooms fall or winter.

Height and spread: *C. japonica* grows 6 to 12 feet by 6 to 12 feet or more, to 25 feet high with great age. Can be maintained at 3 feet. *C. sasanqua* grows 4 to 6 feet high. Spread varies from upright to prostrate. Grows to 15 feet high with great age. Can be maintained at 3 feet. For both, growth rate is slow to moderate.

Uses: *C. japonica*—plant 2 to 4 feet apart for sheared or shaped hedge. Plant 4 to 6 feet apart for screen. Background. Containers. *C. sasan-*

Buxus sempervirens—common boxwood

qua—plant 1-1/2 to 2-1/2 feet apart for sheared or shaped hedge. Plant 3 to 4 feet apart for screen. Background. Containers. Espalier. Topiary.

Valued for: Long life, elegance and attractive foliage and flowers.

There are thousands of cultivars, species camellias and rare varieties. Most are available only from specialty nurseries. Those listed are widely available. All are reliable, with upright growth.

Cultivars: *C. japonica:* Zones 8 to 10 except as noted.

'Ace of Hearts', red, semidouble, tolerates hot, dry locations. 'Berenice Boddy', to Zone 7, light pink, semidouble, vigorous growth. 'Covina', rose-pink, semidouble, tolerates hot, dry locations. 'Debutante', to Zone 7, light pink, peony form, vigorous growth with profuse flowers. 'Glen 40', to Zone 7, deep red, formal double, slow, compact growth. One of the best. Excellent cut flowers. 'Herme' or 'Jordan's Pride', to Zone 7, mixed pink and white, semidouble. 'Magnoliaeflora', blush pink, semidouble, compact form. Does well in warm, interior valleys. Excellent cut flowers. 'Mathotiana', crimson-red, double. 'Nuccio's gem', exceptional, white, double flowers, dense form. 'Purity', white, rose form to double flowers. Vigorous growth. 'Scentsation', silvery pink, fragrant flowers. 'Swan Lake', to Zone 7, white, peony form, show-quality flowers. Vigorous growth.

Cultivars: *C. sasanqua:* All are adapted to Zones 7 to 10, in full sun or part shade:

'Cleopatra', rose-pink, semidouble, compact form. 'Hino de Gumo', single white flowers with pink edge. 'Hiryu', deep, crimson-red, double or rose form. Tall and erect with narrow green leaves. 'Jean May', shell-pink, double, outstanding glossy foliage. 'Setsugekka', white, semidouble, with ruffled petals and yellow stamens. Showy, excellent cut flowers. 'Sparkling Burgundy', ruby-rose, peony form, excellent for espaliers. 'Yuletide', deep red, single flowers with yellow stamens. Blooms at Christmas. Upright and tough. One of the best for hedges. Popular.

Planting and care: Plant balled and burlapped or from containers in rich, well-drained soil. Acid conditions are best. Tolerant of dense shade. Sasanquas take full sun and dry air or almost full shade and humidity.

Japonicas usually need part shade and more humidity. Plant high and apply a mulch over root zone. Ample water at first, then little is necessary after plant is established. Head back tops to encourage bushiness or prune back sides to encourage upright growth. Right after flowering, shear or selectively prune back branches one by one to previous season's pruning scar. Both procedures stimulate heavy budding. Thin buds for show-quality flowers. For no flowers, shear at least twice a year. Fertilize after flowering. Do not overfertilize. Iron chelates correct chlorosis. Locate plants away from drying winds and protect from winter sun in northern limits of range. Excellent in large containers. Soil mix should be acid, composed of 50% organic material.

Caragana arborescens
Siberian pea tree
Deciduous shrub or small tree
Zones 2 to 9
Native to Manchuria and Siberia

Leaves are yellow-green to gray-green, finely cut into leaflets. Fine texture. Spring flowers are small, yellow and pealike. Fruit forms in pods. Form is upright. Leaves drop early.

Height and spread: 12 by 6 feet. Can be maintained at 3 feet.

Uses: Plant 1 to 2 feet apart for sheared hedge. Plant 2-1/2 to 3 feet apart for shaped hedge. Windbreak or shelterbelt. *Caragana arborescens lorbergi* makes a fine espalier.

Valued for: Windbreaks and sheared hedges in the most difficult climates, drought tolerance and adaptation to difficult soil conditions.

Dwarf peashrubs make low hedges that require little pruning. *Caragana aurantiaca* and *C. pygmacea* have gray-green leaves. *C. frutex* has green leaves. All are fine textured, produce small, yellow, pealike flowers and are tolerant of drought and alkaline soil.

They grow 2 to 3 feet high by 1-1/2 to 2 feet wide. Plant 12 to 15 inches apart for sheared or shaped hedge. Low, thorny barrier.

Planting and care: Plant from seeds, cuttings or containers in well-drained soil. Full sun. Drought tolerant after plant is established. Becomes scraggly if not clipped. Forms dense branches to plant base in full sun with shearing. Cut to the ground to renew hedge.

Camellia japonica—camellia

Carissa grandiflora
(C. macrocarpa)
Natal plum
Broadleaf evergreen shrub
Zones (9) and 10
Native to South Africa

Natal plum is an effective, thorny barrier or formal-looking sheared hedge. An attractive, informal screen with little maintenance that has close-up interest year-round. Plant in containers for a movable screen or espalier. Leaves are dark green, 3 inches long, oval, thick and shiny. Coarse texture. Abundant, white, fragrant flowers are shaped like small stars. Small, red, plum-shaped fruit taste sweet and tart at the same time. Eat fresh, or add to salads or sauces. Flowers and fruit often appear on the plant simultaneously.

Height and spread: 7 by 7 feet. May reach 15 feet with best conditions. Dwarf cultivars are available.

Uses: Plant 1-1/2 to 4 feet apart for sheared or shaped hedge. Plant 4 to 5 feet apart for screen. Plant dwarf natal plums 6 to 18 inches apart for low hedge. Barrier. Background. Espalier. Containers.

Valued for: Coastal planting, elegant foliage and flowers, edible fruit and fast, low-maintenance growth.

Cultivars: 'Fancy' grows to 6 feet high. It is noted for its profuse flower and fruit production. Excellent screen or espalier. 'Ruby Point' grows to 6 feet high. It is noted for the red color of new foliage. 'Boxwood Beauty'

grows 2 by 2 feet, similar to *C. grandiflora* but thornless. Form is exceptionally compact and easily shaped. Little pruning is necessary. 'Tomlinson' is thornless, growing slowly to 2-1/2 feet high by 3 feet wide. Leaves have russet tinge. Large flowers, wine-colored fruit.

Planting and care: Plant from seeds or containers after danger of frost has passed. Average to poor soil. Needs exposure to full sun for best flowers and fruit. Accepts shade. Drought tolerant near the coast. Needs regular irrigation inland. Freezes at 28F (−2C). Usually recovers from frost damage quickly. Prune heavily in early spring or any time to control growth.

Carpinus betulus
Hornbeam, European
hornbeam, Yokebeam
Deciduous tree
Zones 4 to 10
Native to Europe and Asia Minor

This is one of the classic hedge plants of Europe. It is used for hedgerows in England and for spatial definition in the great gardens of the United States, France, England and Italy. Lumber milled from hornbeam is one of the toughest known, used by Romans for chariots, and by generations since the Middle Ages for oxen yokes. Upper branches are often *pleached,* woven, into a dense ceiling. Or side branches

are pleached to form an impenetrable barrier. See page 113 for more information on pleaching. Leaves are dark green, 1-1/2 to 3-1/2 inches long, toothed at the edges. Coarse texture. Flowers are inconspicuous. Fruit are formed in 5-inch-long clusters. Fall color is usually yellow, occasionally red. Leaves turn brown, often cling to branches through winter.

Height and spread: 40 to 60 feet by 30 to 40 feet. Usually about 20 to 30 feet high. Can be maintained at 4 to 6 feet. Slow to moderate growth rate.

Uses: Plant 2 to 4 feet apart for sheared or shaped hedge. Plant 4 to 10 feet apart for screen. Space narrow forms closely together. Barrier. Noise buffer. Background. Pleaching. Canopy.

Valued for: Long life, ability to be sheared or pleached, dense foliage and resistance to pest damage.

Cultivars: 'Fastigiata' grows to 30 feet high by 12 feet wide. It occasionally reaches 50 feet, spreading to an oval shape with age. 'Pyramidalis' is similar. Both are popular. 'Columnaris' is more spreading. American hornbeam, *C. caroliniana,* also makes an excellent hedge. It resembles European hornbeam but prefers light shade and moisture.

Planting and care: Plant balled and burlapped or from containers in any well-drained soil in spring. Do not plant in fall. Best with full sun and average water. May be sheared, but dense growth makes this unneccessary with large-scale screen plantings.

Carissa grandiflora—natal plum

Carissa grandiflora—natal plum

Ceratonia siliqua
Carob, St. John's bread
Broadleaf evergreen tree
Zones 8 to 10
Native to the Mediterranean

Carob makes an excellent, large-scale, hedgewall or dense, broad screen. Branches reach to the ground. Leaves are dark green, divided into 2-inch-long, round, glossy leaflets. Medium texture. Flowers are male and female on separate plants. Fruit on females is a long, brown pod. It has high sugar content and a chocolatelike taste. It can be ground into carob powder and used in baking. Roots may heave pavement. Trees create heavy shade.

Height and spread: 30 to 40 feet by 30 to 40 feet. Can be held to 8 feet. Slow to moderate growth rate.

Uses: Sheared hedge planted 6 to 15 feet apart. Screen planted 15 to 20 feet apart. Background. Windbreak. Canopy when pruned up. Food source. Noise buffer. Highway planting. Firebreak.

Valued for: Dark, dense foliage and carob pods, tolerance of desert or coastal conditions, heat, drought, wind, poor soil and low maintenance.

Planting and care: Plant from seeds or containers in any well-drained soil. Full sun to part shade. No water after plant is established, but deep, infrequent irrigation produces faster growth. Do not overwater. Subject to crown rot. Young trees need winter protection in colder areas. Shear any time.

Chaenomeles
(C. speciosa, C. lagenaria, Cydonia japonica)
Flowering quince,
Burning bush
Deciduous shrub
Zones 4 to 10
Native to Japan and China

Flowering quince has long been one of the most popular barrier hedges. Many named cultivars of all sizes and colors are available. They are also well suited to informal espalier forms. Leaves are 1-1/2 to 3 inches long, dark green, shiny and bronzy when young. Medium texture. Flowers bloom in early spring. They are white through shades of pink to red, usually single and showy. Small, yellow quince fruit follow. They can be made into a delicious, spicy jelly. Interesting winter character is created by unusual branching pattern. Most varieties have sharp thorns.

Height and spread: 5 to 7 feet by 5 to 7 feet. Can be maintained at 4 feet. Smaller cultivars are available.

Uses: Plant 1 to 1-1/2 feet apart for border. Plant 2-1/2 to 4 feet apart for sheared or shaped hedge or screen. Barrier. Espalier.

Valued for: Flowers, attractive branching and ease of growth.

Cultivars: Many cultivars are available. Here are some of the most common.

1 to 1-1/2 feet: *Chaenomeles japonica* 'Alpina', orange.

2 to 3 feet: 'Jet Trail', white. 'Cameo', apricot-pink, double. 'Phyllis Moore', pink, semidouble. 'Pink Lady', rose-pink, buds are redder. 'Rowallane', red. 'Texas Scarlet', scarlet. Japanese quince, *Chaenomeles japonica,* orange-red flowers. 'Stanford Red', scarlet with a few thorns.

5 to 7 feet: 'Snow', white, upright. 'Nivalis', white. 'Apple Blossom', white and pink. 'Pink Beauty', pink, upright. 'Enchantress', shell-pink. 'Coral Sea', coral-pink. 'Clarke's Giant Red', red. 'Rubra Grandiflora', red, upright. 'Boule de Feu', red, semidouble. 'Minerva', red. 'Hollandia', red, blooms spring and fall. 'Toyo Nishiki', all colors, which bloom on plant at same time. 'Falconet Charlot', salmon-pink, double, thornless. 'Red Ruffles', red, ruffled and thornless.

Planting and care: Plant balled and burlapped, bare root or container-grown plants in light to heavy soil. Will not tolerate alkaline conditions, common in the Southwest. Best with full sun and average water. Tolerates heat and cold, but may not bloom where winters are warm. Prune any time. Flowers are produced on the previous season's growth, so prune in early spring.

*Ceratonia siliqua—*carob

Carpinus betulus 'Fastigiata'—upright hornbeam

Chamaecyparis lawsoniana
Port Orford cedar, Lawson false cypress
Needled evergreen tree
Zones (5) to 9
Native from northwest California to southwest Oregon

Port Orford cedar makes a dense, tight hedge when sheared and topped at 10 feet. A relatively narrow, large-scale screen plant with branches to the ground. Pyramidal form. Scalelike needles are dark blue-green. Cultivars are available in other colors. Coarse texture. Inconspicuous, red male cones appear at tips of needles. Female cones look like juniper berries.

Height and spread: 70 by 30 feet. Can be maintained at 10 feet. Smaller cultivars are available. Fast growth rate.

Uses: Plant 2 to 3 feet apart for sheared or shaped hedge. Plant 6 to 10 feet apart for screen. Windbreak. Noise buffer. Background.

Valued for: Fast growth, dense, evergreen, low-maintenance screen.

Cultivars: 'Allumii', blue cypress, also scarab cypress, is narrow to 30 feet high. It has blue-green or metallic blue foliage. Useful for hedges. 'Forsteckensis' grows 6 feet high, spreading 4 feet wide. Dark-green leaves have mossy texture. Makes a compact screen. 'Nidiformis' ('Nestoides'), bird's-nest cypress, grows 6 feet by 3 to 5 feet, and has dark-green leaves. Top is depressed into a nest shape. Similar cultivars with bluish-green foliage include 'Grandi' and 'Tamariscifolia'. All three are used for informal screening or hedging. 'Elwoodii' grows slowly to 8 feet high and 3 feet wide. Dense, columnar form, silvery blue color, medium texture. 'Minima Glauca' is a dwarf to 3 feet high and 2-1/2 feet wide. Blue-green, soft texture, compact and neat.

Planting and care: Plant from containers in moist, well-drained soil in full sun. Prefers cool, coastal conditions. Plant in partial shade in hot, inland valleys. Regular water. Prune large branches any time. Shear in early spring. Susceptible to root rot in poorly drained soils. Where soil is infested with the fungus *Phytophthora lateralis,* root rot, substitute *Thuja, Juniperus, Chamaecyparis pisifera* or *Chamaecyparis thyoides.*

Citrus
Citrus
Broadleaf evergreen shrubs or small trees
Zones 9 and 10
Hybrids of species originally from southeast Asia and the Malay Peninsula

Citrus include some of the finest hedge, screen, espalier, barrier or background plants for mild-winter areas. Plants can be grown in containers for a movable screen. Bringing plants in containers indoors before temperatures drop in cold climates is an old tradition. Citrus also work well as espaliers on a fence for screening in limited spaces. Espalier citrus on a south-facing wall with an overhang and wind protection to take advantage of warm microclimates, especially in zones that are typically too cold. Prolonged, frequent cold temperatures are more damaging than an occasional brief frost.

Leaves are medium to dark, shiny green, and range from small to large, depending on variety. Medium texture. Flowers are small with white, waxy petals. They have a sweet, powerful fragrance, especially on

Chamaecyparis species — Port Orford cedar

warm evenings. Fruit is edible, decorative and loaded with vitamin C. Most varieties have thorny branches.

Uses: Food source. Shaped or sheared hedge. Screen. Barrier. Background. Espalier. Topiary. Containers. Noise buffer. Small spaces.

Valued for: Long life, great elegance, fragrance and delicious fruit.

Planting and care: Plant from containers in slightly acid to slightly alkaline soil that is well drained. Best in full sun to light shade. Regular deep irrigation is needed for best fruit quality. Feed with commercial, slow-release citrus fertilizer. Don't fertilize the first year and take care not to overfertilize. Head back tops of young plants to encourage bushiness. Pinch to shape. Heavy pruning reduces fruit production. Remove suckers and deadwood. Choose a variety or a grafted dwarf that will grow to the mature height you desire.

Any citrus will grow in a large container. In cold-winter areas, this is the only way they can be grown. When temperatures drop below freezing, the containers can be moved to a warmer location. Many gardeners follow a schedule each year, moving plants indoors, then outdoors, in tune with the seasons. Dwarfs are perhaps the best suited to containers, but full-size trees will be naturally dwarfed by the limited root space.

Citrus aurantifolia
Lime

Limes grow to 12 to 15 feet tall and as wide, with small, medium-green leaves. Fruit color varies from green to orange. The classic bartender's lime is 'Mexican', a cultivar with green fruit. It is tender to cold, suitable for growth only in a warm microclimate in Zone 10. It is most reliable as a dwarf in containers.

Uses: Plant 'Bearss' 6 to 8 feet apart for large-scale screen. Plant 'Rangpur' 2 to 6 feet apart for sheared or shaped hedge. Can be maintained at 3 feet high. 'Rangpur' can be espaliered.

Cultivars: 'Bearss' lime is bushy with yellow fruit, but with true lime flavor. Vigorous growth. Best as a large-scale screen or in containers. 'Rangpur' lime is not a true lime but the fruit is sour. Leaves are dull, dark green. New leaves have a purplish tint. Fruit is small and orange. Tolerates severe pruning.

Citrofortunella mitis
Calamondin and Dwarf calomondin

Calamondin is a kumquat hybrid that is cold tolerant and easy to grow. It is one of the best citrus for containers indoors. Dwarfs grow 8 to 10 feet high, spreading 6 to 8 feet wide, with dense, compact bushy form. Small leaves. Full-size, columnar trees grow to 35 feet by 15 feet. Difficult to find. Sour-tasting fruit is orange, 1-1/2 inches wide. It can be used like a lemon to flavor food and drinks. Relatively few thorns.

Uses: Plant dwarfs 2 to 4 feet apart for sheared or shaped hedge. Plant 4 to 5 feet apart for screen. Plant full-size trees 5 to 10 feet apart for large-scale screen.

Citrus aurantium
Sour orange

Sour orange is an exceptional ornamental. Its orange-colored, sour fruit is used in marmalade and to flavor Cointreau and Curacao liquers. Cultivars with willowlike leaves are occasionally available. Flowers of 'Bouquet des Fleurs' have the most elusive and penetrating fragrance. Oil is used in French perfumes. Exceptional as a low-maintenance screen because of minimal pruning requirement.

Uses: Plant 'Bouquet des Fleurs' 5 to 6 feet apart for screen. Plant 3 feet apart for shaped hedge. Containers. 'Chinotto' and 'Myrtifolia' grow 6 to 7 feet tall, sometimes to 10 feet. Plant 2 to 3 feet apart for sheared or shaped hedge. Plant 3 to 5 feet apart for screen.

Cultivars: 'Seville' grows to 15 to 20 feet high and spreads 10 to 15 feet wide. Vigorous, upright growth may reach 30 feet. Leaves are dark green, to 4 inches long. Plants are exceptional for large-scale screening. Plant 1 to 4 feet apart for sheared or shaped hedge. Plant 5 to 8 feet apart for screen. 'Bouquet des Fleurs', also known as 'Bouquet', grows to 8 to 12 feet high with dense, dark-green, round leaves that have a ruffled appearance. 'Myrtifolia' has smaller leaves than others and is excellent for sheared hedges, or as a substitute for *Pittosporum* species. Minimum pruning is required.

Citrus x paradisi, grapefruit, as an espalier.

Citrus sinensis
Sweet orange
Blood orange

Orange, or sweet orange, grows to 15 to 20 feet high, spreading 20 to 24 feet wide, with large, dark-green leaves. Form is dense and bushy. Fruit are orange and sweet. Grows vigorously.

Uses: Plant 4 to 8 feet apart for large-scale shaped hedge. Plant 8 to 10 feet apart or more for screen. Espalier. Containers.

Cultivars: 'Valencia' is easy to grow. Although fruit have seeds, it is sweeter and juicier than navel fruit. Other sweet oranges include 'Trovita', 'Diller' and 'Shamouti'—a smaller tree form with seedless oranges. 'Robertson' navel has a slow growth rate. 'Washington' navel is a favorite. 'Summernavel' has an open, spreading form.

Known as the *connoisseur's citrus*, blood orange grows to 18 feet high and as wide, with broad, rounded form and narrow, dark-green leaves. Orange fruit have a red blush and dark-red flesh. Taste has raspberry overtones but is otherwise similar to a sweet orange. Juice is a deep-red color.

'Moro' is the best blood orange for desert areas, and has the deepest red flesh. 'Sanguinelli' is a smaller tree and the best choice for coastal situations. 'Tarocco' is the largest tree. It is well suited to warm, interior valleys.

Uses: Same as sweet orange. One of the best citrus to espalier.

Murraya paniculata
Orange jessamine

Orange jessamine grows 6 to 15 feet high, spreading as wide with glossy, dark-green leaves that are divided into small leaflets. White, bell-shaped flowers are small and have a strong citrus fragrance. Plant blooms at least twice a year. Not a true citrus, but a close relative.

Plant has open form. Pinch or shear to keep it dense. Does not require reflected heat. Needs partial shade, rich soil and ample water. Dwarf variety is slower growing and generally inferior.

Uses: Plant 2 to 3 feet apart for sheared or shaped hedge. Espalier. Topiary.

Fortunella margarita
Kumquat and
Dwarf kumquat

Kumquat is an exceptional ornamental. Grows 6 to 25 feet high, spreading 6 to 25 feet wide, with small, narrow leaves and few thorns. Bright-orange fruit are round or oval, 1-1/2 inches in diameter. Skin is sweet and flesh is tart. Eat the entire fruit without peeling, or use them in preserves and fruit salads. Resistant to cold, but fruit sets only in warm-summer areas. Tolerates severe pruning.

Uses: Plant 3 to 5 feet apart for sheared or shaped hedge. Can be maintained at 3 feet or plant dwarfs 2 to 4 feet apart. Plant 6 to 8 feet apart for screen. Espalier. Containers.

Cultivars: 'Nagami' is the most common cultivar, but 'Meiwa' has the best fruit.

Citrus limon
Lemon

Lemon is the fastest-growing citrus and the one most suited to espalier training and heavy pruning. It grows to 25 feet high and 22 to 26 feet wide, with large, dark-green leaves and sour, yellow fruit.

Uses: Plant 2 to 5 feet apart for sheared or shaped hedge. Can be maintained at 5 or 6 feet, but best as large-scale planting. Use 'Improved Meyer' for 3- to 6-foot-high hedges. Plant 5 to 10 feet apart for screen. Espalier. Containers.

Cultivars: 'Lisbon' is the best variety for espalier purposes. It has the densest foliage and greatest tolerance to frost. 'Eureka' is the commercial lemon variety. 'Improved Meyer' is smaller and is an excellent ornamental with few thorns. Fruit is yellow tinged with orange. It has a slightly sweet flavor. Can be maintained at 3 feet.

Citrus espalier

Citrus reticulata, mandarin, as a container espalier.

HEDGES: 3 TO 4 FEET HIGH
Kumquat
'Improved Meyer' lemon
'Rangpur' lime

HEDGES: 4 TO 6 FEET HIGH
Lemons
'Bearss' lime
Mandarin
Orange jessamine

LARGE-SCALE HEDGES AND SCREENS
Blood orange
Calamondin
Grapefruit
Lemon
Navel orange
'Seville' sour orange
'Valencia' sweet orange

SCREENS REQUIRING MINIMAL PRUNING
Calamondin
'Improved Meyer' lemon
'Chinotto', 'Myrtifolia' and
   'Bouquet des Fleurs' sour orange

BEST SUITED FOR SHEARING
Orange jessamine
'Myrtifolia' and 'Seville'
   sour orange

ESPALIERS
Blood oranges
   especially 'Tarocco'
True lemon
'Rangpur' lime
Orange jessamine
'Summernavel' orange

FORMAL ESPALIER OR CORDON FENCE
True lemon only

CONTAINER PLANTING
Dwarf calamondin
Kumquat
'Improved Meyer' lemon
Dwarf lime
'Rangpur' lime
Mandarin
'Valencia', 'Summernavel' and
   'Shamouti' orange

Citrus x paradisi
Grapefruit

Grapefruit grows to 20 feet high, spreading 20 to 24 feet wide with large, dark-green leaves. Easy, fast growth, but heat is required for sweet fruit. Ideal in the desert, or plant where it receives reflected heat, such as espaliered against a south wall. Excellent for an informal hedge.

Uses: Plant 5 to 10 feet apart for large-scale, shaped hedge. Plant 10 feet apart for screen. Espalier.

Cultivars: 'Marsh Seedless' has yellow fruit. 'Redblush' has pink fruit.

Citrus reticulata
Mandarin, Tangerine

Mandarin grows at a moderate rate to 12 to 15 feet high by 16 to 20 feet wide, with a rounded form and small, narrow leaves. It is an exceptional small tree when pruned. Produces small, but beautiful tangerine fruit. Prefers heat.

Uses: Plant 3 to 4 feet apart for shaped hedge. Can be maintained at 6 feet. Plant 6 to 10 feet apart for screen. Containers.

Cultivars: 'Clementine', 'Dancy', 'Fairchild', 'Kara' and 'Kinnow' are popular cultivars. Plant several for cross-pollination. Dwarf trees are available for containers, or shape them into low hedges.

Cocculus laurifolius
Cocculus, Laurel-leaf cocculus
Broadleaf evergreen shrub
or small tree
Zones 8 to 10
Native to Himalayas and
southern Japan

Multiple stems of cocculus produce dense foliage. Leaves are dark green, shiny and attractive. They are 2-1/2 to 6 inches long with three veins running end to end. New leaves are light green. Medium to coarse texture. Greenish flowers are inconspicuous, followed by small, black berries.

Height and spread: 15 to 25 feet by 15 to 25 feet. Can be maintained at 6 feet. Slow growth rate when young; faster after plant is established.

Uses: Plant 1-1/2 to 4 feet apart for sheared or shaped hedge. Plant 4 to 10 feet apart for screen. An elegant background hedge or screen where water is not a limited resource. Espalier.

Valued for: Lustrous, dark-green leaves and low maintenance.

Planting and care: Plant from containers in average, well-drained garden soil. Full sun to dense shade. Supply with ample water.

Cocculus laurifolius—cocculus

Cocculus laurifolius—cocculus

Cornus mas
Cornelian cherry
Deciduous shrub or small tree
Zones 4 to 9
Native to Asia, central and southern Europe

Twiggy, bushy form may be sheared into a handsome, box-shaped hedge, but flowers and fruit will be reduced. Best to prune selectively or let plant grow naturally. Leaves are shiny, medium to dark green, 4 inches long or less. Medium texture. Tiny, yellow flower clusters cover plant before leaves appear. Fruit are sour, bright red, less than 1 inch long. They remain on twigs into winter. Birds love the fruit, which can be made into a tasty preserve. Brilliant yellow or red leaf color is attractive in fall.

Height and spread: 15 by 15 feet, usually 5 by 5 feet. Can be maintained at 3 feet. Slow growth rate.

Uses: Plant 18 inches apart for sheared hedge. Plant 1-1/2 to 3 feet apart for shaped hedge or screen. Espalier.

Valued for: Year-round interest, edible fruit, early spring flowers and few pests.

Cultivars: 'Flava' has yellow fruit.

Planting and care: Plant bare root, balled and burlapped. Cuttings or from containers. Tolerates most soils, including alkaline. Full sun or light shade. Ample to average water. Little pruning is necessary. Shear or prune after bloom. Flowers form on previous year's growth.

Cornus stolonifera
(C. sericea)

Red-osier dogwood
Deciduous shrub
Zones 2 to 10
Native to much of North America

This shrubby, twiggy plant spreads by *stolons,* underground runners, to form clumps. Leaves are medium green, fresh looking, to 2-1/2 inches long. Medium texture. Tiny flowers are creamy white in 2-inch-wide clusters. Small berries are white or bluish white. Fall leaf color is brilliant red. Bark is red or yellow, which contrasts vividly with snow.

Cornus alba, tatarian dogwood, produces an effect similar to *C. stolonifera.* 'Siberica' and 'Siberica Bloodgood' have exceptionally red twigs. 'Coral' has coral-red twigs. Culture and recommended zones are the same as red-osier dogwood.

Height and spread: 15 by 15 feet, but most often 7 by 7 feet. Fast growth rate.

Uses: Plant 1-1/2 to 3 feet apart for shaped hedge. Plant 2 to 4 feet apart for screen.

Valued for: Year-round interest and ability to grow in wet locations.

Cultivars: 'Flaviramea', yellow twig dogwood, and 'Lutea' have vivid yellow twigs and branches, providing interest in winter. They grow 6 to 7 feet high, spreading as wide. Zones 2 to 7. *C. s. baileyi* has brilliant red twigs, 8 by 8 feet maximum. 'Isanti' has red twigs. Growth habit is naturally compact, requiring little pruning. Space plants 18 inches apart. 'Kelseyi' is a dwarf to 2 feet high, with red twigs. Other varieties are available locally where plants are native.

Planting and care: Easy to propagate from cuttings, by ground layering or by planting suckers. Plant bare root or from containers. Tolerates a range of soil types, thriving in wet, poorly drained areas. Full sun or part shade. Requires ample water. Prune in early spring while plant is dormant. Remove old stems to force more colorful new growth.

Corylus avellana
Hazel, European filbert, Cobnut
Deciduous shrub
Zones 5 to 9
Native to Europe

Hazel is one of the traditional, British hedgerow shrubs. Pliable branches pruned from the hedgerow are woven along the top of hedges for a traditional finish known as *ethering.* See *Crataegus.* Freshly cut branches are also used to make woven fences. Large leaves are yellow-green with serrated edges. Coarse texture. Flowers are decorative catkins that last into winter. Fruit is a delicious nut similar to commercial filbert, *Corylus maxima.* Form is broad and upright, occasionally leggy. Yellow fall color.

Height and spread: 10 to 15 feet by 10 to 15 feet. Can be maintained at 3 feet. Moderate growth rate.

Uses: Plant 3 to 6 feet apart for shaped hedge. Plant 6 feet apart for screen.

Valued for: Traditional hedgerow planting, woodland look, edible nuts.

Planting and care: Plant from seeds or containers in average soil. Full sun to part shade. Average water. Prune to keep the shrubs within bounds. Accepts shearing but looks coarse.

Cotoneaster lucidus
(C. acutifolia)

Hedge cotoneaster
Deciduous shrub
Zones 4 to 10
Native to Siberia and northern Asia

Hedge cotoneaster is often grown as a hedge, but the upright form is excellent as a screen. Popular in cold-winter areas. Susceptible to fireblight. It is not always long-lived, but is attractive and tough while it lasts. Leaves are dark green, shiny, 1/2 to 2 inches long. Medium texture. Fine texture when sheared. Flowers are small and pinkish. Berries are black, attractive to birds. Yellow or red fall color is exceptional. Twiggy and dense winter appearance.

Cotoneaster acutifolia is similar, but has dull leaves. It is often sold by nurseries as hedge cotoneaster.

Height and spread: 5 to 15 feet by 3 to 10 feet. Can be maintained at 2 feet. Moderate growth rate.

Uses: Plant 1 to 1-1/2 feet apart for sheared hedge. Plant 3 to 6 feet apart for screen. Windbreak.

Valued for: Tolerance of cold, shade, coastal winds and poor soils. Attractive foliage and fall color. Low maintenance and ability to be sheared.

Planting and care: Plant balled and burlapped, from seeds, cuttings or containers in any well-drained soil. Full sun to almost full shade. Little water is required after plants are established.

Cornus mas—Cornelian cherry

Crataegus
Hawthorn, Thorn apple
**Deciduous shrubs or
small trees
Zones 3 to 10 as indicated**

Hawthorn is the principal British hedgerow plant. It has been used to enclose fields since the Middle Ages. In fact, the word hedge is derived from *haga,* the Saxon word for *haws* or hawthorn fruit. Plants make exceptional barriers because of their hard thorns, dense growth and their ability to be *pleached,* woven into a living fence. Pleached hawthorns or hawthorns planted 6 inches apart make a impenetrable barrier. All have clusters of applelike flowers and small fruit. Plants are easy to grow, and are not fussy about cultural requirements. Many species are susceptible to fireblight. *Crataegus phaenopyrum,* Washington thorn, described on page 114, is fireblight resistant.

Uses: Plant 2 to 3 feet apart for sheared or shaped hedge. Plant 3 to 6 feet apart for screen. Barrier. Espalier. Pleaching.

Planting and care: Difficult to transplant in fall. Not available bare root. In spring, plant them balled and burlapped or from containers. Adapted to acid to slightly alkaline soil that is well drained. Full sun, average water. Prune when trees are dormant—during winter to early spring. For a traditional pleached hedge, use *Crataegus monogyna.* Space plants 2 to 3 feet apart. Cut the main stems in half almost down to the ground in dormant season. Bend one cut stem, the *plasher,* at a 30° angle into the next upright stem. Tie in place. Remove ties when the branches have grown and bonded together in a natural graft. Prune yearly into box shape. Weave hazel, *Corylus* species, or other pliant branches along the tops for a traditional finish known as *ethering.*

Crataegus grus-galli
Cockspur thorn
**Deciduous shrub or small tree
Zones (3) to 10
Native to Quebec through Michigan
to North Carolina**

Cockspur makes a dense screen. Leaves are dark green, glossy and toothed, to 3 inches long. Coarse texture. Flowers are white. Fruit are orange-red and remain on the plant all winter. Excellent red and yellow fall color. Thorns grow to 3 inches long.

Height and spread: 20 to 35 feet by 15 to 20 feet. Can be maintained at 10 feet.

Valued for: Great hardiness, horizontal branching pattern and shiny leaves.

Cultivars: 'Inermis' is thornless, with abundant white flowers. Grows to 20 feet high. Adapted to Zones 4 to 7.

Crataegus monogyna and Crataegus laevigata
Common hawthorn and English hawthorn
**Deciduous small trees
Zones 5 to 9
Native to Europe**

Common hawthorn and English hawthorn have medium green, 2-inch-long, lobed leaves. Plants have a coarse texture, but respond well to shearing. Both accept pleaching well. Neither should be planted where fireblight is commonly a problem. Both do best in cool, dry-summer areas such as the Pacific Coast.

Common hawthorn, also known as *hedgerow hawthorn* and *English hawthorn,* has white, single flowers and 1-inch-long thorns. Red fruit may be made into jelly. Cultivars of English hawthorn are widely planted for their showy, colorful flowers.

Height and spread: 15 to 30 feet by 15 to 20 feet. Can be maintained at 5 to 10 feet by 30 feet.

Valued for: Long life, barrier planting, pleaching and flowers.

Cultivars: *C. monogyna* 'Stricta' is a thornless, columnar form growing 35 feet high, spreading 9 feet wide. *C. laevigata* 'Paul's Scarlet', also 'Paulii', is an old favorite with double, rose to red flowers.

Cornus stolonifera—red-osier dogwood

Crataegus grus-galli—Cockspur thorn

Crataegus phaenopyrum
(C. cordata)
Washington thorn
Deciduous small tree
Zones 4 to 9
Native to southeastern United States

This is an elegant hawthorn with year-round interest, and the best *Crataegus* for beautiful, orange-to-scarlet fall color. Glossy leaves are medium green, to 3 inches long, with pointed lobes. Coarse texture. White flowers. Fruit is bright red, attractive, remaining on the plant long into winter.

Height and spread: 15 to 25 feet by 10 to 20 feet. Can be maintained at 6 feet.
Valued for: Resistance to fireblight, borers and scale. Good fall color, refined flowers and ability to thrive in city conditions.

Cupressocyparis leylandii
Cupressocyparis
Needled evergreen tree
Zones 6 to 9
Hybrid of Cupressus macrocarpa and Chamaecyparis nootkatensis

Pyramidal form requires no pruning when young, but growth becomes open with age. Often grown as a quick screen. Best when sheared. Needles are dark green, short and scalelike. Fine texture. Small cones are not produced until tree is old.

Height and spread: 30 to 60 feet by 8 to 20 feet. Can be maintained at 4 feet. Fast growth rate.
Uses: Plant 2 to 4 feet apart for sheared or shaped hedge. Plant 4 to 8 feet apart for screen. Background. Windbreak.
Valued for: Fast, evergreen growth, ability to be sheared and narrow, upright form.
Cultivars: 'Castelwellian Gold' has a yellowish cast to the green foliage.
Planting and care: Plant from cuttings or containers in almost any soil. Full sun. Average water. Shear any time.

Cupressus glabra
Arizona cypress
Needled evergreen tree
Zones 6 to 10
Native to southwestern United States and northern Mexico

Pyramidal form of Arizona cypress should be given room to spread. Choose cultivars that are uniform in color and growth habit. Needles are scalelike, ranging in color from green to gray-green or silvery. Fine texture. Small cones.

Height and spread: 20 to 40 feet by 15 to 25 feet. Fast growth rate.
Uses: Screen when planted 15 feet apart. Background. Windbreak. Highway planting.
Valued for: Quick screening, tolerance to heat, drought and poor soil.
Cultivars: 'Gareei', silvery blue-green, holds well in winter. Not too large. 'Greenwood' and 'Pyramidalis' are similar in color.
Planting and care: Plant from containers in any soil. Full sun to part shade. Do not plant in cool or humid areas or in shade. Plants may be bothered by juniper blight. No water required after plant is established. Mulch with manure once a year for faster growth.

Cupressus sempervirens 'Stricta'
Italian cypress
Needled evergreen tree
Zones 8 to 10
Native to southern Europe and western Asia

Strict, strong, vertical form used in the great Italian Renaissance gardens for spatial definition, formal allees and emphasis. Makes a peerless, large-scale, hedgewall or screen, requiring *no* pruning. Windbreak qualities are even effective when there are gaps be-

Crataegus phaenopyrum—Washington thorn

Crataegus phaenopyrum—Washington thorn

tween trees. A planting of several trees dominates the landscape. Taste and imagination are required to use plants effectively. Best suited to large properties. Needles are rich, dark green, short and scalelike with a dull cast. Fine texture. Flowers and cones are inconspicuous.

Height and spread: 30 to 40 feet by 3 to 6 feet, 100 by 10 feet with great age. Can be maintained at 6 feet high, but not recommended. Moderate growth rate.

Uses: Plant 6 inches apart for shaped hedge. Plant 3 to 10 feet apart for screen. Background. Windbreak.

Valued for: Long life, vertical, columnar form and stately proportions, low maintenance and drought tolerance.

Planting and care: Plant balled and burlapped or from containers in any well-drained soil. Best in non-humid climates. Full sun.

Cydonia oblonga
Fruiting quince
Deciduous shrub or small tree
Zones 5 to 9
Native to Asia

Fruiting quince is exquisite in spring, with its grayish-green foliage and pink flowers. Thornless, twisted branches give winter interest. Susceptible to fireblight. Needs 100 to 450 hours of winter chilling. These are hours below 45F (7C), necessary to break the plant's rest period. Leaves are dark green with white undersides, to 4 inches long. Coarse texture. Flowers are showy, white or pink, up to 2 inches across, single and roselike. Fruit are edible, look like large, somewhat misshapen apples. They are golden yellow and fragrant, and are usually not eaten fresh, except for 'Pineapple'. Fruit can be made into excellent preserves, or baked and served with cream.

Height and spread: 12 to 15 feet by 12 feet. Slow growth rate.

Uses: Plant 4 feet apart for screen. Espalier.

Valued for: Fruit, form and flowers.

Cultivars: 'Pineapple', 'Champion', 'Smyrna', 'Apple' and 'Cooke's Jumbo'.

Planting and care: Plant from containers or bare root in any well-drained soil. Tolerates wet situations and some shade. Full sun is required for best fruit. Average water requirement. Prune only to shape and stimulate growth. Fruit forms at end of new growth. Branches that are cut back do not bear fruit.

Dodonaea viscosa
Hopbush
Broadleaf evergreen shrubs or small trees
Zones 8 to 10
Native to Arizona through South American and warm regions of the Old World

Exceptionally fast growth and drought tolerance makes this plant a Western favorite. 'Green' is elegant when clipped. 'Saratoga' is deep purple. 'Purpurea' is lighter purple turning greenish in the shade. Leaves are willowlike to 4 inches long. Medium texture. Flowers are inconspicuous. Pinkish, winged seeds are decorative.

Height and spread: 15 by 12 feet. May reach to 40 feet under best conditions. Can be maintained at 4 feet.

Uses: Plant 2 to 4-1/2 feet apart for sheared hedge. Plant 3-1/2 to 4-1/2 feet apart for shaped hedge. Plant 6 to 9 feet apart for screen. Windbreak. Background—'Green' only. Espalier.

Valued for: Fast, low-maintenance growth, drought tolerance, color and willowy appearance.

Planting and care: Plant from containers in any soil after danger of frost has passed. Full sun to partial shade. Does best in improved soil. Provide with deep, spaced irrigation.

Cupressocyparis leylandii—cupressocyparis

Dodonaea viscosa 'Purpurea'—purple hopbush

Elaeagnus angustifolia
Russian olive
Deciduous small tree
Zones 2 to 10
Native to southern Europe and West through Central Asia

Russian olive is one of the most popular, drought-tolerant, cold-area windbreak trees or barrier screens. Bushy form is more suited to screen or shaped-hedge planting, but can be sheared. Leaves are silvery gray, willowlike, to 3-1/2 inches long. Medium texture. Small, yellow flowers are not showy but fragrant. Round, yellow berries are 1/2 inch in diameter. Twisted branches and brown bark are attractive in winter.

Height and spread: 25 by 25 feet. Can be maintained at 4 or 6 feet.

Uses: Plant 2 to 4 feet apart for sheared or shaped hedge. Plant 4 to 6 feet apart for screen. Windbreak. Shelterbelt. Barrier. Canopy when pruned.

Valued for: Ability to stand the most adverse conditions.

Planting and care: Plant in any well-drained soil in full sun. Water is generally not required after plant is established. Prune in winter or early spring. Subject to wilt and borer damage.

Elaeagnus pungens
Silverberry
Broadleaf evergreen shrub
Zones 6 to 10
Native to Japan

Silverberry is easily sheared into formal shapes. Closely spaced planting makes an impenetrable barrier. Loose, sprawling, natural form is attractive. Leaves are 2 to 4 inches long and wavy. From a distance, they appear to be olive colored, but actually are green with rusty spots. Medium to coarse texture. Cultivars with variegated leaves are popular. Flowers are inconspicuous but fragrant. Fruit are edible, 1/2-inch red berries.

Height and spread: 8 to 15 feet by 6 to 15 feet. Can be maintained at 3 feet.

Uses: Plant 1-1/2 to 2 feet apart for sheared or shaped hedge. Plant 2 to 4 feet apart for screen. Windbreak. Barrier. Background. Espalier.

Valued for: Fragrance, ability to be sheared and ease of growth.

Planting and care: Plant from containers in any soil. Little fertilizer is required. Full sun or part shade. Average water requirement but accepts some drought. Tolerates wind and high heat. Few pests. Prune any time.

Eriobotrya japonica
Loquat, Japanese plum
Broadleaf evergreen shrub
or small tree
Zones 9 and 10
Native to China and Japan

Multistemmed, dense, shrubby form suited to large-scale screening, as long as plants are selected before nurseries prune them into tree forms. Espalier hedges are useful in narrow spaces or as espaliers on chain-link fence or wall. Leaves are dark green, toothed, rusty brown underneath, 6 to 12 inches long. Coarse texture. White clusters of fragrant flowers are not particularly showy. They bloom in fall. Yellow, gold or orange fruit are delicious—tartly sweet. Fruit are smaller than an apricot and has a large, brown seed. Use fruit fresh or in salads.

Eriobotrya deflexa, bronze loquat, is similar but smaller and more shrublike with bronze leaves and showier flowers. Growth is fast, but no fruit are produced and plants are not drought tolerant. Good for an espalier.

Height and spread: 15 to 30 feet by 15 to 30 feet.

Uses: Plant 4 to 8 feet apart for screen. Espalier. Canopy—prune up

Eriobotrya japonica—loquat espalier

for a dense ceiling. Containers.

Valued for: Edible fruit, tropical appearance and ease of maintenance.

Planting and care: Easy to grow from seeds. Begins to bear fruit after four years. For consistent form and fruit quality, plant named cultivars from containers. Grows in any well-drained soil. Full sun to almost full shade. Accepts some drought after plant is established, but best with average water. Prune and shape in early spring. Thin fruit to increase size of individual fruit left on tree. Espaliers cannot tolerate heat, so do not plant them against south-facing walls. Fruit are damaged at 15F to 28F (−10C to −20C).

Escallonia rubra
Escallonia
Broadleaf evergreen shrub
Zones 9 and 10
Native to Chile and South America

Compact, upright growth of escallonia requires little pruning. It accepts shearing well. Sheared hedges make an excellent background because flow-ers are less abundant. Leaves are 1 inch long, dark green and glossy. Medium texture. Showy clusters of red, applelike blooms are on the plant through most of the summer.

Height and spread: 6 to 15 feet by 3 to 6 feet. Can be maintained at 3 feet. Fast growth rate.

Uses: Plant 2 to 4 feet apart for sheared or shaped hedge. Plant 4 to 6 feet apart for screen. Windbreak. Barrier. Background. 'Balfouri' and 'Fradesii' ('Frades') can be used for espaliers. Coastal planting.

Valued for: Lush foliage, flowers, low maintenance and drought tolerance.

Cultivars: 'Apple Blossom', 5 by 5 feet or more with pinkish-white flowers. 'Fradesii' ('Frades'), 6 by 6 feet, pink to rose flowers. 'Jubilee', compact and dense to 6 feet high. Pink to rose flowers bloom sporadically all year. 'C. F. Ball' grows just short of 3 feet high. Space 1-1/2 feet apart.

Planting and care: Plant from containers or cuttings in any soil except alkaline soil. Full sun or part shade. Average water, tolerates some drought after established. Recovers quickly from frost damage. Prune or shear after flowering. Tip-prune any time.

Escallonia rubra—escallonia

Elaeagnus pungens—silverberry

Escallonia rubra—escallonia

Eucalyptus

Eucalyptus, Gum, Mallee
Broadleaf evergreen trees and shrubs
Zones 8 to 10 as indicated
Native to Australia

Eucalyptus are popular plants in mild-climate regions. Most are fast growing, and make excellent evergreen screens. Most people think of trees when they think of Eucalyptus. But don't overlook adapting smallish or slower-growing eucalyptus, including *E. erythrocorys*, red-cap gum, and *E. torquata*, coral gum. Both bloom well. Large-scale screens and windbreaks often need to be supplemented with low shrubs at their base.

Uses: Screen. Windbreak. Background. Highway or beach planting. Noise buffer. Espalier.

Valued for: Low maintenance, drought and soil tolerance, fast growth and freedom from pests or diseases. Some tolerate wet soils.

Planting and care: Easy to grow from seeds or plant from 1-gallon cans. Tolerates most soils. Full sun or light shade. Little water required after plants are established. Head back *E. erythrocorys* and *E. torquata* when planting and once or twice after growth begins. This encourages bushiness and keeps them dense. Occasional hard freezes damage eucalyptus or kill them to the ground. Recovery is usually rapid.

SHRUBBY AND SMALL SCALE

Eucalyptus caesia. Zones 9 and 10. Attractive, weeping habit makes a lovely screen. Also makes a fine espalier. Needs wind protection. Rose-colored flowers bloom all winter.

Eucalyptus erythrocorys, red-cap gum. Zones 9 and 10. Attractive, red bud caps and yellow flowers appear for a long period. Plant 10 to 12 feet apart. Can be trained as an espalier.

Eucalyptus lehmannii, bushy yate. Zones 8 to 10. One of the best. Dense, broad form, 20 to 30 feet by 20 to 30 feet or more, with branches to the ground. Yellow-green leaves have a russet tint. Medium texture. Good noise buffer. Plant 15 to 25 feet apart or prune for a canopy. 'Max Watson' is more compact.

Eucalyptus spathulata, swamp mallee. Zones 9 and 10. Gold and cream flowers appear on plant for a long period. Tolerates wet soils. Plant 6 to 15 feet apart.

Eucalyptus stellulata, black Sally. Zones 8 to 10. Pendulous branches and smooth, gray-green bark. Plant 15 to 25 feet apart.

Eucalyptus torquata, coral gum. Zone 10. Attractive coral and yellow flowers. Narrow form. Can be planted close together or farther apart, depending on desired screen density.

LARGE-SCALE ONLY

Eucalyptus camaldulensis, red gum. Zones 8 to 10. Fine in desert areas. Fast growth. Plant 15 to 20 feet apart.

Eucalyptus globulus 'Compacta', dwarf blue gum. Zones 9 and 10. Not overly attractive, but its dense, vase-shaped form can be held to 10 feet, or sheared. Not for desert areas but fine at the beach or as a highway noise buffer. Plant 10 to 15 feet apart.

Eucalyptus gunnii, cider gum. Zones 8 to 10. Withstands cold to about 5F (−15C.) Vigorous growth. Plant 10 to 20 feet apart.

Eucalyptus microtheca. Zones 8 to 10. Popular in desert areas. Stake for vertical trunks. Plant 10 to 15 feet apart.

Eucalyptus erythrocorys—red-cap gum

Eucalyptus lehmannii—bushy yate

Eucalyptus torquata—coral gum

Eucalyptus sideroxylon 'Rosea', pink ironbark. Zones 9 and 10. Weeping foliage, pink to red flowers and dark, rust-colored bark. Plant 10 feet apart for dense screen, up to 20 feet apart for screen effect.

Euonymus alata
Winged burning bush
Deciduous shrub
Zones 3 to 10
Native to Japan and China

Winged burning bush has a broad, flat-topped form. Best as an informal, unclipped screen but withstands heavy shearing. Stems develop corky ridges called *wings*. Fall color is stunning against an evergreen backdrop. Leaves are medium green, 1-1/2 to 2 inches long, medium texture. Flowers are inconspicuous. Small, red capsules split open to reveal orange seeds that attract birds. Fall color is brilliant, claret-red, rosy pink in shade. Twigs hold snow for winter interest.

Height and spread: 9 to 15 feet by 9 to 15 feet.

Uses: Plant 1-1/2 to 2-1/2 feet apart for sheared or shaped hedge. Plant 3 to 4 feet apart for screen. Background. Espalier.

Valued for: Fall color, ease of growth and ability to withstand difficult situations.

Cultivars: 'Compacta', also 'Compactus', is dense and upright, 4 to 10 feet by 4 to 10 feet. Requires little clipping, grows well in shade and has long season of fall color. More attractive branching pattern than the species. Plant 2 to 3 feet apart for an informal screen.

Planting and care: Plant bare root, balled and burlapped, from cuttings or containers in any soil. Full sun or part shade. Little water is required after plants are established.

Euonymus fortunei
(E. vegetus)
Wintercreeper
Broadleaf evergreen vining shrub
Zones 5 to 10
Native to China

Leaves of wintercreeper are dark green, glossy, to 1 inch long. Medium texture. Variegated cultivars are available. Flowers are inconspicuous. Small, orange berries split open to reveal decorative, orange seeds.

Height and spread: 5 by 5 feet. Can grow to 20 feet as a climbing vine if given support.

Uses: Plant 2 to 2-1/2 feet apart for sheared or shaped hedge or screen. Background. Espalier. Containers. Wall cover. Border.

Valued for: Fast, evergreen growth, and adaptability to shade and cold.

Cultivars: Many are available. 'Sarcoxie' is upright to 6 feet high. It requires little pruning and may be espaliered. 'Golden Prince' has golden new growth. For compact, low borders, space them 6 to 18 inches apart. 'Emerald Gaiety' grows to 5 feet high. It has green foliage edged in white. 'Emerald n' Gold' has green foliage edged in yellow.

Planting and care: Plant from containers, cuttings or balled and burlapped. Does best in moist, well-drained soil. Full sun to full shade. Average to ample water. Prune any time. Not adapted to humid climates.

Euonymus alata, winged burning bush, sheared, deciduous form

Euonymus alata, winged burning bush, fall color

Euonymus japonica
Evergreen euonymus
Broadleaf evergreen shrub
Zones 6 to 10
Native to Japan

Densely branching, upright form. Leaves are dark green, 1 to 2-1/2 inches long, glossy and tough. Medium texture. Flowers are inconspicuous. Variegated cultivars are available.

Height and spread: 8 to 10 feet by 6 feet.

Uses: Plant 6 to 12 inches apart for border. Plant 1 to 2 feet apart for sheared or shaped hedge. Plant 3 feet apart for screen. Background. Espalier. Topiary.

Valued for: Tolerance of heat and poor soil, and its ability to maintain neat appearance with minimal pruning.

Cultivars: 'Grandifolia' has larger, darker green leaves than species. Often sheared into topiary forms. 'Aureo-marginata', golden euonymus, has green leaves edged in yellow. 'Microphylla' and 'Microphylla Improved', formerly 'Pulchella', are compact, no taller than 2 feet. Small, fine-textured leaves are dark green. Rarely need pruning.

Planting and care: Plant in any soil in full sun or part shade. Average water.

Prune any time. Can be kept to any height. Susceptible to mildew. To reduce mildew problems, plant in a breezy, sunny site. High humidity can cause problems. Does well in the Pacific Northwest, right up to the coastline.

Euonymus kiautschovica 'Manhattan'
Broadleaf evergreen shrub
Zones 6 to 10

Leaves are dark, medium green, 1-1/2 inches long. New leaves are shiny and lighter green. Compact form. Medium texture. Flowers are inconspicuous. Typical, showy euonymus fruit.

Height and spread: 6 by 6 feet.

Uses: Plant 1-1/2 to 2 feet apart for sheared or shaped hedge. Plant 3 feet apart for screen. Noise buffer. Background. Espalier. Topiary.

Valued for: Attractive foliage, tolerance of shade and desert conditions.

Planting and care: Plant from containers in average garden soil. Tolerates full sun to almost full shade. Average water.

Fagus sylvatica
Beech, European beech
Deciduous tree
Zones 5 to 10
Native to central and southern Europe

This is one of the classic hedge plants of Europe, used for ancient hedgerows in England and for spatial definition as tall hedgewalls on great estates. Broad, pyramidal form can be sheared to fit narrow spaces. Branches sweep to the ground. Leaves of the species are glossy dark green, 2 to 4 inches long. Coarse texture. Cultivars with copper or purple leaves are popular. Flowers are inconspicuous. Bears small nuts, which are edible. Birds and squirrels love them. Fall color is a fine, golden bronze. Tree doesn't look bare in winter because leaves hang on, usually until new growth appears in spring.

Height and spread: 70 to 80 feet by 60 feet. Can be maintained at 6 feet. Slow growth rate.

Uses: Plant 2 to 4 feet apart for sheared or shaped hedge. Plant 4 to 10 feet apart for dense screen. Good noise buffer. Background. Prune canopy for a leafy ceiling. Field enclosure. Pleaching.

Valued for: Long life and its ability to be sheared or pleached.

Euonymus japonica 'Aureo-marginata'

Euonymus japonica 'Aureo-marginata'

Cultivars: The famous copper beech is 'Atropunicea', also a popular English hedge plant. Color is bronzy green to bronzy purple. Sometimes identified as 'Purpurea'. 'Riversii' is a grafted, dark-purple variety sold as River's purple beech. 'Asplenifolia' has green, fernlike foliage. 'Pendula' is a green, weeping form useful for large-scale screening. Green 'Fastigiata' is good for screening in narrow spaces.

Planting and care: Plant balled and burlapped or from containers. Well-drained soil is essential. Prefers slightly acid soil pH—5.0 to 6.5. Do not plant deeper than the level at which they were grown in containers. Full sun. Average water. Prune in summer or fall. Winter or spring pruning cuts may "bleed" in cold climates. For high, formal hedges, construct a rough, wooden framework and train branches on this support. Framework can be removed or allowed to decay naturally after hedge reaches full height.

Feijoa sellowiana
Pineapple guava
Broadleaf evergreen shrub
or small tree
Zones 8 to 10
Native to Brazil

Shrubby form is easily shaped to any size. Makes an elegant espalier and a silvery screen. Sheared plants have fewer flowers and fruit. Leaves are 2 to 3 inches long, medium green, glossy with chalk-white undersides. Medium to coarse texture. Flowers are showy—petals are white outside and maroon inside with dark-red stamens. Fruit are oval, grayish green, 3 inches in diameter. Eat fruit fresh or in preserves, or as a flavoring in applesauce. Plants in coastal areas have fruit with best flavor. Flower petals can be eaten in fruit salads. Birds and bees are attracted to plants.

Height and spread: 15 to 25 feet by 15 to 25 feet. Can be maintained at 3 feet high.

Uses: Plant 1-1/2 to 4 feet apart for sheared or shaped hedge. Plant 5 to 6 feet apart for screen. Espalier. Containers.

Valued for: Attractive flowers and edible fruit, low maintenance and drought tolerance.

Cultivars: 'Pineapple Gem' and 'Coolidge' are self-fertile with reliable fruit and form.

Planting and care: Plant from seeds or from containers. Seedlings vary. Several plants are needed in an area for pollination. Tolerant of any well-drained soil. Full sun, reflected heat or part shade. Average water requirement. Accepts drought after plant is established. Prune in late winter. Shear any time. Fruit are ripe when they drop to the ground.

Fontanesia fortunei
Fontanesia
Deciduous shrub
Zones 5 to 10
Native to China

This is a vigorous, upright plant, recently introduced to nurseries. Related to privet. Glossy leaves are whitish green, 1 to 4 inches long. Medium to coarse texture. Flowers are small, greenish white, not unlike privet. Fruit is a flat-winged nutlet.

Height and spread: 10 to 15 feet high, upright form. Can be held to 4 feet.

Uses: Plant 1-1/2 to 3 feet apart for shaped hedge. Plant 3 to 6 feet apart for screen.

Valued for: Graceful form, willowlike foliage, ease of propagation.

Planting and care: Plant bare root or from seeds, cuttings or containers in almost any soil. Full sun or part shade. Tolerates drought after it is established. Prune once in early spring and once in summer. Pliable twigs may be difficult to cut with electric shears. Quick recovery from winter damage.

Fagus sylvatica—beech

Feijoa sellowiana—pineapple guava

Forsythia x intermedia

Forsythia, Showy border forsythia, Golden bells
Deciduous shrub
Zones 4 to 9
Hybrid of Forsythia suspensa and Forsythia viridissima

Fountainlike form of forsythia is best suited to large-scale screening on large properties. Allow plenty of room for plants to spread. Shearing reduces flowering and makes plants unattractive when out of leaf. Pick branches in midwinter and bring them indoors to enjoy their bloom. Leaves are medium green, 2 to 3 inches long. Medium texture. Flowers are showy, pale yellow to deep, brassy gold. Few flowers are produced in Zone 4.

Height and spread: 6 to 8 feet by 10 feet or more.

Uses: Space according to ultimate size. See following. Shaped hedge or screen. Formal or informal espalier.

Valued for: Early yellow flowers, arching, graceful branches, flowers forced into early bloom indoors.

Cultivars: 'Spring Glory' has pale-yellow flowers. 'Spectabilis' has golden-yellow flowers. 'Beatrix Farrand' has large, gold flowers with orange throats. Grows to 10 feet high.

'Arnold Dwarf' has few flowers, deep-green foliage. Grows 2 feet high and spreads 4 feet wide. Makes a low, compact hedge in cold areas. Few pests. Little pruning is required. *Forsythia ovata* 'Ottawa' grows to 3 to 4 feet by 4 feet or more with pale-yellow flowers and reddish-purple fall color. Hardier and blooms earlier than *Forsythia x intermedia*.

Planting and care: Plant bare root or from cuttings or containers in any soil. Full sun or light shade, average water requirement. Prune immediately after flowers fade. Cut one-fourth to one-third of the stems to within 4 inches of ground. Cut entire plant to the ground if it grows out of bounds. Flowers appear on previous season's growth. Fertilize and groom often.

Gardenia jasminoides

Gardenia
Broadleaf evergreen shrub
Zones 8 to 10
Native to China

Upright form, clean foliage and fragrance makes this a special hedge or espalier worth planting where it is adapted. Plants are generally smaller in desert areas. Leaves are shiny, medium to dark green, up to 4 inches long. Medium to coarse texture. Flowers are double, white, to 3 inches in diameter.

Height and spread: Varies by cultivar. Maximum is 8 by 4 feet.

Uses: Plant 1 to 2 feet apart for shaped hedge. For a screen, space according to plant's ultimate spread. See following. Background. Espalier.

Valued for: Fragrance, beautiful flowers and foliage.

Cultivars: 'Veitchii' is easiest to grow and widely available. Upright to 4-1/2 feet high, with many flowers. 'Veitchii Improved' has slightly larger form and flowers. 'Mystery', 6 to 8 feet high, has large flowers. It is widely available and popular. 'August Beauty' grows 4 to 6 feet high. It is bushy and blooms summer through fall.

Planting and care: Plant from containers in slightly acid, well-drained, moisture-retaining soil. Crowns of plants should be planted slightly above ground level and mulched. Plant in full sun on the coast, in part shade in hot areas. Thrives with humidity and warmth. Needs ample water. Prune to shape. For impressive results, feed once a month with acid plant food or gardenia fertilizer.

Gardenia jasminoides—gardenia

Gardenia jasminoides—gardenia

Hibiscus rosa-sinensis

Tropical hibiscus, Chinese hibiscus
Broadleaf evergreen shrub
Zones (8, 9) to 10
Native to Asia

Tropical hibiscus is most effective in Zone 10 as an informal screen. Growth habit varies, but it is usually a broad-spreading shrub. Benefits from regular pinching of growing tips. Plantings look best as a single flower color.

Sheared hedges produce few flowers but make outstanding, dark-green backgrounds in tropical gardens. Leaves are dark green and glossy. Their size varies by cultivar. Coarse texture. Flowers are showy, at least 4 inches across, single or double. Red is the most common flower color but hundreds of cultivars in many colors are available. Check with local nurseries for pink, yellow, white, apricot, orange and mixtures.

Height and spread: Often 6 by 8 feet, occasionally 15 feet high in subtropical areas. Grows to 30 feet high in the tropics.

Uses: Plant 2 to 4 feet apart for sheared or shaped hedge. Plant 4 to 6 feet apart for screen. Background. Espalier. Containers.

Valued for: Flowers, fast growth and tropical effect.

Planting and care: Plant in well-drained soil. Full sun to part shade. Best near the coast. Locate plant where it will receive afternoon shade in hot, dry areas. Protect from wind. Requires ample water, but allow soil to dry out before the next watering. Established old-time, red varieties are drought tolerant. Pinch tips in spring and summer to shape plant. Do major pruning in early spring. Remove one-third of old wood and any frost damage. If plants freeze to the ground, cut back damaged growth, wait until spring then feed and water. For fastest growth, feed monthly from spring to early fall. Container plants require fertilizer regularly.

Hibiscus syriacus

(Althea syriacus)
Rose of Sharon,
Shrub althea, Mallow
Deciduous shrub
Zones 5 to 10
Native to India and China

Rose of Sharon is most effective as an informal, shaped hedge of one variety of single flowers. Upright form spreads with age if not pruned. Leaves appear in late spring. They are gray-green to medium green, 2 to 3 inches long. They may be toothed, simple or have three lobes. Coarse texture. Flowers are 2-1/2 to 4 inches wide, single or double. White, pink, red, blue, purple and mixtures are available. Singles produce capsule-shaped seed pods.

Height and spread: 8 to 12 feet by 6 to 10 feet. Can be maintained at 3 feet.

Uses: Plant 2 to 3 feet apart for shaped hedge. Plant 3 to 6 feet apart for screen. Espalier.

Valued for: Late blooming, showy flowers and ease of growth.

Cultivars: 'Diana' has pure-white flowers with few seed pods. Widely available and often considered the best. 'Blue Bird' has azure-blue flowers with red throats. 'Woodbridge' ('Woodedge') has magenta-rose flowers with red throat. 'Red Heart' has white flowers with red throat. 'Lady Baltimore' has pink flowers with red throat. 'Double Red' has double-red flowers. 'Jeanne d'Arc' flowers are white with pink blush. 'Paeoniflorus' has pink flowers. 'Collie Mullens' has lavender flowers.

Planting and care: Plant from containers or cuttings in well-drained soil. Full sun. Likes moisture but tolerates some drought after it is established. Frost may damage young plants. Prune dead tips in spring and prune to shape any time. For largest flowers, prune previous season's growth down to three buds during dormant season. Shearing is not recommended because flowers are produced on current season's growth.

Hibiscus rosa-sinensis—tropical hibiscus

Hibiscus rosa-sinensis—
tropical hibiscus

Ilex aquifolium—holly

Ilex crenata 'Convexa'—Japanese holly

Ilex cornuta—Chinese holly

Ilex
Holly
**Most evergreen shrubs
and small trees
Zones 3 to 10 as indicated**

Evergreen hollies are among the most outstanding hedge, screen, barrier and background trees and shrubs. Thousands of cultivars and hybrids, with and without berries, are available for a variety of soil and climate conditions. Deciduous hollies are not widely planted, simply because there are many other superior deciduous shrubs.

Most hollies have rich green leaves, but cultivars with variegated leaves are also available. Flowers are inconspicuous, with male and female flowers on separate plants. Berries are usually showy red, with some yellow and white varieties. Species with black berries are less showy. Typically, a male plant must be within 300 feet of a female plant, usually much less, before the female will bear fruit. Birds flock to fruiting hollies.

Uses: Plant 1 to 4 feet apart for sheared or shaped hedge. Plant 3 to 10 feet apart or more for screen, depending on ultimate spread of plant. Spiny-leaf varieties as barrier. Background. Noise buffer. Topiary. Espalier. Dwarfs are excellent for containers.

Planting and care: Plant balled and burlapped or from containers. Most hollies do best in slightly acid, well-drained soil, but note exceptions in lists and descriptions. Full sun to part shade. For most species, part shade essential in hot, dry climates.

Plant in wind-protected sites in cold climates to avoid damage from frost. Average to ample water is best, even for varieties that are drought tolerant. If berries are desired, choose a self-fertile cultivar, or plant at least one male for every 10 females for pollination. Male branches may be grafted to female plants to provide pollination. If you do this, identify them on the plant so you will not prune them out berry production.

Shearing greatly reduces berry production and can eliminate berries completely. Shape or shear once a year in late spring after growth is complete. Prune in winter only in Zone 10. The shrubby species may be cut to within 18 inches high to renew leggy growth, but do not prune single-trunk tree forms this way.

Hollies appreciate a light mulch around the roots to keep them cool. Occasional, light fertilizing produces bigger berries and faster growth. Avoid overfertilizing. Most young plants grow slowly. Prune tops periodically until dense side growth is achieved.

Ilex x altaclarensis 'Wilsonii'
Wilson holly
**Broadleaf evergreen shrub
or small tree
Zones 6 to 10
Hybrid of Ilex aquifolium and Ilex perado**

One of the best hollies because of its vigor and tolerance of a wide range of growing conditions. Leaves are dark green, spiny and glossy, 3 to 5 inches long. They turn a darker color in shade. Coarse texture. Females are self-fertile. Berries are bright red, borne in profusion. Green bark. Form is slender and pyramidal.

Height and spread: 6 to 8 feet by 3 to 5 feet. Or grows as a 20-foot-high tree. Can be maintained at 4 feet. Moderate growth rate.

Valued for: Warm-climate planting and tolerance of wind, poor soils, some drought and shade.

'Camilliaefolia' is another popular *I. altaclarensis* cultivar, but 'Wilsonii' is the most widely available.

FOR WARM, DRY AREAS
Ilex x altaclarensis 'Wilsonii'
Ilex x aquipernyi
Ilex crenata
Ilex cornuta 'Burfordii'
Ilex 'Lydia Morris'
Ilex 'Nellie R. Stevens'
Ilex pernyi
Ilex vomitoria

TOLERANT OF SWAMPY SOIL
Ilex glabra
Ilex opaca, in its native habitat only
Ilex verticillata
Ilex vomitoria

TOLERANT OF POOR SOILS
Ilex x altaclarensis
Ilex x aquipernyi
Ilex cornuta
Ilex crenata
Ilex 'Nellie R. Stevens'
Ilex pernyi
Ilex vomitoria

FOR COLD CLIMATES
Ilex x meserveae

Ilex aquifolium
Holly, English holly, Christmas holly
Broadleaf evergreen shrub
or small tree
Zones (6) to 9
Native to the British Isles, Europe, northern Africa and China

One of the classic, British hedgerow plants known in that country simply as *holly*. Plants spaced 6 inches apart will make an impenetrable fence. Tall, pyramidal form. *I. aquifolium* is one of the best screening plants, but its slow growth rate makes close spacing necessary for quick coverage. Best in partial shade, especially in hot areas. Tolerates partially clay soil. Should not be planted in windy locations.

Spiny leaves are shiny dark green, 1-1/2 to 4 inches long. Medium to coarse texture. Profuse berries are red. Both male and female plants are necessary for berry production.

Cultivars with smooth leaves, variegated leaves or yellow berries are available.

Height and spread: 6 to 60 feet high, depending on cultivar. Spreads slightly more than half the height. Slow growth rate.

Valued for: Long life, bright-red berries, shiny, toothed foliage.

Cultivars: Hundreds of cultivars are available. Many are better for hedges than the species because of dense foliage and form. These are some of the best.

'Augustifolia' has finer-textured leaves than the species, with a narrow, pyramidal form. 'Balkans', female and non-fruiting male, is reliably cold tolerant to Zone 6. Foliage is smooth, dull green, not shiny. Dense, upright form with many red berries. Popular since its introduction from Yugoslavia in 1934. 'Boulder Creek' is noted for large, blackish-green leaves and red berries. 'Sparkler' is noted for its large crop of red berries that set when the plant is young. Vigorous, upright, medium size. 'Teufel's Little Bull' is a widely available, non-fruiting male with small leaves and compact, upright form.

Ilex aquifolium 'Argentea-marginata' — variegated English holly

Ilex cornuta 'Burfordii' — Burford's holly

Ilex x aquipernyi
**Broadleaf evergreen shrub
or small tree
Zones (5) to 10
Hybrid of Ilex aquifolium and Ilex pernyi**

Neat, dense appearance. Upright, pyramid form. Somewhat drought tolerant. Leaves are dark green, 1-1/2 to 2 inches long and spiny. Medium texture. Berries are borne on self-fertile plants.

Height and spread: 10 to 30 feet by 10 to 20 feet.

Valued for: Tolerance of most soil conditions, refined appearance. Bright-red berries are formed without having both male and female plants.

Cultivars: 'Brilliant' grows to 10 feet high with leaves 2 to 4 inches long. Most popular and widely available. 'San Jose' is similar but more reliably cold tolerant. Cold-hardy in much of Zone 5.

Ilex cassine
**Dahoon holly
Broadleaf evergreen small tree
Zones 7 to 10
Native to southeastern United States**

Narrow, conical form. Not widely planted outside of the South but excellent for hedges. Leaves are spineless, growing 2 to 3 inches long. Medium texture. Berries are dull red, occasionally yellow.

Height and spread: 15 to 25 feet by 8 to 10 feet. Moderate to fast growth rate.

Valued for: Vigorous growth and smooth, soft foliage.

Ilex cornuta
**Chinese holly, Horned holly
Broadleaf evergreen shrub
or small tree
Zones (6) to 10
Native to eastern China**

The species form of this pyramid-shaped plant is rarely grown, but its cultivars are among the most popular hollies. Clean, glossy leaves almost look like plastic. Some are rectangular. They are spiny, dark green, 2 to 3 inches long. Medium texture. Large berries are red. Male plants must be near the species for females to set fruit, although this is not required of most of its cultivars.

Height and spread: 4 to 20 feet by 4 to 10 feet, depending on cultivar. Moderate to fast growth rate.

Valued for: Tolerance of dry heat and slightly alkaline soils, Glossy foliage, large berries and low maintenance.

Cultivars: Hardy in most of Zone 6. Self-fertile except as noted.

'Berries Jubilee' has mounded, compact form. Slow growth to 8 feet high but usually much smaller. Large, spiny, rectangular leaves grow to 4 inches long. Coarse texture. Begins bearing many, large, red berries at an early age. Decorative and showy.

'Burfordii' has the best heat and drought tolerance of all hollies, and is easy to maintain. It grows 12 to 20 feet high and 8 to 15 feet wide. Most often 6 feet high by 4 feet wide. Growth rate is rapid to slow, depending on amounts of water and fertilizer supplied to plant. Leaves are glossy dark green, 1-1/2 to 3 inches long, with a sharp tip. Edges turn in and are usually smooth but some have spines. Medium texture. Berries are produced in profusion. Upright, rounded form and unfussy, heat-tolerant growth makes this the most popular holly for southern California, high-desert areas and the South. Not suited to low-desert areas. Flowers are produced on old wood, so pruning will lessen or eliminate berry production. Even so, it is most attractive as a shaped or sheared hedge. Prune before new growth appears in early spring. Excellent espalier. Add iron sulfate to alkaline soils.

'Burfordii Nana', also known as 'Dwarf Burford', is excellent as a low hedge or container planting. It has the same qualities as 'Burfordii'. Some plants grow to 5 or even 10 feet high but are easy to maintain at any size. Slower growth rate than 'Burfordii', with smaller, darker green leaves.

'Carissa' is noted for its spineless leaves and low-maintenance requirements. It has a spreading, mounded form with erect branches. Grows to a maximum height of 5 feet but usually much less. Use as low hedge or container planting. Few if any berries. Minimal pruning required.

'China Girl' and 'China Boy' are heat and cold tolerant—to $-20F$ ($-29C$). They are compact and can be held to any size. Rapid growth rate. Female bears fruit. Male is a fruitless pollinator that also makes a fine shrub. Both can be grown in protected areas of Zone 5.

Ilex cornuta 'D'Or'—Chinese holly cultivar

'Dazzler' produces large, red berries in abundance. Upright and compact to 8 to 12 feet high but usually less. Some leaves are spiny.

D'Or' produces large, yellow berries in abundance. Upright, rounded form to 10 to 15 feet high. Some leaves are spineless, some are rectangular. Showy when loaded with yellow fruit. Best used as a screen.

'Rotunda' grows as rounded, compact, mounded form, requiring minimum pruning. Usually grows 2 feet high and as wide. Sometimes reaches 5 feet. Produces few if any berries. Low-maintenance requirement.

'Willowleaf' is noted for small leaves that are unlike those of typical hollies. They are narrow, dark green, with a pointed tip and a slight twist. Broad, dense form to 8 or 10 feet high, spreading wider. Produces many red berries. Medium texture. May become a small tree.

Uses: Plant 12 to 15 inches apart for border or low hedge. Topiary. Containers.

Valued for: Long life, elegance in sheared or natural form, fine texture and ability to withstand formal shaping.

Cultivars: 'Black Beauty' is compact with dark-green leaves. Exceptional cold tolerance. Zone 5 in protected locations. 'Compacta' is a superior, compact form with dark-green leaves. Minimal pruning requirement. May reach 6 feet high but usually much lower. 'Convexa', 'Convexa Bullata', is noted for small, shiny, cupped leaves and cold tolerance. Slow growth to 5 or 8 feet high, spreading much wider. Can be sheared to any dimension. Zone 5 in protected locations. 'Glory' is a fruitless male. Use it as a pollinator or alone. It has tiny, oval leaves. Makes an excellent border or sheared, low hedge. 'Green Island' grows in a loose, mounding form to 2 feet high, spreading twice as wide. 'Green Lustre' is noted for its minimal pruning requirement and fine texture. Grows as 2- by 2-foot, dense, rounded form. 'Helleri' has

low-maintenance requirement and a slow growth rate. One of the most popular for borders with broad, rounded form. Stays 1 foot high for years. Eventually grows to 4 feet high, spreading much wider. Dark-green, slightly toothed foliage. Fine texture. Blue-black berries are produced when male plant is nearby. Will not tolerate wet situations. 'Hetzi' has deep-green, cupped leaves similar to 'Convexa', but spreading, rounded form grows vigorously to 6 to 8 feet high—perfect for hedges and screens in most residential areas. Black berries are produced when a male plant is nearby. 'Latifolia' is noted for its vigorous, cold-tolerant growth, and large, 1-1/2-inch-long leaves. 'Microphylla' has a stiff, compact form, growing to 6 feet high. Small leaves. Zone 5 in protected locations. 'Rotundifolia' grows fast and vigorously to 6 to 12 feet tall. Round, upright form. Oval leaves have sawtooth edges, grow to 1-1/4 inches long. 'Stokes' is a male plant noted for minimum pruning requirement and neat appearance. It grows upright and rounded to 5 feet high. Dense, compact growth.

Ilex crenata
Japanese holly,
Asiatic holly
Broadleaf evergreen shrub
Zones (5, 6) to 10
Native to Japan and Korea

Neat, dense, rounded form accepts shearing well. Sides can be pruned vertical. The species form of *Ilex crenata* is rarely grown, but its many cultivars are popular and reliable broadleaf evergreen plants. Often substituted for *Buxus*, but its form is not as billowy. Moderately drought tolerant. Excellent as low hedge or low-maintenance screen. Ancient Japanese hedges of *I. crenata* are so dense people can walk on them. Leaves are smooth, deep, medium-green, shiny, to 1/2 to 1 inch long. They sometimes have a slight, sawtooth edge. Fine texture. Berries are black and usually inconspicuous. Male and female plants are necessary for berry production, although plants are not valued for their berries. Some cultivars are rarely available that have yellow fruit.

Height and spread: 1 to 8 feet or more, by 12 feet. Can be maintained at any size. Dwarf cultivars are available. Slow growth rate except as noted.

Ilex crenata—Japanese holly

Ilex 'Emily Bruner'
Broadleaf evergreen shrub or small tree
Zones 6 to 10
Hybrid of Ilex cornuta and Ilex latifolia

'Emily Bruner' is a recently developed holly. It grows in a pyramidal form, best as a tall screen or shaped hedge. It can also be grown as an espalier. Leaves are dark green, shiny, 4 to 6 inches long and spiny. Coarse texture. Berries are bright red. A male plant is required nearby to produce berries.
Height and spread: Estimated at 15 feet by 8 to 10 feet. Rapid growth rate.
Valued for: Vigorous growth and large, lustrous leaves.

Ilex 'Foster's No. 2'
Broadleaf evergreen tree
Zones 7 to 10
Hybrid of Ilex cassine variety and Ilex opaca

Pyramidal form of 'Foster's' No. 2' is superior to many *Ilex opaca* cultivars. It has glossy foliage and longer-lasting berries, but cut branches do not hold up as well for decorations. Use for large-scale screening. Leaves are dark blue-green, glossy, 1-1/2 to 3 inches long, spiny and narrow. Medium texture. Berries are bright red and appear in profusion.

Height and spread: 15 to 20 feet by 12 to 15 feet. Moderate growth rate.
Valued for: Tolerance of varying soil, light and moisture conditions, attractive foliage.

Ilex glabra
Inkberry, Gallberry
Broadleaf evergreen shrub
Zones (3) to 10
Native to swampy areas from Nova Scotia to Florida

Upright, rounded form is excellent for hedges. Shear to keep it dense. Tolerates heavy shade, but form will be more open. The only holly to spread by underground stems or stolons. Cut to within 12 inches of soil to renew screen plantings that have gotten "leggy" with age. Leaves are lustrous dark green with light-colored undersides, 1 to 2 inches long, thin and usually spineless. Medium texture. They are more like *Buxus* than holly. Often yellow-green in summer, occasionally purplish in coldest winters. Berries are inky, blue-black, often hidden within foliage, but more showy than *Ilex crenata*. Male plant must be near females to bear fruit.
Height and spread: 3 to 8 feet by 5 to 10 feet or more. Slow growth rate.

Valued for: Ability to grow in cold or wet locations. Tolerance to shade and rapid recovery from heavy pruning.
Cultivars: 'Compacta' is noted for compact, dense form to 4 feet high. One of the hardiest broadleaf evergreens—to Zone 3. 'Ivory Queen' is noted for its showy white berries. May be difficult to find. It is more cold-tender than the species.

Ilex latifolia
Lusterleaf holly
Broadleaf evergreen tree
Zones 7 to 10
Native to Eastern China and Japan

Upright, pyramidal form is best used as a large-scale screen with occasional shaping to keep it dense. Makes an elegant espalier. Crush leaves to release pleasant fragrance. Leaves are dark green, glossy, 4 to 9 inches long with sawtooth edges. Coarse texture. Flowers are creamy white or yellow. Berries are dull red. Male plant must be near females to bear fruit.

Tolerant of a range of soil conditions. Full sun, except in hot, dry areas where part shade is required.
Height and spread: 15 to 60 feet by 8 to 30 feet. Moderate growth rate.
Valued for: Extremely large, aromatic leaves and treelike proportions.

Ilex latifolia—lusterleaf holly

Ilex latifolia—lusterleaf holly

Ilex 'Lydia Morris' and 'John Morris'

**Broadleaf evergreen shrubs
or small trees
Zones 6 to 10
Hybrids of Ilex cornuta and Ilex pernyi**

'Lydia Morris' is more open in form than John Morris, and is most available. Both are compact and pyramidal. Leaves are dark green, small and spiny. Fine to medium texture. Female produces red berries when a male pollinator is present.

Height and spread: 10 feet by 6 feet or more.

Valued for: Handsome, upright form, and tolerance of limited drought, vigorous growth.

Ilex x meserveae

**Blue holly, Meserve holly
Broadleaf evergreen shrub
Zones (5) to 9
Hybrid of Ilex aquifolium and Ilex rugosa**

Blue holly hybrids are popular for cold-climate areas. They will freeze to the ground in windy locations in Zone 5. Leaves are lustrous, dark green or bluish green, spiny, 1-1/2 inches long or more. Medium texture. Berries are red and showy. Male plant must be near female to bear fruit. Twigs are purple or bluish. New foliage is often slightly red.

Height and spread: 6 to 7 feet by 6 to 7 feet or more. Moderate growth rate.

Valued for: Exceptional cold and wind tolerance, and ability to survive in poor soils. 'Dragon Lady' makes a good small-space planting.

Cultivars: 'Blue Angel', compact, rather small. 'Blue Prince', fast growth, broad pyramidal shape, twiggy look. 'Blue Princess', deep green, attractive and showy. 'Blue Stallion', vigorous growth with spineless leaves. Use alone or as a pollinator. 'Dragon Lady'—upright blue holly, noted for unique, columnar form with dense foliage. To 12 or 15 feet by 4 feet with minimal pruning. Plant 1-1/2 to 3 feet apart for a narrow, low-maintenance screen. Needs a male plant nearby to set fruit.

Ilex 'Nellie R. Stevens'

**Broadleaf evergreen shrub
or small tree
Zones 7 to 10
Hybrid of Ilex cornuta and Ilex aquifolium**

Conical, upright form spreads with age. Excellent as a screen or shaped hedge. A female plant. Popular holly in California. Widely available. Leaves are dark green, 2-1/2 to 3-1/2 inches long with few spines. Leaf edges are rolled under. Medium to coarse texture. Berries are orange-red, produced in profusion at an early age.

Height and spread: 8 to 20 feet by 5 to 20 feet or more. Fast growth rate.

Valued for: Tolerance of dry heat, drought and vigorous growth in less than desirable soil conditions.

Ilex opaca

**American holly
Broadleaf evergreen tree
Zones (5) to 9
Native to central, southern and eastern United States**

Ilex opaca grows as an upright, pyramidal form. It is a classic screen and hedge plant in the southern and eastern United States. Fine, old specimens can be seen at Mount Vernon and Williamsburg. For uniform, sheared hedges, plant a quality cultivar and shape to force bushiness. Leaves vary considerably. Generally, they are thin and pliable, lacking the stiff feel, deep color and gloss of English holly, *Ilex aquifolium*. Still, they are attractive. Surface may be shiny or dull, 2 to 4 inches long, with spiny edges. Medium texture. Berries are small and red, rarely yellow. Male plant must be nearby for female to bear fruit.

Birds have spread this tree in its native range to swampy or dry soils. Out of its natural habitat, however, it must have slightly acid, well-drained soil.

Height and spread: 8 to 50 feet by 5 to 30 feet. May reach to 100 feet. Slow to rapid growth rate. Size and growth varies by cultivar.

Valued for: Long life, ability to be sheared.

There are over 1,000 cultivars and varieties. Many nurseries offer their own cutting-grown plants selected for their cold tolerance, ability to be sheared and dense, pyramidal form. Cold-tolerant cultivars will survive in Zone 5 in locations protected from the wind. All are reliable in Zones 6 to 9 if planted in cool sites with acid soil.

Cultivars: 'Christmas Carol' is cold tolerant and fast growing. 'Croonenburg' also grows fast, and produces abundant amounts of large berries. Grows to 10 or 15 feet high. Pyramidal form, but doesn't fill out until plant is older. Dark green, spiny leaves. 'Cumberland' has the glossiest

Ilex opaca—American holly

leaves. It is fast growing and cold tolerant. 'East Palatka' is fast growing with lustrous, medium-green, 2-inch-long leaves that have a pointed tip but few spines. Shrubby, pyramidal form to 15 to 25 feet. Small, red berries in abundance. Excellent as sheared hedge. 'Greenleaf' is noted for its narrow form and cold tolerance. Useful in small spaces. Grows to 30 feet high with dense, spiny, medium-to-dark-green foliage. Produces few berries. 'Hume No. 2' is noted for large, shiny leaves to 3-1/2 inches long. Leaves have a pointed tip but no spines. Form a dense pyramid with many red berries. 'Jersey Knight' is cold tolerant and produces an abundance of inconspicuous male flowers. Rutgers University rates it high as a pollinator. Dark-green leaves. 'Old Heavyberry' has exceptional cold tolerance and produces abundant amounts of red berries. Slow growth rate. 'Santa Claus' is a popular male pollinator and is cold tolerant. 'Savannah' has large, smooth, light-green leaves, 3 or 4 inches long but not spiny. Showy, deep-red berries are produced in abundance. Pyramidal form to 6 feet tall, sometimes much more. Popular in the South. 'Wyetta' grows fast and has showy berries. Ex-

ceptional cold tolerance. Moss-green, non-glossy leaves are shaped like English holly. Forms a tall, narrow pyramid. *Ilex opaca* var. *xanthocarpa* has yellow berries but is difficult to find. 'Canary', 'Morgan Gold' or 'Yellow Jacket' produce yellow berries, and are occasionally available.

Ilex paraguariensis
Maté
Broadleaf evergreen tree
Zone 10
Native to Paraguay, Argentina and Brazil

Maté is a popular tealike beverage in South America. The plants make an excellent espalier or sheared hedge. Rare in nurseries, but it is easy to grow from seeds. Leaves are dark green, leathery and spiny, 1 to 5 inches long. Medium to coarse texture. Berries are red. Leaves are dried to make an herbal tea, which contains a stimulant similar to caffein.
Height and spread: 20 by 15 feet.
Valued for: Herbal tea, leaves and attractive foliage.

Ilex pernyi
Perny holly
Broadleaf evergreen shrub or small tree
Zones 6 to 10
Native to central China

Perny holly is not too fussy about soil conditions, and is moderately drought tolerant. Cut branches are ornamental. Prune yearly for neat appearance. Not as popular as its hybrids, such as 'Lydia Morris' and 'John Morris', but useful as a tough, evergreen screen. Leaves are medium to dark green, 1/2 to 1-1/2 inches long and spiny. Medium texture. Berries are produced in profusion if both male and female plants are present.
Height and spread: 8 to 20 feet by 4 to 10 feet. Moderate growth rate.
Valued for: Tolerance of soil conditions, heavy production of large, red berries, hybridizing with other hollies.

Ilex verticillata
Winterberry, Firebush, Black-alder
Deciduous shrub or small tree
Zones 4 to 8
Native to eastern North America

Rounded, multistem shrub form may be shaped into a hedge. Best as an in-

Ilex verticillata—winterberry

Ilex verticillata—winterberry

formal screen or massed near highways. Birds flock to the plants. Faster growth rate with fertilizer and regular water. Cuttings root easily. Oval leaves are deep, rich green, 1-1/2 to 3 inches long, with slight, sawtooth edges and downy undersides. Showy, bright-red berries are borne in profusion. Male plant must be nearby for female to set berries. Fall color is blackish or bronze early in season. Winter look is attractive because of twigs and clinging berries.

Height and spread: 6 to 9 feet by 6 to 9 feet, 30 by 30 feet with age. Slow growth rate.

Valued for: Cold tolerance, ability to survive in swampy or shady locations and abundance of red berries.

Cultivars: 'Chrysocarpa' is rare, producing yellow berries. 'Nana' is a small female plant that produces large berries if male plant is nearby. 'Winter Red' is full size with bronze fall color.

Ilex vomitoria
Yaupon
Broadleaf evergreen shrub
or small tree
Zones 7 to 10
Native to southern United States

Open, irregular, twiggy form is best when shaped or sheared to create a neat, dense appearance. A popular landscape plant in the Southwest, California and high-desert areas. Dwarf cultivars are favored for low, formal hedges. Plants hold their sheared form well, reducing maintenance. Plants are easy to control. They are attractive in small-space areas, such as entryways, atriums or near pools. Oval leaves are medium to dark glossy green, 1/2 to 2 inches long, with sawtooth edges. Fine texture. Berries are small, shiny and red. No male pollinator is required. Dwarf cultivars bear no fruit.

Height and spread: 12 to 20 feet by 12 to 20 feet. Slow to moderate growth rate. Can be maintained at any size. Dwarf cultivars are available. Plant them 12 to 18 inches apart for border. Topiary. Containers.

Valued for: Fine texture and ability to be sheared, tolerance of alkaline soils, drought, heat, full sun, dry or swampy locations and low maintenance.

Cultivars: 'Nana', dwarf yaupon, remains a compact mound 1-1/2 feet high and 3 feet wide for years. Eventually reaches 5 or 6 feet high if left unsheared. Produces no berries. 'Pride of Houston' is upright to 10 to 15 feet. Unsheared form is irregular. Small, dark-green leaves. Produces berries. 'Stokes' is smaller and more compact than 'Nana', with rich, dark-green foliage. No berries.

Juniperus
Juniper
Needled evergreen shrubs or trees
Zones 2 to 10 as indicated

The popularity of junipers is based on their ease of maintenance and the evergreen look they provide in difficult situations. Low-spreading forms may be used for borders. Shrubby forms make sprawling screens.

Needles are short and scalelike, spiny when young. Medium to fine texture. Female berries are chalky, blue-green, turning brown in two years. Tiny male cones appear on tips of branchlets.

Uses: Plant 3 feet or more apart for sheared or shaped hedge or screen. Windbreak. Background. Noise buffer. Containers. Topiary. Espalier.

Valued for: Dependable, easy growth, low maintenance and sculptural form.

Hundreds of cultivars are available in many shades of green, blue and gray. A few quality species with columnar forms are presented in the following.

Planting and care: Plant all junipers as balled and burlapped or from containers in any well-drained soil. They tolerate a wide range of soils but cannot survive in wet conditions. Full sun. Little water is needed after plants are established.

Juniperus chinensis 'Hetzii Columnaris'

Juniperus species, juniper, trimmed as hedge.

Juniperus chinensis
Chinese juniper
Zones 4 to 10
Native to China and Japan

A common hedge plant in Japan, this juniper is excellent in hot, dry sites and coastal areas. Tolerates drought. Often espaliered. Shearing is usually not necessary.

Cultivars: 'Columnaris', also Pyramidalis', 'Columnaris Glauca', Zones 4 to 10, parts of Zone 3. Fast growth from 12 to 20 feet high, spreading 3-1/2 feet wide. Gray-green leaves. 'Hetzii Columnaris', Zones 4 to 10, is dense growing to 6 to 15 feet high. 'Keteleeri', Zones 5 to 10, fast growth to 10 to 20 feet high, loose form. 'Spartan', Zones 5 to 10, fast growth to 20 feet high, narrow and dense. 'Kaizuka' ('Torulosa'), Zones 5 to 10, sculptural, twisted form to 15 to 30 feet high. Rich, dark-green foliage. Not suited to shearing. It makes a unique, three-dimensional screen when spaced 4 to 10 feet apart.

Juniperus scopulorum
Rocky Mountain juniper
Zones 5 to 9
Native to Rocky Mountain region

Best juniper for western Kansas, Oklahoma, Texas and high-desert areas. Tolerates drought. Not recommended in the southeastern United States or Zone 10. Often sheared to make the texture more fine and for a more dense appearance.

Cultivars: 'Cologreen' grows to 15 feet high with an upright, broad, pyramidal form. 'Columnaris' grows 20 feet high and 3-1/2 feet wide. 'Gray Gleem' grows slowly to 20 feet high. Silvery gray foliage is dense.

Juniperus virginiana
Eastern red cedar
Zones 2 to 9
Native to central and eastern United States

This is the best juniper for Northeast conditions. Plant 12 to 15 inches apart for a hedge, 10 feet apart for a screen. Foliage turns brownish in winter.

Juniperus canaerti is similar. It reaches 30 by 15 feet with somewhat open, twisted branches. Holds its dark-green color in cold temperatures.
Cultivars: 'Cupressifolia', Zones 5 to 9, grows to 7 feet high. Narrow, dark-green leaves have fine texture. More dense when sheared. 'Skyrocket', Zones 4 to 9, grows to 15 feet high with an extremely narrow form. Space closely. Somewhat silvery green foliage.

Laurus nobilis
Grecian laurel, Sweet bay
Broadleaf evergreen shrub
or small tree
Zones 8 to 10
Native to the Mediterranean

This is a classic hedge plant used by the Romans and later in the great Renaissance gardens of Italy. It is easily shaped into tall walls for formal

Juniperus chinensis 'Pfitzerana Aurea'

Juniperus chinensis 'Pfitzerana Aurea'

spacial definition. It is an elegant plant that makes an exceptional background or informal screen. Multiple stems, broad and conical form and dense foliage.

This is the herb *bay leaf,* used in cooking. Leaves are dark green, 2 to 4 inches long and 1 inch wide. Pungent when crushed. Medium texture. Flowers are borne in small, inconspicuous, yellow clusters. Small, black, inedible berries follow.

Height and spread: 15 to 40 feet by 10 to 20 feet. Slow to moderate growth rate. Can be maintained at 4 feet.

Uses: Plant 1 to 2-1/2 feet apart for sheared or shaped hedge. Plant 6 to 10 feet apart for screen. Background. Containers. Topiary.

Valued for: Long life, aromatic foliage, sophisticated appearance and ability to withstand city conditions.

Planting and care: Plant from containers in any well-drained soil. Full sun or part shade. Part shade required in desert areas. Drought tolerant after plant is established. Prune selectively in summer. Or, allow new shoots to reach 3 to 4 inches and then shear. New growth quickly covers sheared leaves.

Lavandula
Lavender
Broadleaf evergreen shrub
Zones 5 to 10
Native to the Mediterranean

Classic, low, border plant for flower gardens or edging pathways. Leaves are silvery gray or gray-green, less than 2 inches long, fragrant. Medium texture. Flowers of species are lavender, clustered on spikes. They bloom in summer with a heady fragrance. Attractive to bees. Make sachets from young flowers by removing stems and drying flowers in a cool closet.

Height and spread: Up to 4 feet by 4 feet. Dwarfs are available.

Uses: For border, space according to ultimate width of cultivar. For a shaped hedge, plant unnamed species 2 to 3 feet apart.

Valued for: Aromatic flowers, gray edging, low maintenance and tolerance of drought. Old-fashioned elegance.

Cultivars and varieties: Lavender-colored flowers: *Lavandula angustifolia,* English lavender, is listed by some

nurseries as *L. officinalis, L. spica, L. vera* and *L. latifolia.* Plants grow 3 to 4 feet high and spread 3 to 4 feet wide. 'Compacta' and 'Compacta Nana' grow to only 8 inches high and 12 to 15 inches wide. 'Munstead' grows 18 inches and as wide. Flowers are dark, bluish lavender. Early bloomer. *Lavandula dentata,* French lavender, is more greenish gray with toothed foliage. It grows 3 feet high and as wide. Flower spikes are shorter and bloom for a longer period.

Dark-blue flowers: 'Hidcote' grows slowly to 12 inches high and as wide. Foliage is gray.

Pink flowers: 'Jean Davis' grows 15 inches high and as wide. Pale-pink flowers fade to white in summer heat. Foliage is blue-green.

Planting and care: Plant from 4-inch pots or containers in loose, well-drained soil. Full sun. Tolerates drought, but not adapted to wet conditions. Needs little or no fertilizer. Remove spent flower spikes and shear occasionally for neat appearance. Loves heat.

Lagerstroemia indica
Crape myrtle
Deciduous shrub or small tree
Zones 7 to 10
Native to China

Some abhor the practice of shearing crape myrtle, but larger and more

Lavandula dentata—French lavender

flowers result. For most attractive appearance, choose a cultivar that reaches the height desired and tip-prune into a screen. Flowers will be more than adequate. Young leaves are bronzy. Mature leaves are glossy dark green, to 2 inches long. Flowers are profuse and showy, in large clusters of pink, white, red, purple, shell, rose or orchid. Fall color is yellow, orange or red. Seed capsules hang on the tips of bare branches for winter interest.

Height and spread: Varies by cultivar. Trees reach 20 feet by 12 to 15 feet. Slow to moderate growth rate.

Uses: For border, plant 'Crape Myrtlettes' 12 to 18 inches apart. For sheared hedge, plant them 2 to 3 feet apart or more. For shaped hedge, plant 2 to 6 feet apart. For screen, plant large varieties at least 6 feet apart. Espalier.

Valued for: Long flowering period, sculptural branches and mottled bark.

Cultivars: 3-to 4-foot height: 'Crape Myrtlettes' with dark red through rose, pink, lavender or white flowers. Bloom begins when plant is 12 inches tall. Plant seeds or from containers for a neat hedge or espalier.

4- to 5-foot height: 'Petite Snow', white. 'Petite Red Imp', red. 'Petite Embers', rose red.

5- to 7-foot height: 'Petite Pinkie', pink. 'Petite Orchid', dark orchid. 'Snow White', white. 'Petites', pink, white or red.

6- to 10-foot height or more: 'Rosea', deep rose-magenta. 'Select Purple', purple. Many shrubby, large-scale tree forms are available.

Mildew-resistant—Indian Tribe Series: 'Catawba', dark purple and compact. 'Potomac', medium pink and upright. 'Cherokee', red and spreading. 'Seminole', medium pink and spreading. 'Powhatan', medium lavender, dense and globelike.

Planting and care: Plant balled and burlapped or from containers in almost any well-drained soil. Cuttings root easily. Full sun to part shade, does well in reflected heat. Average water requirement. Tolerates some drought. Current-season's growth bears flowers. Prune to shape from dormant season until early spring. For best flower production, head back tree forms 12 to 18 inches. This increases bushiness, but ruins the natural form. Selectively cut back to major branches and remove twiggy growth.

For a second or third bloom, remove faded flowers before seeds form. Leave as much foliage and stem as possible. Repeat when second flowers fade. Ample water, fertilizer and disease control also increase flowering. Powdery mildew is a serious problem in cool-damp or shady-humid locations. Indian Tribe cultivars are resistant to powdery mildew.

Ligustrum
Privet
Deciduous, semideciduous and evergreen shrubs or small trees
Zones 3 to 10 as indicated

Privets are popular, pest-free hedge plants. If plants are not sheared regularly, they produce flowers with a fragrance many people find objectionable. In addition, many people are allergic to the pollen.

Deciduous and semideciduous privets have a great deal in common. Leaves are glossy, medium green, 1 to 3 inches long. Medium texture. Flowers are tiny and white and grow in 1- to 3-inch-long clusters. Fruit are small, black, poisonous berries that form in clusters. These privets are overused and need constant shaping, have no fall color and are short-lived. Only regal privet is attractive in its natural form. The rest are best sheared as formal hedges or backgrounds, or maintained as low hedges. The popularity of privets is based on their fast growth rate and tolerance of poor soils, city conditions and occasional drought.

Evergreen privets have many virtues. They are discussed in more detail in the following. Planting and care for both are generally the same.

Planting and care: Deciduous varieties may be planted bare root. Plant evergreen species from containers. Both are tolerant of a wide range of soil types, from mildly acid to alkaline, and dry to wet. Will not tolerate extremely wet conditions. Full sun to half shade. Average water requirement. Somewhat drought tolerant after plant is established. Early shaping is essential to prevent "legginess." Shear tops immediately after planting. Continue to shear tops and sides frequently to keep the base wider than the top. Shear any time, unless flowers are desired. If so, wait until flowers fade before shearing. This prevents formation of berries. Cut to the ground to renovate.

Ligustrum amurense
Amur privet
Deciduous shrub
Zones 3 to 10
Native to northern China

This is the most cold-tolerant privet, often used in the Midwest. Not as attractive as *Ligustrum ibolium,* which is also quite hardy. Olive-green leaves. Grows to 15 feet high and spreads to 10 feet wide. Plant 1 to 2 feet apart for hedge.

Ligustrum x ibolium
Ibolium privet
Deciduous shrub
Zones (4) to 10
Hybrid of Ligustrum ovalifolium and Ligustrum obtusifolium

Fairly cold tolerant with attractive foliage. Widely planted on the East Coast. Grows 8 to 10 feet high. Spreads 5 to 8 feet wide. Plant 1 to 2 feet apart for hedge.

Ligustrum japonicum
Japanese privet, Waxleaf privet
Broadleaf evergreen shrub
Zones 7 to 10
Native to Japan and Korea

Japanese privet is one of the most popular hedge plants in mild-winter areas. Available from nurseries as a standard tree, often clipped into decorative globes, columns and topiary shapes. Excellent in containers for movable screens. Handsome and distinguished. Needs part shade and ample water in desert areas. Easy to transplant. Glossy or waxy leaves are medium to dark green, 2 to 4 inches long, thick and spongy. Medium texture. Flowers are showy.

Height and spread: 6 to 12 feet by 6 to 10 feet. Can be maintained at 1 foot high or less. Moderate growth rate.

Uses: Border. May be sheared low or to narrow dimensions at 6- to 12-inch spacing. Plant 1 to 3 feet apart for sheared hedge. Plant 3 to 4 feet apart

Lagerstroemia indica—crape myrtle

Lagerstroemia indica—crape myrtle

for screen. Background. Containers. Topiary. Small spaces. Espalier.

Valued for: Great elegance, rich foliage, compact form and acceptance of formal shaping.

Cultivars: 'Coriaceum' or 'Rotundifolia'—curly leaf privet. Upright to 4 or 5 feet. Leaves have inrolled edges, some of which are round. Needs shade in hot, dry areas. 'Silver Star' is a compact, variegated form with deep-green, mottled leaves edged in white. Other variegated forms are available.

Ligustrum texanum, waxleaf privet, is actually a cultivar of *L. japonicum,* but is often sold as a separate species. Foliage is more lush, dense and upright. Plant grows 6 to 9 feet by 4 to 7 feet. Moderate growth rate. Shear to any size. Can be used as a windbreak.

Ligustrum 'Suwanee River' is a hybrid of *L. japonicum.* Erect, compact form with twisted, dark-green leaves. Produces no berries. Grows 3 to 4 foot by 2 or 3 feet. Can be maintained at 18 inches. Slow growth rate.

Ligustrum lucidum
Glossy privet
Broadleaf evergreen shrub or small tree
Zones 8 to 10
Native to China, Korea and Japan

Glossy privet is a popular, handsome privet where winters are mild. Broad form has branches that grow to the ground, which makes an effective windbreak or screen. Darker green and larger in scale than Japanese privet, but often confused with it at nurseries. Leaves are not thick and spongy like those of Japanese privet. Fairly drought tolerant after plant is established. Don't buy standards unless you want tree form. Leaves are dark green, 2 to 6 inches long, glossy and crisp. Medium to coarse texture. Flowers and berries are borne in profusion.

Height and spread: 30 feet by 20 feet. Can be maintained at 3 feet, or to 12 feet. Moderate growth rate.

Uses: Plant 1 to 3 feet apart for sheared hedge. Plant 5 to 10 feet apart for screen. Background. Windbreak. Noise buffer. Canopy when pruned. Containers.

Valued for: Clean, dark foliage, for high, formal hedgewalls, and drought-tolerant, low-maintenance screen.

Ligustrum ovalifolium
California privet
Semideciduous shrub
Zones (5) to 10
Native to Japan

This is the most popular privet. Deciduous in cold winters. Recovers quickly from frost damage. Evergreen in mild-winter areas. To encourage the leaves to stay on branches, feed and water regularly. Cut to the ground to renovate.

Height and spread: 12 to 15 feet by 8 to 10 feet. Can be maintained at 6 inches.

Uses: Plant 9 inches apart for border. Plant 9 to 19 inches apart for sheared hedge. Plant 4 to 6 feet apart for screen. Background.

Valued for: Glossy, semievergreen foliage and heat tolerance.

Ligustrum obtusifolium var. regelianum
Regal privet
Deciduous shrub
Zones 3 to 10
Native to Japan

Regal privet grows to 12 feet high and spreads 15 feet wide. In its natural form, it makes an acceptable background screen. Foliage turns russet or purplish in fall. Has a tendency to get leggy. Attractive, horizontal, arching branches. Popular for mass planting in cold-winter areas. Most attractive as an unclipped screen. Cut to the ground wherever it gets out of bounds. Shearing ruins the form. A low-maintenance shrub.

Height and spread: 4 to 5 feet by 6 to 9 feet

Uses: Plant 1-1/2 to 2 feet apart for sheared hedge. Plant 4 feet apart or more for shaped hedge or screen. Background. Highway planting in the East.

Ligustrum japonicum—Japanese privet

Ligustrum japonicum—Japanese privet

Ligustrum x vicaryi

Vicary golden privet
Deciduous shrub
Zones (4, 5) to 10
Most are hybrids of Ligustrum
obtusifolium or Ligustrum ovalifolium

Vicary golden privet is such a striking, even gaudy plant, it difficult to use in the landscape, except as a carefully planned accent. For bright-yellow color, plant in full sun. Many privets bear the name ''vicaryi'' or ''vicari.'' Dwarf forms are available.

Height and spread: 6 to 10 feet by 4 to 8 feet

Uses: Plant 1 to 2 feet apart for sheared hedge.

Ligustrum vulgare

Common privet,
European privet
Deciduous shrub
Zones (3) to 10
Native to Europe and North Africa

This deciduous privet is highly susceptible to anthracnose twig blight, but remains popular in the Midwest because of its cold tolerance. Cheyenne privet, 'Cheyenne', is a particularly cold-hardy cultivar. Not recommended in northern section of Zone 3.

Height and spread: 12 to 15 feet by 10 feet.

Uses: Plant 18 inches apart for sheared hedge.

Valued for: Extreme cold tolerance.

Lonicera korolkowii var. zabeli

Zabel's honeysuckle
Deciduous shrub
Zones 3 to 10

This is probably the best honeysuckle in cold climates for a tall, clipped hedge. Arching, natural form is used in shelterbelt plantings. Leaves are dark, blue-green, to 2 inches long. Medium texture. Showy flowers are dark-rose. Berries are bright red and attract birds. Leaves stay on branches late into fall.

Height and spread: 8 to 12 feet by 8 to 12 feet.

Uses: Plant 2 to 3 feet apart for sheared or shaped hedge. Plant 3 to 4 feet apart for screen. Windbreak. Background. Shelterbelt.

Valued for: Low maintenance, tolerance of cold and desert conditions, and attractive flowers.

Planting and care: Plant from cuttings, balled and burlapped or from containers in any well-drained soil. Full sun to part shade. Average water requirement.

Lonicera nitida

Box honeysuckle
Broadleaf evergreen shrub
Zones 7 to 10
Native to China

When neatly sheared, this plant resembles a boxwood, *Buxus* species, more than honeysuckle. It has an erratic branching pattern if not shaped or sheared. Leaves are shiny, dark-green ovals, 1/2 inch long. Fine texture. Flowers are small, white and fragrant. Purplish-blue berries are translucent. Foliage turns bronze in cold weather.

Height and spread: 6 by 6 feet. Can be maintained at 2 feet. Fast growth rate.

Uses: Plant 1 to 3 feet apart for sheared or shaped hedge. Plant 3 to 5 feet apart for screen. Background. Espalier.

Valued for: Fine texture, dark-green foliage, tolerance of coastal conditions.

Planting and care: Same as *Lonicera korolkowii.*

Lonicera tatarica

Tatarian honeysuckle
Deciduous shrub
Zones 3 to 8
Native to central Asia and southern Russia

Upright stems create an arching form. Most effective as a tall, fast-growing screen. Neater form when shaped. Oval leaves are bluish green or dark green, to 2 inches long. Medium texture. Trumpet-shaped flowers are showy white, pink or red. Attractive to hummingbirds. Decorative red berries attract birds. Birds spread the seeds, which gives the plant a reputation of being an invasive pest. Winter appearance is twiggy and unattractive.

Height and spread: 10 to 12 feet by 10 to 12 feet. Fast growth rate.

Uses: Plant 2 feet apart for sheared hedge. Plant 2 to 3 feet apart for shaped hedge. Plant 3 to 6 feet apart for screen. Background. Shelterbelt snowcatch. Windbreak.

Valued for: Hardy, background greenery, fragrant flowers and low maintenance.

Cultivars: 'Arnold Red' grows 6 feet high and as wide, with deep-red flowers. Most readily available. 'Alba' grows 10 feet high and as wide with

Lonicera tatarica—tatarican honeysuckle

white flowers. 'Nana' is slow growing to 3 feet high and as wide with pink flowers. Plant 'Nana' 1-1/2 to 2 feet apart for sheared or shaped hedge.

Planting and care: Easy to grow from seeds, but flower color and form will vary. Plant bare root, balled and burlapped, from cuttings or containers in any soil. Full sun to part shade. More graceful growth but fewer flowers in shade. Average water requirement. Tolerates drought after plant is established. Prune to remove dead wood after flowering. Cut to the ground to renew growth.

Lonicera x xylosteoides
'Clavey's Dwarf'
Deciduous shrub
Zones (4) to 10

This plant is useful as an unclipped, low hedge, and tolerates heavy shearing. Leaves are blue-green, to 1-1/2 inches long. Medium texture. Flowers are yellow, but non-showy. Red berries are attractive to birds.

Height and spread: 3 by 3 feet or wider, may reach 6 by 6 feet. Slow growth rate.

Uses: Border. Plant 1-1/2 to 2 feet apart for sheared hedge. Plant 1 to 3 feet apart for shaped hedge.

Valued for: Low maintenance and cold tolerance. Compact form requires little pruning.

Planting and care: Plant bare root, balled and burlapped, from cuttings or containers. Accepts any soil except wet soil. Full sun or partial shade, few flowers in shade. Average water requirement.

Magnolia grandiflora
Southern magnolia
Broadleaf evergreen tree
Zones 7 to 10
Native to southeastern United States

Southern magnolia is a classic plant to espalier. It also makes a noble, large-scale screen if shrubby plants are selected. Young form is pyramidal, then plant becomes rounded with age. Can be maintained at narrow width with constant pruning. Leaf and petal drop can be messy, but plant generally requires little maintenance. Leaves are narrow, leathery ovals, dark green, up to 9 inches long. They are shiny with bronzed, velvety undersides. Coarse texture. Flowers are white, up to 9 inches wide, and are richly fragrant. Seeds are formed in a large, conelike structure.

Height and spread: 60 to 100 feet by 30 to 50 feet. Can be held to 8 feet. Slow to almost fast growth rate depending on moisture and whether magnesium is available in the soil.

Uses: Plant 10 to 25 feet apart for screen. Plant 5 to 8 feet apart for shaped hedge. Espalier. Background. Containers.

Valued for: Magnificent presence in the landscape, foliage and fragrant flowers, ease of espalier and pest-free growth.

Cultivars: Many are available. 'St. Mary' is a popular, grafted selection. It is compact and bushy—approximately 20 by 20 feet—one of the best for containers. 'Edith Bogue' is probably the most cold tolerant.

Planting and care: Plant from containers in rich, moist soil. Full sun to heavy shade. Avoid reflected heat in desert areas. Average to ample water. Branches may break in windy locations. If grown as an espalier with morning shade, wind protection and an overhang, magnolia can be grown well out of its adapted climate zones.

Magnolia grandiflora—magnolia

Magnolia grandiflora—magnolia

Mahonia aquifolium
Oregon grape, Holly grape
Broadleaf evergreen shrub
Zones 5 to 10
Native to West Coast

Oregon grape has an erect form. It is a good choice for a natural screen, especially in shady areas. Plant cultivars for uniform height and for little pruning. Dark-green leaves are bronzy when young, especially when exposed to full sun or cold. Glossy, 1- to 2-inch-long, toothed leaflets are holly-like. Medium texture. Flowers are bright yellow in showy clusters. Dark-blue berries appear in clusters and can be made into jelly.

Height and spread: 4 to 8 feet by 2-1/2 to 5 feet. Can be maintained at 3 feet. Dwarf cultivars are available. Moderate growth rate.

Uses: Plant 1 to 2-1/2 feet apart for shaped hedge or screen. Barrier. Background.

Valued for: Shade and drought tolerance, low maintenance, fine fruit, flowers and foliage.

Cultivars: 'Compacta' makes a low hedge to 2 feet high. Spreads to become a ground cover if not pruned. 'Golden Abundance' is erect and

Mahonia aquifolium—Oregon grape

dense, to 9 feet high or more. It has bright, medium-green leaves and showy yellow flowers. Introduced by Rancho Santa Ana Botanic Garden in Claremont, California. 'Orange Flame' grows to 5 feet high. New growth is orange, contrasting with mature green leaves. Winter color is bright red if plants are grown in full sun.

Planting and care: Plant balled and burlapped, from cuttings, divisions or from containers in average soil. Full sun to full shade on the coast. Needs shade inland. Avoid placing plants in cold, windy sites. Average water requirement. Becomes drought resistant after plant is established. Prune errant growth any time. Annual pruning promotes bushiness. Cut to the ground to renovate.

Malus pumila
Apple
Deciduous hybrid trees
Zones 4 to 10

The apple is a classic fruit. Plants were espaliered in medieval monastery gardens to save space and to take advantage of favorable microclimates. Cordon fences and espalier hedges are useful for limited space screening. Espaliered semidwarfs in containers on city balconies have the potential to produce several bushels of fruit each year.

Leaves are medium green. Although leaf size varies, texture is usually coarse. Flowers are single, pink to white, 1 to 1 1/2 inches wide and slightly fragrant. Fruit is yellow, green, red or blended colors, and comes in many sizes and flavors.

Height and spread: 4- by 4-foot dwarf on M.27 rootstock, 9- by 7-foot dwarf on M.9 rootstock, 12- by 9-foot dwarf on M.26 rootstock, 15- by 12-foot semidwarf on M.7 rootstock, 30- by 20-foot on standard. Moderate growth rate.

Uses: Food source. Border-espaliers 1-foot high in the French manner. For cordon, space dwarfs 1 to 3 feet apart. For espalier-hedge, plant 2 to 8 feet apart. Espalier against a wall. For a canopy when pruned up, space according to ultimate spread, or plant closer and pleach. Containers.

Valued for: Long life, edible fruit and attractive flowers.

Cultivars: Apples are suitable to a wide range of climates and tastes.

Most popular varieties are grown in Zones 5 to 7. 'Anoka', 'Wealthy', 'Harlson' and 'Secor' are hardy in Zone 4. In cold areas, espalier on a south-facing wall with an overhang and wind protection to take advantage of warm microclimate. 'Beverly Hills', 'Gordon', 'Pettingill' and 'Winter Banana' are low-chill apples suitable for Zones 8 to 10. "Old" apple varieties are available from specialty nurseries. Favorites to espalier include: 'McIntosh', 'Golden Delicious', 'Fameuse', 'Cortland' and 'Jonathan'.

Planting and care: Planting several varieties with staggered fruit maturity times extends the season and helps ensure necessary cross-pollination. Check with local nurseries to find out which apples are best for your area. Plant bare root or from containers in average, well-drained soil. Be certain graft is above soil level. When planting, prune off all but three or four of the most vigorous, well-arranged branches or begin to train in espalier or cordon pattern. See page 64. Full sun to light shade. Average water. Do not overfertilize young trees. Thin fruit after natural fruit drop that occurs in early summer. Space fruit 6 inches apart along the branch or leave one fruit per spur. Be careful not to damage spurs when thinning or picking fruit.

Malus baccata 'Columnaris'
Columnar Siberian crabapple
Deciduous tree
Zones 2 to 9
Native to Russia and Asia

This plant produces a strong, vertical effect, similar to a Lombardy poplar. Older trees become more vase shaped. Leaves are green, 2 to 4 inches long. Coarse texture. Flowers are white, fragrant, up to 1 inch wide. Small, yellow, waxy fruit are attractive to birds. Susceptible to fireblight but resistant to rust disease. Suited to high-desert areas but not to low deserts.

Height and spread: 25 by 4 feet when young, 30 by 8 feet when old. Fast growth rate.

Uses: Plant 2 to 4 feet apart for screen.

Valued for: Upright form, flowers, rust resistance and hardiness.

Planting and care: Plant bare root or from containers in slightly acid to slightly alkaline soil that is well drained. Full sun. average water requirement.

Malus sargentii
Sargent crabapple
Deciduous small tree
Zones 5 to 9
Native to Japan

Form is shrubby with many horizontal branches. Plant a row of standard crabapples behind a row of Sargent crabapples for a spectacular, tall, colorful screen. Leaves are dark green, occasionally lobed, 2 to 4 inches long. Medium to coarse texture. Showy, fragrant flowers are small and white, massed on branches. Small fruit are dark red, loved by birds. Suited to high-desert areas but not to low deserts.

Height and spread: 6 to 10 feet high. Spread is usually twice the plant height. Can be maintained at 3 or 4 feet. Slow growth rate.

Uses: Plant 2 to 4 feet apart for sheared or shaped hedge. Plant 4 to 10 feet apart for screen. Espalier.

Valued for: Profuse flowers, disease resistance, ease of growth and decorative, scarlet fruit.

Cultivars: 'Rosea' has pink buds, pinkish-white flowers. 'Tina' grows to 5 feet high, is the most disease resistant.

Planting and care: Plant bare root or from containers in slightly acid to slightly alkaline soil that is well drained. Tolerates some wetness. Full sun. Average water requirement. Prune or shear hedges after flowering. Next season's buds set in summer. No need to prune screens except to shape.

Myrica californica
Pacific wax myrtle
Broadleaf evergreen shrub
Zones 9 and 10
Native to West Coast

This versatile, Western native is an erect, multistem shrub, best in light shade with moisture. Extremely dense when sheared or pruned. Form is more open without clipping. Leaves are dark green, 3 to 4 inches long, narrow, toothed and glossy. Pale undersides. Coarse texture. Sheared plants have fine texture. Deepest green color in shade. More yellow in sun. Inconspicuous flowers are bunched on stems. Waxy, purplish nuts attract birds. Not adapted to hot, dry climates.

Planting and care: Plant from containers in well-drained soil. Full sun to part shade. Ample to little water. Tolerates drought after plant is established. Hardy to 18F (−8C).

Height and spread: 10 to 30 feet by 10 to 15 feet. Naturally smaller when exposed to coastal winds. Can be maintained at 5 feet.

Uses: Plant 3 to 4 feet apart for sheared hedge. Plant 4 to 6 feet apart for shaped hedge or screen.

Valued for: Clean, lustrous foliage, ability to be sheared, and low maintenance where adapted.

Malus pumila—apple 'Golden Delicious'

Myrtus communis
Myrtle, True myrtle
Broadleaf evergreen shrub
Zones 9 and 10
Native to western Asia

This is one of the ancient, Roman hedge plants, cultivated in Europe since the 16th century. Compact, rounded form makes an excellent formal hedge or a neat, dependable background screen. A warm-climate classic. Shiny leaves are dark green, 1 to 2 inches long. Fine to medium texture. Flowers are small, white or pinkish with showy stamens. Small berries are bluish black.

Height and spread: 6 feet by 5 feet, 15 by 20 feet with great age. Can be maintained at 3 feet. Moderate growth rate.

Uses: Plant 6 to 24 inches apart for border. Plant 1-1/2 to 3 feet apart for sheared hedge. Plant 3 to 4 feet apart for screen. Background. Formal shaping.

Valued for: Long life, dark, dense, aromatic foliage, low maintenance, heat and drought tolerance. Tolerates many soil types.

Cultivars: 'Compacta' grows 3 feet high and 2 feet wide. Slow growth rate, good for low hedges or edging.

Small, dense form. 'Microphylla' grows 2 feet high and 1-1/2 feet wide. Fine texture, makes an excellent border plant. Variegated cultivars are occasionally available.

Planting and care: Plant from containers in any well-drained soil. Full sun to part shade. After plant is established, little water is required. Plant thrives in moist soil that has excellent drainage. Shear any time.

Myrsine africana
African boxwood
Broadleaf evergreen shrub
Zones 8 to 10
Native to the Azores to China and Taiwan

The form of African boxwood is rounded and dense, irregular when young. It is often mistaken for *Buxus* species, boxwood. It is an excellent substitute where water is limited. Leaves are dark green, 1/2-inch long, glossy with round tips. Ultra-fine texture. Flowers are insignificant. Stems and twigs are red. Unfortunately, it is scarce in nurseries.

Height and spread: 3 to 8 feet by 3 to 8 feet. Can be held to 3 feet. Moderate growth rate.

Uses: Plant 1-1/2 to 3 feet apart for sheared or shaped hedge. Plant 3 feet apart for screen. Background. Containers. Topiary.

Valued for: Lush, fine-textured look and tolerance to drought and smog.

Planting and care: Plant from containers in any well-drained soil. Full sun or part shade. Accepts drought after plant is established. Pinch to shape or shear.

Nandina domestica
Nandina, Heavenly bamboo
Broadleaf evergreen or
semideciduous shrub
Zones 6 to 10
Native to China

Nandina has an upright form, with an Oriental look reminiscent of bamboo. It is an exceptional container plant or informal hedge. Competes well with tree roots. Leaves are medium green in shade, yellow-green with red highlights in sun. Many, 1- to 2-inch, pointed leaflets appear on branches. Fine texture. White flowers are small, appearing in clusters. Red berries are ornamental, most evident in part shade. Birds eat them. Winter leaf color is often bright red.

Nandina domestica—heavenly bamboo

Nandina domestica—heavenly bamboo

Height and spread: 4 to 6 feet by 2 to 3 feet. Can be held to 3 feet. Cultivars range from 1 foot high to 8 feet high. Moderate to fast growth rate.

Uses: Plant dwarfs 12 to 18 inches apart for border. Plant 1-1/2 to 2-1/2 feet apart for shaped hedge or screen. Background. Container planting. Feature planting.

Valued for: Delicate appearance, minimal pruning requirement, small spaces, tolerance of full shade, drought, low maintenance.

Cultivars: 'Alba' has white berries. 'Compacta' grows to 4 to 5 feet high. 'Nana' and 'Nana Purpurea' are more red than species, with a mounding form to 12 to 18 inches high by 15 inches wide. Useful as borders. 'Umpqua Warrier' grows tall and fast with attractive winter color. It may be hard to find.

Planting and care: Plant from containers in most soils. Full sun to full shade. Little water required after plant is established. Lush, fast growth with ample water and fertilizer. Cannot tolerate hot soils. Add a mulch over root zone in warm-summer areas. Avoid planting in parking-lot planting strips. In desert areas, locate plants where they will receive afternoon shade. Do not shear.

Strip and thin canes for graceful silhouette. Feed with iron to correct chlorosis. Deciduous at 10F (-12C). Quick recovery from winter damage. Little bother from pests.

Nerium oleander
Oleander
Broadleaf evergreen shrub
Zones 8 to 10
Native to southern Europe, Asia Minor and North Africa

This is a warm-climate classic, cultivated in ancient Persia and by the Moors in Spain's great gardens. Bushy form branches to the ground. Leathery leaves are dark green, narrow, 4 inches or longer. Coarse texture. Flowers are showy, profuse, 2 to 3 inches wide, waxy, usually single and occasionally fragrant. Available in pure white, pink, salmon, rose or dark red. For a refined look, plant white, single-flower varieties as sheared hedges, or dwarfs as low hedges. Others are best as a large-scale background or roadside screen.

All plant parts are poisonous. Do not burn clippings. Deer won't eat this shrub.

Height and spread: 12 feet by 12 feet, more or less depending on cultivar. Fast growth rate.

Uses: Plant dwarfs 2 to 3 feet apart for border. Plant 2 to 2-1/2 feet apart for sheared hedge. Plant 3 to 6 feet apart for shaped hedge. Plant up to 9 feet apart for screen. Windbreak. Background. Containers. Highway screening.

Valued for: Flowers, ease of growth, lush appearance in difficult areas, and tolerance to heat, drought and alkaline soil.

Cultivars: Many are available; these are only a sampling. All have single flowers except as noted.

Dwarfs, 3 to 5 feet high, easily held to less: 'Petite Pink' and 'Petite Salmon'. Zones 9 and 10.

To approximately 6 feet: 'Mrs. Roeding', double salmon. 'Casablanca', white. 'Algiers', dark red.

Large scale: 'Sealy Pink', pink. 'Red Single', red. 'Cherry Ripe', rose-red. 'Sister Agnes', white, to 20 feet.

Planting and care: Plant from containers in any soil and full sun. Little water is required after plant is established. Tolerates average garden irrigation. Prune in early spring. Shear or tip-prune any time. Cut out old wood to rejuvenate mature plants.

Nerium oleander—oleander

Nerium oleander—oleander

Osmanthus fragrans
**Sweet osmanthus,
Sweet olive
Broadleaf evergreen shrub
Zones 8 to 10
Native to eastern Asia**

Compact, rounded form requires little pruning. Easily sheared into narrow, formal shape. Flowers are inconspicuous, white and sweetly scented. Use to screen windows or enclose patios. Leaves are dark green, 2-1/2 to 4 inches long, glossy and leathery. Edges are usually smooth. Coarse texture. Bring cut branches indoors for powerful, sweet fragrance. Blooms almost all year in mild-winter areas.

Height and spread: 10 feet by 10 feet, 15 feet or more with age.
Can be maintained at 5 feet or less. Moderate growth rate.

Uses: Plant 1-1/2 to 3 feet apart for sheared hedge. Plant 3 to 4 feet apart for shaped hedge. Plant 5 to 6 feet apart for screen. Background. Espalier. Containers.

Valued for: Great fragrance, lush foliage and neat, easy-care growth in most soils.

Planting and care: Plant balled and burlapped, or from containers in any soil. Full sun to part shade. Best in part shade with deep, infrequent watering. Drought tolerant after plant is established. Tip-prune for bushiness. Shear any time. Do any major shaping in early spring. Feed with gardenia food in nutrient-poor soils.

Osmanthus heterophyllus
**(O. ilicifolius)
False holly
Broadleaf evergreen shrub
Zones (6) to 10
Native to Japan and Taiwan**

Handsome, compact, rounded form. Easily sheared. Shiny leaves are dark green, 2 inches long, spiny and leathery. Variegated cultivars are used to brighten shady corners. Medium texture. Fragrant, yellow flowers are inconspicuous.

Height and spread: 15 feet by 15 feet, easily maintained at 5 feet. Moderate growth rate.

Uses: Same as *Osmanthus fragrans.*

Valued for: Hollylike foliage, fragrance, neat, easy-care growth in shade and most soil types.

Cultivars: 'Gulftide' is upright to 15 feet high. Leaves are slightly longer than species. 'Ilicifolius' is upright from 8 to 20 feet high. 'Variegata' grows slowly to 4 to 5 feet high. Leaves are edged in white. 'Aureus' is similar to 'Variegata' but smaller.

Planting and care: Culture is same as *Osmanthus fragrans.* Tolerates more shade. Drought tolerant after plant is established.

Philadelphus x virginalis
**Mock orange
Deciduous shrub
Zones 5 to 9
Hybrids of European species**

Upright, arching form of mock orange is best as an informal screen. Leaves are dull, medium-green, 1 to 3 inches long. Coarse texture. Showy, white flowers are profuse and sweetly scented. Brief, early summer bloom period.

Philadelphus x virginalis—mock orange

Osmanthus fragrans—sweet osmanthus

Flowers are prized for wedding bouquets.

Height and spread: 7 to 8 feet by 5 to 6 feet. Fast growth rate.

Uses: Plant 2 to 5 feet apart for shaped hedge or screen. Windbreak.

Valued for: Fragrant flowers, vigorous, low-maintenance growth and resistance to pests and diseases.

Cultivars: 'True Strain' sometimes blooms all summer. 'Minnesota Snowflake' tolerates temperatures to −30F (−34C). Zones 4 to 8.

Planting and care: Plant bare root, balled and burlapped, from cuttings or containers in well-drained soil. Full sun to light shade. Average water requirement, but does best with lots of moisture. Prune yearly after flowering. Remove portions of stems that have borne blossoms. Tends to get leggy. Cut old wood and unwanted shoots to the ground.

Photinia x fraseri
Photinia
Broadleaf evergreen shrub
Zones (7) to 10
Hybrid of Chinese species

Photinia has a broad, dense form with branches that reach to the ground. Often sheared to stimulate new growth, which is bright bronze-red. New, red growth is striking on hedge plantings. Shaped hedge in part shade is darker green, more refined in appearance. Mature leaves are glossy, dark green, 3 to 5 inches long. Coarse texture. Flowers are profuse and showy, borne in clusters in spring. Cut branches are used by florists for arrangements.

Height and spread: 12 feet by 12 feet. Can be maintained at 4 feet by 3 feet. Moderate to fast growth rate.

Uses: Plant 3 to 4 feet apart for sheared or shaped hedge. Plant 6 to 10 feet apart for screen. Background. Highway planting. Espalier.

Valued for: Red foliage, flowers, low maintenance and tolerance of drought, heat and neglect.

Planting and care: Plant from containers in average soil. Full sun to part shade. Little water is required after plant is established, but it thrives with ample moisture. To harden growth in cold-winter areas, decrease water in late summer, and do not shear plants at this time. Otherwise, remove errant branches and shape or shear any time.

Physocarpus opulifolius 'Nanus' and 'Dart's Gold'
Dwarf ninebark and Golden ninebark
Deciduous shrubs
Zones 2 to 7
Hybrids of species native to northeast United States

Both of these cultivars have dense, rounded forms, and are popular in cold-winter areas as low, clipped hedges. 'Nanus' leaves are medium green. Leaves of 'Dart's Gold' are golden yellow. Both have a coarse texture. Flowers are light pink, borne in clusters. Fruit are brown or reddish, maturing to decorative seed pods.

Height and spread: 3 feet by 3 feet. Can be maintained at 2 feet.

Uses: Plant 1-1/2 to 2-1/2 feet apart for sheared or shaped hedge.

Valued for: Hardiness and neatness with few pest problems.

Planting and care: Plant bare root or from containers in any soil except highly alkaline soil. Full sun. Average to ample water. Drought in winter will damage plants. Regular shearing keeps plants dense.

Photinia x fraseri—photinia

Photinia x fraseri—photinia

Picea abies
(P. excelsa)
Norway spruce
Needled evergreen tree
Zones 2 to 10
Native to northern and central Europe

Norway spruce grows in a pyramidal form with branches to the ground that become more pendulous with age. Screen plantings should be placed well away from paths to allow room for spread. Plants decline in attractiveness after about 30 years. Needles are dark, shiny green, 1/2 to 1 inch long. Medium texture. Cones are 4 to 7 inches long and pendulous.
Height and spread: 50 feet by 30 feet, to 100 feet or more. Greatly spreading with age if grown in best cultural conditions. Can be maintained at 6 feet. Fast growth rate.
Uses: Plant 3 feet apart for sheared or shaped hedge. Plant 15 to 25 feet apart for screen. Windbreak. Background. Noise buffer.
Valued for: Dark-green foliage and fast, cold-tolerant growth.
Planting and care: Plant balled and burlapped or from containers in rich, moist soil. Full sun. Best in cool, moist locations. Shear or prune in early spring to shape.

Picea glauca
White spruce
Needled evergreen tree
Zones 2 to 10
Native to northern United States and Canada

White spruce shears well as a hedge, but foliage color varies, so it does not make a good, neutral background plant. For uniform hedge color, select plants individually or select cultivars. Needles are pale green or grayish green, 1/2 inch long. Medium texture. Cones are 1 to 2-1/2 inches long.
Height and spread: 75 to 90 feet by 12 to 15 feet or more. Can be maintained at 6 feet. Moderate to fast growth rate.
Uses: Plant 3 feet apart for sheared or shaped hedge. Plant 8 to 10 feet apart for screen. Windbreak. Shelterbelt. Noise buffer.
Valued for: Cold and drought tolerance and fast, evergreen growth.
Cultivars: 'Conica', dwarf Alberta spruce, is *very* slow growing to 8 feet high. Light-green needles turn grayish with maturity. No pruning is necessary. 'Densata', Black Hills spruce, grows slowly to 20 to 40 feet high. Needles are dark, bluish green. Excellent in the Plains States. Withstands heat, drought, cold and wind. Both are more dense and compact. Plant 2 feet apart for hedges.
Planting and care: Plant balled and burlapped or from containers in rich, well-drained, moist soil. Full sun. Drought tolerant after plant is established. Shear or prune to shape in early spring.

Pinus eldarica
(P. halapensis eldarica)
Mondell pine, Blue eldarica
Needled evergreen tree
Zones 6 to 10
Hybrid of southern European species or native to Afghanistan, southern Russia

Form is symmetrical, pyramidal and dense from the base up. Mondell pines are often grown for Chrismas trees. Needles are dark blue-green, medium texture.
Height and spread: 30 to 80 feet by 12 to 35 feet. Very fast growth rate.
Uses: Screen planted 8 to 15 feet apart or more. Windbreak. Background. Noise buffer. Highway planting.
Valued for: Drought and heat tolerance, fast, pest-free growth, tolerance of desert or coastal conditions, poor soil and low maintenance.

Pinus mugo mugo—mugo pine

Pinus mugo mugo

Mugo pine
Needled evergreen shrub
Zones 2 to 10
Native to Balkan states and eastern Alps

Mugo pine forms a tight mound with upright branches. Spreads with age. Bristly needles are dark green, 1 to 2 inches long. Fine texture. Cones are rounded, 2 inches wide, somewhat inconspicuous.

Pinus mugo, Swiss mountain pine, is much more variable in size, shape and color. It grows much larger, reaching up to 30 feet high with optimum conditions.

Height and spread: 4 feet by 4 feet or more. Can be maintained at 1 foot high. Slow growth rate.
Uses: Border. Plant 1-1/2 to 3 feet apart for shaped, low hedge. Containers.
Valued for: Symmetrical, mounded, dense form that requires little pruning.
Planting and care: Plant balled and burlapped or from containers in well-drained soil. Full sun to light shade. Drought tolerant after plant is established. No fertilizer is necessary. Pinch back to shape once a year in spring, or trim tops by shearing.

Pinus nigra

Austrian pine
Needled evergreen tree
Zones 5 to 10
Native to central Europe

Form is dense and pyramidal, eventually broad and flat-topped. Needles are dark green, 3 to 6 inches long. Medium to coarse texture. Unlike most pines, it is suited to almost any soil type. Will not tolerate dry winds or drought.

Height and spread: 40 feet by 20 feet. Moderate growth rate.
Uses: Plant 10 to 15 feet apart for screen.
Valued for: Extreme cold and wind tolerance, ability to survive in city conditions and most soils.

Pinus strobus

White pine
Needled evergreen tree
Zones (2) to 8
Native to eastern North America

White pine is useful as a sheared, evergreen hedgewall in cold areas. Locate screen plantings well away from paths. Needles are blue-green, 3 inches long or less. Fine, delicate texture. Cones are 3 to 8 inches long. Old, unclipped trees are open and irregular in form. Will not tolerate air pollution. Needles may be burned when exposed to strong winds. Pleasant pine scent.

Height and spread: 80 to 100 feet by 50 to 70 feet. Can be maintained at 5 feet or 25 feet. Slow growth at first, then grows rapidly.
Uses: Plant 2 to 6 feet apart for sheared or shaped hedge. Plant 6 to 20 feet apart for screen. Background. Noise buffer. Windbreak.
Valued for: Ability to be sheared, tolerance of cold and light shade and soft, blue-green color year-round.
Cultivars: 'Fastigiata', pyramidal white pine, is narrow and dense to 60 to 70 feet high. Columnar form. Zones 3 to 10. 'Pendula', weeping white pine, grows 40 to 50 feet high with weeping branches that sweep the ground. Do not shear. Zones 3 to 10.
Planting and care: Plant balled and burlapped or from containers in well-drained soil. Prefers sandy loam but tolerates most types. Full sun to light shade. Average water requirement. No fertilizer is necessary. To groom hedges, shear candles back in early spring. Take care not to cut into twiggy growth below needles. Severe pruning will produce unattractive appearance, but dense foliage covers stubby branches within a few years.

Pinus strobus—white pine

Pinus strobus—white pine

Pittosporum
Pittosporum
Broadleaf evergreen shrubs or trees
Native to Australia except tobira

Pittosporum are lush, low-maintenance plants that have many uses. Clean foliage and small, waxy flowers in clusters are partly hidden by leaves. Small, round fruit often split open to reveal sticky seeds.

Planting and care: Plant from containers in average garden soil. Full sun to part shade or dense shade as noted. Drought tolerant after plant is established. Best with occasional, deep irrigation and annual spring or summer fertilizing.

Pittosporum crassifolium
Karo
Broadleaf evergreen shrub
or small tree
Zones 9 and 10

Leathery leaves are greenish gray, 2 inches long. Rounded tips taper to stems. Medium to coarse texture. Maroon flowers are inconspicuous.

Height and spread: 25 feet by 15 feet. Can be maintained at 5 feet by 3 feet. Fast growth rate. Dwarf cultivars are available.
Uses: Plant dwarfs 1-1/2 to 3 feet apart for border. Plant 1-1/2 to 3 feet apart for sheared or shaped hedge. Plant 5 feet apart for screen. Background. Windbreak. Containers.
Valued for: Gray color and tolerance of ocean winds.
Cultivars: 'Nana' and 'Compacta' make dense, 3- by 3-foot mounds, perfect for shaped borders, low hedges or containers.

Pittosporum eugenioides
Lemonwood
Broadleaf evergreen tree
Zones 9 and 10

Excellent as a dense, sheared hedge or umbrella-shaped canopy tree against background plants with dark-green foliage. Close spacing and frequent topping are required for a compact hedge. Leaves are yellow-green with light, wavy edges, 2 to 4 inches long. Medium texture. Flowers are yellow and fragrant, but rarely present on sheared hedges.
Height and spread: 40 feet by 25 feet. Can be maintained at 4 feet by 3 feet. Fast growth rate.
Uses: Plant 1-1/2 to 3 feet apart for sheared hedge. Plant 5 to 10 feet apart for screen. Windbreak. Canopy when pruned up.
Valued for: Sheared, yellow-green hedges, screens and canopies.

Pittosporum tenuifolium
(P. nigrans, P. nigricans)
Black-stemmed pittosporum
Zones 9 and 10

Erect form and clean foliage make an exceptional, large-scale hedge. Leaves are oval, pale green, 1 to 1-1/2 inches long. Fine to medium texture. Flowers are dark purple, inconspicuous. They bloom occasionally on sheared hedges. Stems and twigs are almost black.
Height and spread: 15 feet by 8 feet. Can be maintained at 6 feet by 3 feet. Moderate growth rate.

Pittosporum eugenioides—lemonwood

Pittosporum tobira 'Variegata'—variegated tobira

Pittosporum crassifolium—karo

Uses: Plant 1-1/2 to 3 feet apart for sheared hedge. Plant 3 to 5 feet apart for screen. Background. Windbreak.
Valued for: Fresh color, narrow, upright form with little pruning and tolerance of coastal winds.

Pittosporum tobira
Tobira, Mock orange
**Broadleaf evergreen shrub
or small tree
Zones 8 to 10
Native to China and Japan**

Mounded form is easily shaped into a hedge but shearing results in ragged appearance. Makes a dark background. 'Variegata', with light leaves, is excellent for brightening dark areas. Tolerates cold, heat, alkaline soils, coastal winds and heavy shade. Tip-prune to encourage dense growth. Leathery leaves are dark, blue-green, 2 to 3 inches long. Rounded tips curve in and taper toward stems. Medium to coarse texture. Yellowish-white flowers are fragrant.
Height and spread: 6 to 15 feet by 8 to 20 feet. Can reach 30 feet high. Can be maintained at 6 feet by 3 feet. Slow to moderate growth rate.
Uses: Plant dwarfs 2-1/2 feet apart for border. Plant 2 to 3 feet apart for shaped hedge. Plant 3 to 8 feet apart for screen. Background. Windbreak. Containers.
Valued for: Shade tolerance, dark, glossy foliage, sweet fragrance and lush appearance.
Cultivars: For Zones 9 and 10 only: 'Wheeler's Dwarf' grows to 2-1/2 feet by 5 feet, usually much less. Easily controlled. Dense with small, glossy leaves. Needs part shade and ample water in desert areas. 'Variegata' grows to 5 by 5 feet. Looks fresh with gray-green foliage with white edges and splotches. One of the best variegated plants. Exceptional in part shade.

Pittosporum undulatum
Victorian box
**Broadleaf evergreen tree
Zones 9 and 10**

One of the most outstanding and versatile broadleaf evergreen trees. Tall hedgewalls make peerless backgrounds or screens. Shear each year in early spring for straight, vertical sides. New growth quickly covers ragged leaves. Shape with hand pruning for best appearance. Prune up for dense, umbrella-shaped canopy with graceful, multiple stems. Leaves are dark, blue-green, 2 to 4 inches long. Medium texture. Flowers are creamy white, powerfully fragrant, especially on warm evenings. Tolerates considerable shade and neglect.
Height and spread: 30 by 30 feet to 60 feet high in certain locations. Can be maintained at 8 feet by 4 feet.
Uses: Plant 5 to 8 feet apart for sheared or shaped hedge. Plant 8 to 12 feet apart for screen. Background. Windbreak. Canopy when pruned up. Containers. Noise buffer.
Valued for: Dark, glossy foliage, sweet fragrance, excellent overhead screening.

Plumbago auriculata
(P. capensis)
Plumbago, Cape plumbago
**Broadleaf evergreen or
semideciduous shrub or vine
Zones 9 and 10
Native to South Africa**

Plumbago is excellent when trained and tied against a wall or fence, and sheared for a fine-textured, flowery hedge. Makes a large, sprawling screen without support. Briefly deciduous or damaged by heavy frost, but plant recovers quickly. Leaves are medium green, 1 to 2 inches long. Fine texture. Flowers are blue or white in large, round clusters. Hot sun bleaches flower color. Blooms all year in mild climates.
Height and spread: 4 to 6 feet by 8 to 10 feet. Spreads much further as an espalier. Can be maintained at 2 feet. Slow growth at first, then rapid. A small shrub in desert areas.
Uses: Plant 3 to 4 feet apart for sheared or shaped hedge. Plant 4 to 8 feet apart for screen. Espalier. Containers.
Valued for: Abundant, true-blue flowers, fast, easy-care growth, lush, cool look with tolerance to heat, drought and poor soil.
Cultivars: 'Alba' has white flowers.
Planting and care: Plant from cuttings or containers in any well-drained soil. Full sun to part shade. Little water required after plant is established. For fastest growth, feed with complete fertilizer once each spring. Shear or shape any time.

Plumbago auriculata, plumbago, as sheared espalier.

Podocarpus gracilior
(P. elongatus)
Podocarpus, Fern pine
Needled evergreen tree
Zones 9 and 10
Native to east Africa

Podocarpus makes a slow-growing screen or elegant hedge planting. Young plants are dark green and gawky. Branches are often pendulous. Pointed leaves are blue-green with a hint of gray, 1 to 2 inches long. Pine-like texture. Plants are excellent where cleanliness is desired. There is little leaf drop. They are commonly used near pools or in entryways where leaf drop would be undesirable.

Height and spread: 30 feet by 30 feet, to 60 feet with great age. Can be maintained at 4 feet. Slow growth rate.

Uses: Plant 1 to 2-1/2 feet apart for sheared or shaped hedge. Plant 3 to 10 feet apart for screen. Background. Noise buffer. Espalier. Containers. Close-up viewing.

Valued for: Soft, sophisticated look, fresh color, resistance to pests and shade tolerance.

Planting and care: Plant from cuttings or containers in average garden soil. Full sun to heavy shade. Should have part shade in hot climates. Average to ample water. Stake young, floppy trees and encourage one main shoot. Shear as necessary.

Podocarpus macrophyllus
(P. macrophylla)
Yew pine
Needled evergreen shrub or tree
Zones 7 to 10
Native to Japan

Yew pine makes an exceptionally narrow, tall, sheared hedge, perfect for limited spaces. Columnar form is accentuated by pruning. Leaves are dark green on top and pale beneath. They are stiff, narrow and grow to 4 inches long. Fine to medium texture. Inconspicuous flowers.

Podocarpus macrophyllus maki, shrubby yew pine, has smaller leaves and is slower growing to 6 to 8 feet high. Form is more compact. Usually maintained at 2-1/2 to 4 feet. It is a popular indoor container plant.

Height and spread: 20 feet by 5 feet or more, to 50 by 20 feet with age. Can be maintained at 2 feet high and 1-1/2 feet wide. Slow growth rate.

Uses: Plant 1 to 3 feet apart for sheared or shaped hedge. Plant 3 to 4 feet apart for screen. Background. Noise buffer. Espalier. Containers. Formal shaping.

Valued for: Vertical form, sophisticated look and narrow dimensions as a sheared hedge. Resistance to pests.

Planting and care: Plant from cut-tings or containers in rich, well-drained soil. Full sun to shade, but form is less compact in dense shade. Average to ample water. Limited drought tolerance. Shear two or three times a year in early spring through early fall.

Populus
Poplar
Deciduous trees
Zones 2 to 10 as indicated

Poplars have soft, bright, new foliage, fall color and dense, twiggy appearance in winter to provide year-round interest. Lombardy poplar has been used for centuries. It has the most narrow form. The other poplars featured here have similar tall forms with greater spreads.

Poplars are best suited to large-scale properties away from sewer lines, water lines, septic tanks and leach lines. Greedy, invasive roots can heave nearby pavement. Most poplars sucker profusely and have a relatively short life span. Most decline in appearance and should be replaced after about 30 years. Some live much longer. It is best to plant a permanent screening plant at the same time with the quick-growing poplars. When the poplars decline, the permanent, long-lived trees can take over.

Uses: Screen. Windbreak. Shelterbelt. Highway screening. Accent plant.

Podocarpus macrophyllus—Yew pine

Podocarpus macrophyllus—Yew pine

Valued for: Fast growth, cold tolerance, low maintenance, dramatic silhouette and fall color.

Planting and care: Difficult to plant bare root in fall. Plant balled and burlapped, from cuttings or containers in any soil. Full sun to light shade. Ample to little water. Fastest growth in moist, well-drained soils. Shaping is usually unnecessary. Pruning cuts made in winter or spring may bleed.

Populus nigra 'Italica'
Lombardy poplar
Zones 2 to 10
Native to Mediterranean region and Italy

Lombardy poplar has bright, shiny, medium to yellow-green leaves. Beautiful golden fall color. 'Theves' strain is resistant to stem canker disease. Fewer disease problems in Northern areas and Pacific Northwest. Produces suckers from the roots.

Uses: Space no farther than 8 feet apart for a dense screen. Effective as windbreak when planted 15 to 25 feet apart, but there will be gaps between the trees.

Height and spread: 60 to 80 feet tall, spreading 4 to 15 feet.

Populus alba 'Bolleana'
Bolleana poplar
Zones 3 to 10
Hybrid of species originally from Europe and Asia

Bolleana poplar has leaves that are dark green and maplelike, with silvery undersides. Bronze fall color. Grows in sandy soils right to the coast. May not sucker from the roots.

Height and spread: 50 to 60 feet tall.

Uses: Spaced closely, makes a dense, tall screen.

Valued for: Substitute for Lombardy poplar. It is not as susceptible to canker disease, and produces fewer root suckers.

Populus simonii 'Fastigiata'
Pyramidal Simon poplar
Zones 2 to 10
Hybrid of species originally from northern China

'Fastigiata' has shiny, medium-green leaves and reddish twigs. Said to be resistant to canker disease.

Height and spread: 45 to 60 feet tall.

Uses: Dense, tall screen.

Valued for: Not as upright as Lombardy poplar.

Potentilla fruticosa
Potentilla, Bush cinquefoil
Deciduous shrub
Zones (2) to 10
Native to Northern Hemisphere

Leaves of potentilla are dark or medium green, hairy, and finely cut into 1/2-inch leaflets. Fine texture. Flowers are profuse and showy, characteristically yellow with five petals. They look similar to single, small roses. No fall color. Twiggy winter look with brown, hairy fruit.

Height and spread: 2 to 4 feet by 2 to 4 feet. Fast growth rate.

Uses: Plant 18 inches apart for sheared or shaped hedge.

Valued for: Flowers that bloom all summer and fast, easy, cold-tolerant growth.

Cultivars: 'Jackmanii', Jackman's variety, is probably the best for hedges. Upright, 2 to 4 feet high, spreading 2 to 4 feet wide. It has medium-green leaves and pure-yellow flowers. 'Gold Star' grows 2 to 2-1/2 feet high, spreading wider. It also makes a neat hedge with dark-green leaves and bright-yellow flowers. Many other cultivars are available that have yellow, white, red, rosy pink and tangerine flowers.

Fall color of *Populus nigra* 'Italica'—Lombardy poplar.

Planting and care: Plant from containers in moist, well-drained soil. Full sun or part shade. Average to little water. Shear once a year to remove spent flowers and fruit.

Prunus
Plum, Cherry, Cherry laurel
Deciduous and evergreen trees

The genus *Prunus* includes deciduous purple-leaf plums, Japanese flowering cherries, edible plums and evergreen cherry species known as *laurels*. A characteristic of *Prunus* species is sawtooth leaf edges.

The evergreen cherry laurel species are basic, easy-care landscape shrubs. All have glossy leaves with lighter-colored undersides. Small, ivory flowers are borne on spikes.

Many cultivars of ornamental Japanese flowering cherry and purple-leaf plum make lovely spring-flowering screens. The most useful is the columnar Japanese flowering cherry, *Prunus serrulata* 'Amanogawa'. Its form, like a small Lombardy poplar, makes it valuable in a narrow space or where little pruning is desired.

their abundant crops of sweet fruit makes them good choices for screening if space allows.

European plums have fruit that is so sweet it can be dried as prunes. Japanese plums are larger and juicier. Japanese plums grow vigorously and make the best screens and shaped hedges if their lower branches are not pruned off. Train espalier hedges in informal patterns.

Japanese plums grow vigorously. Plant several varieties to ensure cross-pollination and to extend fruit season. Check with local nurseries for the best plums and pollinators for your area.

Leaves vary in color and size. They are generally medium green with occasional bronze tints. Medium to coarse texture. Flowers are pink or white. Fruit color and flavor vary according to cultivar.

Height and spread: 15 to 22 feet by 15 to 22 feet. Can be maintained at 12 feet. Dwarfs grow 8 to 10 feet by 8 to 10 feet and can be maintained at 4 feet.

Uses: Plant up to 10 feet apart for shaped hedge or screen. Espalier. Containers.

Valued for: Fruit, and ease of growth in most soils.

Cultivars: Hybrid plums for Zones 4 to 8: 'Compass', 'Kaga', a useful pollinator, 'Pipestone', 'Sapa', 'Sapalta', 'Tecumseh', 'Underwood' and 'Waneta'.

Numerous European plum varieties are adapted to Zones 5 to 7. Many need no pollinator. Japanese plums are adapted to Zones 5 to 9. 'Santa Rosa' is the most popular variety. It needs no pollinator. 'Weeping Santa Rosa' makes an excellent espalier high on a wall or fence.

Plums adapted to grow in Zones 5 to 10, right to the coast, include 'Mariposa', 'Santa Rosa' and 'Satsuma' Japanese plums, and 'Green Gage' European plum.

Planting and care: Plant bare root or from containers in most soils. Best in rich, well-drained soil. Full sun to light shade. Little water is required after plant is established, but regular, deep irrigation and regular applications of fertilizer help produce the finest fruit. Prune Japanese plums severely. European plums require little pruning after major framework branches have been selected and cut back by half. Thin fruit along branches to one for every 4 to 6 inches.

Prunus laurocerasus—cherry laurel

Prunus laurocerasus—cherry laurel

Prunus caroliniana
Cherry laurel, Carolina cherry
Broadleaf evergreen shrub
or small tree
Zones 7 to 10
Native to southern and southeastern United States

Form of species is dense and shrubby, and can be weedy and invasive. Cultivars are superior plants. Prune regularly for neat, narrow proportions and to eliminate messy flowers and fruit litter. Don't buy standards unless you want a tree form. Leaves are narrow, dark green, 2-1/2 to 3 inches long. Medium texture. Flowers are not particularly showy. Fruit are small, inedible green cherries that turn black.

Height and spread: 15 to 20 feet by 15 feet, 40 by 25 feet with age. Can be maintained at 3 feet. Fast growth rate.

Uses: Plant 2 feet apart for sheared hedge. Plant 6 to 8 feet apart for screen. Windbreak. Background. Noise buffer Espalier. Topiary. Containers.

Valued for: Fast growth, and for lush, drought-tolerant planting.

Cultivars: 'Bright 'n Tight' and 'Compacta' are smaller than the species with dense, glossy foliage. Growth rate for both is slower.

Planting and care: Plant from containers in well-drained soil. Full sun to part shade. Drought tolerant after plant is established. Best near the coast. In desert areas, plant in part shade, avoid reflected heat and water regularly. Prune vigorously and often. Supply with iron in alkaline soils to prevent chlorosis. Responds to ample water and fertilizer.

Prunus ilicifolia
Hollyleaf cherry
Broadleaf evergreen shrub
or small tree
Zones 8 to 10
Native to California and coastal mountains of Baja California

This is a Western classic, useful for large-scale hedgewalls, especially in areas where water is limited. New leaves are yellow-green in spring. Mature leaf color varies. Because seedlings vary, select plants when they are in leaf for uniform hedge color. Leaves are oval, usually dark green and shiny, 1 to 2 inches long, with hollylike spines. Fine texture. Flowers are not particularly showy.

Fruit are small, edible, green cherries that turn purplish red.

Height and spread: 20 to 30 feet by 30 feet or more. Can be maintained at 3 feet. Moderate to fast growth rate.

Uses: Plant 1 to 1-1/2 feet apart for sheared hedge. Plant 3 to 10 feet apart for screen. Background. Windbreak. Noise buffer.

Valued for: Fine-textured elegance and lush appearance, drought tolerance and low maintenance.

Planting and care: Plant from containers or seeds in any soil. Tolerates rocky soil. Best in well-drained soil, near the coast. Full sun or light shade. Little water is required after plant is established. Fastest growth with deep, infrequent irrigation.

Prunus laurocerasus
Cherry laurel, English laurel, Laurel cherry
Broadleaf evergreen shrub
or small tree
Zones (5, 6) to 9
Native to Asia Minor and southeastern Europe

Cherry laurel is most practical when used as a screen. Hedge plantings need constant shaping. Plants look ragged when first sheared but recover quickly. Invasive root system. Leaves are narrow, dark green, 3 to 7 inches long. Coarse texture. Inconspicuous flowers. Fruit are small, green, inedible cherries that turn purple.

Height and spread: 30 feet by 30 feet. Can be maintained at 3 feet. Fast growth rate.

Uses: Plant 3 feet apart for shaped or sheared hedge. Plant 3 to 10 feet apart for screen. Windbreak. Background. Canopy when pruned up. 'Zabeliana' can be espaliered.

Valued for: Long life, fast, low-maintenance screening and tolerance of clay soils and city conditions.

Cultivars: 'Otto Luykens' is compact to 6 feet or more with smaller leaves. More refined look than species. Widely available. 'Schipkaensis' is cold tolerant to Zone 5. May reach 18 feet tall. Small, narrow leaves. 'Zabeliana' is broad and spreading with angling branches, and narrow, elongated, dark-green leaves. May reach 6 feet tall. Accepts full sun. Espalier. No fruit. Cuttings root easily.

Planting and care: Plant balled and burlapped, from cuttings or containers in any soil. Full sun to part or heavy shade. Needs part shade in hot areas. Average water requirement. Prune to shape. Cut back branches singly for neat, formal hedges. Fertilize generously.

Prunus lusitanica—Portugal laurel

Prunus lusitanica
Portugal laurel
Broadleaf evergreen shrub or tree
Zones 7 to 10
**Native to Portugal, Spain and
Canary Islands**

Dense, shrubby form does not require constant pruning. Best as a shaped hedge or screen. Narrow leaves are dark green, 2 to 5 inches long. Medium to coarse texture. Flowers appear in 5- to 10-inch-long spikes that cover the plant. Fruit are small, borne in long clusters. They are bright red then turn dull red.

Height and spread: 10 to 20 feet by 10 to 20 feet, 60 by 60 feet with great age. Can be maintained at 3 feet. Moderate growth rate.

Uses: Plant 2 to 3 feet apart for shaped or sheared hedge. Plant 3 to 8 feet apart for screen. Windbreak. Background.

Valued for: Lustrous, dark foliage, low maintenance, tolerance of heat, sun, shade and limited drought.

Cultivars: 'Myrtifolia' has smaller leaves.

Planting and care: Plant from containers in average garden soil. Full sun or dense shade. Average to little water.

Prunus maritima
Beach plum
Deciduous shrub
Zones 4 to 10
Native to East Coast

Beach plum is a dense, rounded, pest-free shrub cherished on Cape Cod. Best in Zones 6 to 8 in coastal areas. Plants are not always available, but can be obtained from specialty nurseries on the East Coast. Oval leaves are medium green, 2 inches long, with sawtooth edges. Medium texture. Showy flowers are white, single or double, 1/2 inch wide. Edible fruit are attractive small cherries, dull, purplish red.

Prunus flava is similar. It has yellow fruit that are terrific in preserves.

Height and spread: 6 to 10 feet by 8 to 12 feet. Can be maintained at 4 feet. Moderate growth rate.

Uses: Plant 3 feet apart for shaped hedge. Plant 3 to 6 feet apart for screen. Windbreak.

Valued for: Fruit, and tolerance of sandy soils and coastal winds.

Planting and care: Plant bare root or from containers in well-drained soil. Full sun. Average water. Head back the first year to encourage branching.

Pseudotsuga menziesii
(P. douglasii)
Douglas fir
Needled evergreen tree
Zones 4 to 9
**Native to western North
America—Alaska through Mexico**

The natural form of Douglas fir is pyramidal with drooping branches. Makes an exceptional, sheared hedge equal to *Pinus strobus*. See page 145. Can be used as a barrier plant despite its soft appearance. Needles are stiff, dark green or blue-green, 1 to 1-1/2 inches long. Medium texture. Cones are reddish brown, 3 inches long. Bright, light green, new growth opens from red buds. Best adapted to West Coast, Zones 6 to 9.

Height and spread: 70 to 250 feet by 30 to 60 feet. Can be maintained at 10 feet. Fast growth rate.

Uses: Plant 2 feet apart for sheared hedge. Plant 3 to 5 feet apart for screen. Background. Barrier. Noise buffer. Windbreak. Shelterbelt.

Valued for: Aromatic, dark foliage, tough, low-maintenance growth, and for Christmas trees.

Planting and care: Plant balled and burlapped or from containers in any well-drained soil. Full sun to almost

Pseudotsuga menziesii—Douglas fir

Pseudotsuga menziesii—Douglas fir

full shade. Plant is taller and thinner in shade. Accepts drought after it is established, but best with deep, occasional watering. Top and trim hedges, but avoid shearing in spring to conserve attractive new growth.

Punica granatum
Pomegranate
Deciduous shrub or small tree
Zones 8 to 10
Native to southeast Asia

Arching, fountainlike form is best as a shaped hedge or screen. Cultivated by the ancient Greeks and Romans and by Spanish missionaries in the New World. Useful in desert areas. Tolerates drought, heat, and clay and alkaline soils. Lives up to 200 years. Narrow leaves are bright green to yellow-green, bronzy when young, 1 to 3 inches long. Fine texture. Waxy flowers are profuse and showy, bright orange-red, coral or creamy white. Single or fruitless double forms. Fruit are red, to 3 inches in diameter, full of sweet, pulp-covered seeds. Pressed pulp is the source of ambrosia nectar and grenadine syrup. Fall foliage is bright yellow. Leaves may not turn color and drop in mildest areas of

Zone 10. Twiggy look in winter. Some branches have spiny thorns.

Height and spread: 12 to 20 feet by 12 to 20 feet. Can be maintained at 4 feet. Dwarfs to 3 by 3 feet. Moderate growth rate.

Uses: Plant 'Chico' or 'Nana' 1-1/2 to 2 feet apart for border. Plant others 2 to 4 feet apart for sheared hedge. Plant 4 to 6 feet apart or more for screen or shaped hedge. Barrier. Windbreak. Espalier. Containers.

Valued for: Long life, flowers, fruit and tough, low-maintenance growth in difficult situations.

Cultivars: Single, orange-red flowers and fruit: 'Wonderful' grows 8 to 12 feet tall, with 4-inch-wide flowers. Best fruit, except in coastal areas. 'Nana', 3 by 3 feet, is decorative but produces small, useless fruit.

Fruitless with double, carnationlike flowers: 'Alba Plena', 10 by 10 feet or less, with cream colored flowers. New growth is green, not bronze. 'Chico', to 3 by 3 feet, can be maintained at 1-1/2 feet as a border. Flowers are orange-red. 'Double Red' to 12 by 12 feet. 'Mme. Legrelle' grows to 8 by 8 feet, with coral-colored flowers.

Planting and care: Easy to grow from seeds but fruit quality varies. Plant bare root, from cuttings or containers

in any soil. Full sun or reflected heat. Accepts part shade but flowering is reduced. Drought tolerant after plant is established. Fruit sets on new spring growth. Best fruit quality with steady irrigation in well-drained soil with heat and full sun. Sudden moisture or temperature increase causes fruit to split. Prune in late winter. Shear any time but flowers and fruit will be significantly reduced. Responds to regular applications of fertilizer.

Pyracantha
Pyracantha, Firethorn
Broadleaf evergreen shrubs
or small trees
Zones 5 to 10 as indicated
Hybrids of species originally from
Asia, Japan and southern Europe

Pyracantha has a stiff, angular branching pattern and sharp thorns. Not particularly attractive between the time flowers fade and when berries appear. Plants make elegant espaliers. Narrow leaves are glossy, medium green, 1 to 4 inches long. Fine to medium texture. Flowers are dull, ivory-white. They look like tiny, single roses clustered in great abundance. Berries are orange, red or yellowish and cover the plant. They attract birds.

Punica granatum—pomegranate

Pyracantha species—pyracantha

Height and spread: Hybrids vary in form from dwarf to vertical. Species are basically shrub forms. *Pyracantha coccinea:* 6 to 10 feet by 6 to 10 feet. *P. fortuneana:* 15 feet by 10 feet. *P. koidzumii:* 10 to 20 feet by 6 to 12 feet. All can be maintained at any size or trained as espaliers. Slow growth rate at first, then rapid.

Uses: Plant 1-1/2 to 3 feet apart for border. Plant 2 to 3 feet apart for sheared or shaped hedge. Plant 4 to 6 feet apart or more for screen. Barrier. Background. Windbreak. Espalier. Topiary.

Valued for: Hollylike berries, showy flowers and fast, easy growth.

New cultivars are introduced every year. Here are a proven few.

Cultivars: Low dwarfs: 'Red Elf', Zones 7 to 10, has red berries, grows low and compact. Resists fireblight.

Tall and narrow: 'Teton', Zones 7 to 10, semideciduous in Zones 5 to 7, has yellow-orange berries. Upright, vertical form 12 feet high by 4 feet wide. Requires little pruning. An exceptional screening plant when spaced 3 feet apart. U.S. National Arboretum introduction.

Minimal pruning requirement: *P. coccinea* 'Wyatti', Zones 5 to 10, has orange-red berries. Dense form is superior for hedges.

Excellent espalier: *P. fortuneana* 'Graberi', Zones 7 to 10, large, red berries.

Large and shrubby: 'Mohave' Zones 6 to 10, orange-red berries. Resists fireblight. U.S. National Arboretum introduction. 'Watereri', Zones 6 to 10, large, red berries, thornless. Popular in the Northwest. *P. koidzumii* 'Victory', Zones 7 to 10, has red berries. Popular in desert areas. *P. coccinea* 'Government Red', Zones 6 to 10, has red berries.

Cold-tolerant shrubs: *P. coccinea* 'Kasan', Zones 5 to 10, has red-orange berries. *P. coccinea* 'Lalandei', Zones 5 to 10, has orange berries. Upright form.

Planting and care: Plant from containers in any well-drained soil. Full sun to part shade. More open form with fewer flowers when planted in dense shade. Sometimes available from nurseries already trained in espalier form. Average water requirement. Tolerates limited drought. Does not like wet soil. Pinch to shape. Fast growth rate requires constant attention to shaping. Sheared hedges have few flowers or berries. Unfortunately, plants are susceptible to fireblight. Some of the new hybrids are resistant. Provide iron to prevent chlorosis in alkaline soils.

Pyrus communis
Pear, European pear
Deciduous hybrid tree
Zones 5 to 10

A classic, edible fruit with the same history and uses as apples. Susceptible to fireblight, but many newer varieties are resistant. Leaves are medium to dark green, glossy and leathery, 1-1/2 to 3 inches long. Medium texture. Showy, white blossoms are single, up to 1-1/2 inches wide. Fruit are yellow, green, brown or purplish with exquisite flavor. Yellow foliage color in fall.

Height and spread: 30 feet by 25 feet. Can be maintained at 15 feet. Dwarfs grow to 10 feet by 8 feet. They can be maintained at 4 feet.

Uses: Food source. Border-espaliers one-foot high in the French manner. For cordon, space dwarfs 1 to 3 feet apart. For espalier-hedge, plant 2 to 8 feet apart. Espalier against a wall. For a canopy when pruned up, space according to ultimate spread, or plant closer and pleach. Containers.

Pyrus communis—pear

Pyrus communis—pear

Valued for: Long life, edible fruit, flowers, small spaces, pleaching and for formal or informal espalier.

Cultivars: There are pears for every taste. Most popular varieties are suitable in Zones 5 to 7. 'Orient', 'Starkling Delicious', 'D'Anjou', 'LeConte' and 'Winter Nellis' are blight-resistant varieties that will thrive in Zone 8 as well as Zone 9. 'Seckel' is a blight-resistant, pear suitable for Zones 5 to 10 right to the coast. Favorites to espalier include: 'Bartlett', 'Clapp's Favorite', 'Moonglow,' 'Bosc', 'Kieffer' and 'D'Anjou'.

Planting and care: Virtually the same culture as apples, but soil pH should be almost neutral. When planting, cut back the central leader. Remove all but the best branches and shorten those by half. Or begin an espalier or cordon pattern.

Pyrus kawakamii
Evergreen pear
Evergreen shrub or tree
Zones 9 and 10
Native to Taiwan

Evergreen pear is similar to European pear in form, foliage and flowers. Easy to grow. Tolerates most soil types and some drought after plant is established. May be briefly deciduous with cold winters. Handsome evergreen covered with white flowers in spring. Loose, open growth is perfect for espaliers, but heavy pruning reduces or eliminates flowers. Prune and stake to encourage tree form if canopy shape is desired.

Uses: Espalier. Canopy when pruned up. Plant 3 to 4 feet apart for shaped hedge. Can be maintained at 3 feet.

Valued: Elegant flowering, espalier and overhead screening.

Planting and care: Same as *Pyrus communis.*

Pyrus pyrifolia and Pyrus serotina hybrid
Asian pear, Pear-apple,
Chinese pear
Deciduous tree
Zones 5 to 10

Asian pear is similar to European pear, except fruit are round, crisp and firm, like an apple. They have characteristic, gritty pear texture and are brownish-green in color. They are delicious fresh, in fruit salads or cooked. Leaves are shiny and leathery, and turn purple-red in fall.

Height and spread: 25 feet by 25 feet, or less. Can be maintained at 12 feet.

Uses: Same as European pear.

Cultivars: '20th Century' needs a European pear or Asian pear planted nearby for pollination. 'Shinseiki' is self-pollinating.

Planting and care: Same as European pear, although Asian pear is easier to grow. Tolerates inland head and coastal conditions.

Raphiolepis indica
Indian hawthorn
Broadleaf evergreen shrub
Zones 7 to 10
Hybrids of species native to China

Popular plant with a mounding form, often included as part of the landscaping around shopping centers. Leaves are dark green, bronzy when young, 1 to 3 inches long. Coarse texture. Profuse, showy clusters of pink, white or deep-pink flowers. Many cultivars are available. Blue-black berries. Susceptible to fireblight.

Height and spread: Plants with varied mature sizes are available. See Cultivars. Moderate to fast growth rate.

Uses: Border. Plant 2 to 3 feet apart

Pyrus kawakamii—evergreen pear

Raphiolepis indica—Indian hawthorn

for sheared or shaped hedge. Plant 3 feet or more apart for screen. Background. Containers.

Valued for: Tough, low-maintenance growth in difficult situations, and flowers that bloom winter through spring.

Cultivars: 'Ballerina' grows 2 feet high, spreading 4 feet or less, with rosy pink flowers. Space 1-1/2 to 3 feet apart for a border and pinch to control spread. 'Bill Evans' grows fast to 5 to 7 feet high. Upright, open form needs shaping. Light-pink flowers. 'Snow White' grows to 4 feet high, spreading 4 to 6 feet wide. White flowers and light-green leaves. 'Springtime' grows fast to 4 to 6 feet high. Upright form with deep-pink flowers. 'Majestic Beauty' is a giant hybrid with 4-inch-long leaves. Grows up to 15 feet tall with fragrant, pink flowers in clusters. Coarse texture. Reputed to be a cross with *Eriobotrya* species, so it probably could be espaliered. May prove to be an attractive plant. Space 4 to 8 feet apart for large-scale screen or background.

Planting and care: Plant from containers in average, well-drained soil. Full sun to light shade, especially in desert areas. Little water needed after plant is established, but tolerates ample water. Shape annually after flowers fade. Pinch often to encourage dense, compact form. Pinching side shoots stimulates vertical growth. Shear any time. Bronze new growth quickly covers cut leaves.

Rhamnus alaternus
Italian buckthorn
Broadleaf evergreen shrub or small tree
Zones (7) to 10
Native to the Mediterranean region

One of the best, extremely narrow, low or tall sheared hedges, but requires constant clipping to look neat. Jagged, shrubby form makes an inelegant screen. Easy to grow. Leaves are dark green, 2 inches long or less and glossy. Fine texture when sheared, otherwise medium texture. Flowers are inconspicuous. Fruit are tiny black berries.

Height and spread: 12 to 20 feet by 12 to 20 feet. May get larger. Can be maintained at 3 feet. Fast growth rate.

Uses: Plant 6 to 24 inches apart for sheared hedge. Plant 3 to 10 feet apart for screen. Windbreak. Background. Freeway planting. Formal shaping. Variegated form brightens shady sites.

Valued for: Small spaces, fast, pest-free growth, wind, heat and drought tolerance with lush look.

Cultivars: 'John Edwards' has uniform, green color and size. 'Variegata' has fine, creamy white markings. Some branches may revert to green: Cut them out.

Planting and care: Narrow hedges must be spaced 6 to 12 inches apart. Plant from containers in any soil. Full sun to part shade. No water is needed after plant is established, but it accepts any amount. Invasive. Doesn't do well in wet conditions.

Rhamnus cathartica
Common buckthorn
Deciduous shrub or small tree
Zones 3 to 8
Native to Europe and Asia

Common buckthorn is a shrubby form that can spread to become a noxious weed. Although there are hundreds of better shrubs, this one is valuable for extremely poor, shady sites. Use this only in the most trying conditions. Glossy leaves are dark green, 1 to 2-1/2 inches long. Flowers are inconspicuous. Black berries are attractive to birds. Spiny thorns. Shearing reduces berry production. Birds have spread common buckthorn all over the eastern United States. Harbors a rust disease that damages oat crops. High maintenance is required for a hedge.

Rhamnus cathartica—common buckthorn

Rhamnus cathartica—common buckthorn

Height and spread: 18 to 25 feet by 18 to 25 feet. Can be maintained at 4 feet. Fast growth rate.

Uses: Plant 2 to 3 feet apart for sheared hedge. Plant 3 to 10 feet apart for screen. Windbreak. Barrier.

Valued for: Ability to survive in heavy shade, poor soils, drought, wind or city conditions.

Planting and care: Plant from seeds or bare root in any soil. Full sun to full shade. No water is needed after plant is established. Shear often.

Rhamnus frangula 'Columnaris'

Tallhedge buckthorn
Deciduous shrub
Zones 2 to 8
Hybrid of species originally from Europe and western Asia

Tallhedge buckthorn is one of the most popular, cold-tolerant deciduous hedges or screens. Dense foliage on upright form needs no pruning. Leaves are dark green, 2 inches long and shiny. Medium texture. Flowers are inconspicuous. White berries eventually turn pink and then red. Fall color is unspectacular yellow. Plant can get "leggy." Individual plants within a hedge may die out.

Height and spread: 12 to 15 feet by 4

feet. Can be maintained at 3 feet. Fast growth rate.

Uses: Plant 2 to 2-1/2 feet apart for sheared or shaped hedge. Windbreak. Background.

Valued for: Minimal pruning requirement, low maintenance and fast growth in difficult conditions.

Planting and care: Plant bare root or balled and burlapped in any well-drained soil. Full sun to part shade. Little water is needed after plant is established. Head back when planted. Afterwards, no pruning is required. May be sheared to more narrow dimensions when planted 1 to 1-1/2 feet apart. Cut leggy hedges to the ground to renovate.

Rhododendron

Rhododendron and Azalea
Evergreen shrubs
Zones 4 to 10 as noted

Rhododendron is one of the most popular garden plants. Thousands of hybrids and cultivars are available. Several useful species are featured here, but practically any rhododendron or azalea can be mass-planted as an informal hedge or screen. Ultimate size depends on growing conditions.

Valued for: Flowers, foliage and shade tolerance.

Planting and care: Plant balled and burlapped or from containers in rich, moist, acid soil that is well drained. Part shade, except as noted. Ample water. Add a layer of mulch over root zone. Apply an acid, slow-release fertilizer several times a year. In cold climates, do not fertilize after June 1. Tip-prune to shape plants after flowers fade. Do any major pruning in early spring. If flowers are desired on sheared azalea hedges, shear in early spring and after bloom.

Rhododendron indicum

Southern indica
hybrid azaleas
Evergreen shrubs
Zones 8 to 10
Hybrids of species originally from China

Mounding form of this plant is effective when all one color of a single-flower variety is mass-planted. Vigorous and fairly sun tolerant. Risky below 20F (-7C). Popular in California and the South. Cannot tolerate reflected heat. Leaves are medium to dark green, 2 to 2-1/2 inches long. Medium texture. Flowers are available in white, red, pink, lavender and salmon.

Rhamnus frangula 'Columnaris'—tallhedge buckthorn

Rhamnus alaternus 'Variegata'—variegated Italian buckthorn

Belgian indica hybrids are similar, but are less vigorous and more tender to cold.

Height and spread: 3 feet by 3 feet, up to 10 feet by 8 feet with best conditions. Fairly rapid growth rate.

Uses: Plant 2 to 3 feet apart for shaped hedge. Plant 3 to 4 feet apart for screen.

Valued for: Flowers, vigorous growth and tolerance to both heat and sun.

Rhododendron maximum
Rosebay rhododendron
Evergreen shrub
Zones 4 to 8
Native to eastern North America

Form is loose and open. Shape yearly to encourage dense, bushy growth, and tip-prune often. In unsuitable locations, plant may not grow higher than 3 feet, but can reach 40 feet high in Southern mountains. Narrow leaves are dark green, 4 to 8 inches long. Coarse texture. Flowers are pink to white and partially hidden by foliage. Late bloom season. Able to grow on the shady, north sides of buildings.

Height and spread: 8 to 15 feet tall

with irregular form. Moderate growth rate.

Uses: Plant 4 to 6 feet apart or more for shaped hedge or screen. Background.

Valued for: Cold and shade tolerance, and flowers.

Rhododendron obtusum
Kurume azalea
Evergreen shrub
Zones 6 to 10
Native to Japan

Compact and twiggy azalea. Valued in Japan for dense, tiered form rather than for flowers. Pinch and shape for mounded form. Leaves are dull green and small. Fine texture. Flowers are showy and profuse in salmon, pink, white and many shades of red.

Height and spread: 3 to 4 feet by 3 feet. Slow to moderate growth rate.

Uses: Plant 2 to 3 feet apart for sheared or shaped hedge.

Valued for: Mounded evergreen form, fine texture.

Planting and care: Half-sun ideal but accepts full shade. Plants are often deciduous in Zones 6 and 7. Not all cultivars are able to survive the cold in these zones. Check with local sources.

Rhododendron P.J.M. hybrid
Evergreen shrub
Zones 4 to 8
Hybrid of R. carolinianum and R. mucronulatum

This hybrid has a rounded form with dense foliage. It is best to select plants while they are in bloom to make the best color choice. P.J.M. is an excellent small-leaf variety. Leaves are dark green. Medium texture. Flowers are lavender-pink. Purple fall foliage color. May be briefly deciduous when exposed to extreme cold.

Height and spread: 3 to 6 feet by 4 to 5 feet. Moderate growth rate.

Uses: Plant 2 to 3 feet apart for shaped hedge.

Valued for: Flowers early in the season when there is little color, cold tolerance and evergreen foliage with fall color.

Ribes alpinum
Alpine currant
Deciduous shrub
Zones 2 to 7
Native to Europe

Alpine currant has a dense, twiggy

Sheared azalea hedge

Rhododendron indicum—Southern indica hybrid azaleas

form. Lobed leaves are dark green, 1/2 to 1-1/2 inches long. Fine to medium texture. Both flowers and fruit are inconspicuous.

Height and spread: 3 to 4 feet by 3 to 4 feet. Can be maintained much lower. Slow growth rate.

Uses: Plant 1-1/2 to 2 feet apart for sheared or shaped hedge or border.

Valued for: Good performance in full shade, extreme cold and minimal pruning requirement.

Planting and care: Plant bare root or from containers in slightly acid to slightly alkaline soil. Full sun to dense shade. Average water requirement. Withstands limited drought.

Rosa
Rose
Deciduous and evergreen shrubs and vines

Form, flower and leaf color of roses vary considerably. Polyantha, floribunda, grandiflora and miniature roses are hybrids that require more care than the various species. Flower color and form is indicated in the chart on page 160. Most roses are fragrant and thorny, but this is not always the case. Fruit is a colorful *hip* formed at the base of the flower. It is loaded with vitamin C. Use them in preserves and herbal teas if they have not been sprayed with pesticides. A few roses have attractive fall color.

Roses described in the following are easy-care, basic landscape plants. For maximum impact, use a single variety in a mass planting.

Rosa rugosa tolerates ocean wind. *R. multiflora* is cold tolerant. Both can be used as shelterbelts or for wildlife cover. *R. multiflora* is invasive, so is suitable only for large-scale properties. *R. banksiae* and *R. bracteata,* which tolerate ocean wind and shade, are evergreen climbers for mild-winter areas.

Support these or other climbers on a fence. Or peg down canes for sprawling screens or for wildlife cover on large-scale properties. The shrub or climber form of sweetheart rose, 'Cecile Brunner', is fine textured and remains evergreen in Zone 10. Shear for a neat, flowery hedge.

Valued for: Flowers, fragrance, old-fashioned elegance, long life and large-scale screening.

Uses: Plant miniatures 10 inches apart for borders. Sheared hedge. Informal low hedge. Screen. Barrier planted as closely as 6 inches apart. Shelterbelt. Espalier. Containers.

Planting and care: Plant bare root or from containers in well-drained soil. Amend heavy, clay soils with organic matter. Full sun except as noted. Afternoon shade is acceptable. A breezy site is better than one with humid, still air. Average to little water required after plant is established. Feed miniatures, floribundas, polyanthas and grandifloras in spring with 14-14-14 slow-release fertilizer. In mild-winter areas, Zones 9 and 10, feed again in late summer and prune lightly to encourage second bloom. Peg down long canes of climbers that are planted as screens. Basic pruning or shearing should be done during dormant season. Shearing once a year during dormant season will not reduce flowers, but shearing more often may eliminate them. Species roses and climbers need little care, except for the removal of old deadwood. This is not necessary in large-scale plantings. Prune miniatures, grandifloras, floribundas and polyanthas lightly, removing dead wood, suckers and less than one-third of new growth. Mulch roots, especially miniatures, with 2 or 3 inches of compost or gravel. Or, apply a mulch of decomposed manure in spring and do not fertilize. If your roses have disease or aphid problems, spray or dust with general-purpose, commercial rose product. Most roses listed in the chart are disease resistant.

Rosa—'The Fairy' rose

Rosa banksiae—'Lady Banks' rose

Roses for Borders, Hedges and Screens

Name	Zone	Height	Flower Color	Use
Alfred de Dalmas	4	2-3	Light pink	Hedge
Applejack	4	5-8	Pink	Hedge, screen
Beauty Secret	5	min	Red	Border
Blanc Double de Courbert	4	4-7	White	Sheared hedge, screen
Bo Peep	5	min	Pink	Border
Cathedral	4	2-4	Salmon	Hedge
Cecile Brunner	5	4-6	Pink	Sheared hedge, screen
China Doll	4	1-1/2	Pink	Border
Cinderella	5	1	White	Border
Cricri	5	min	Coral	Border
Elmshorn	4-9	4-5	Red	Hedge
Europeana	4	2-3	Red	Hedge
First Edition	4	2-3	Coral	Hedge, border
Golden Wings	4	4-7	Yellow	Hedge, screen
Hansen's Hedge Rose	3	4-5	Pink	Sheared hedge
Happy	5	1	Red	Border
Iceberg	4	5-7	White	Hedge, screen
Judy Fischer	5	min	Pink	Border
Orangeade	4	3-4	Orange	Hedge
Popcorn	5	min	White	Border
Prairie Charm	3	5-6	Salmon	Screen
Prairie Dawn	3	5-6	Pink	Hedge, screen
Prairie Fire	3	5-6	Red	Screen
Prairie Flower	3	4	Red	Hedge
Puppy Love	5	min	Multi	Border
Queen Elizabeth	3	5-8	Pink	Hedge, screen
Red Imp	5	min	Red	Border
Rise and Shine	5	min	Yellow	Border
Rosa banksiae	6	20	White, yellow	Screen
Rosa bracteata	6	20	White	Screen
Rosa eglanteria	4	6-10	Many	Hedge, screen
Rosa gallica officinalis	4	3-4	Red	Sheared hedge
Rosa glauca	2	6-7	Pink, red	Sheared hedge, screen
Rosa harisonii	4	5-7	Yellow	Hedge, screen
Rosa hugonis	5-9	6+	Yellow	Sheared hedge, screen
Rosa moschata 'Robin Hood'	4	4-5	Red	Sheared hedge, screen
Rosa multiflora	5	9-10	White	Hedge, screen
Rosa nitida	3	3-4	Pink	Hedge
Rosa primula	5	6	Yellow	Sheared hedge, screen
Rosa rugosa	2-7	4-6	Pink	Sheared hedge, screen
Rosa rugosa hybrids	4	4-5	Many	Hedge, screen
Rosa virginiana	2	4	Pink	Sheared hedge
Rose Parade	4	3	Pink	Hedge
Sarabande	4	2-3	Red	Hedge
Sea Foam	4	2	White	Hedge, border
Simplicity	4	2-3	Pink	Hedge
Starina	5	1	Multi	Border
Sunsprite	4	2-3	Yellow	Hedge
The Fairy	5	2-3	Pink	Hedge
Yellow Doll	5	min	Yellow	Border

Zone = minimum climate zone. Maximum is indicated when less than Zone 10. Height is in feet. Min = miniature. Sheared hedges may also be grown as informal plantings.

Rosmarinus officinalis
Rosemary
Broadleaf evergreen shrub
Zones (7) to 10
Native to Asia Minor and
southern Europe

Grayish foliage and stiff form of rosemary look best with shaping. Tolerates heat, drought, alkaline soils and neglect. Deer and rabbits will not eat it. Leaves are needlelike, dark green with gray undersides, less than 1/2-inch long. They are the familiar, pungent cooking herb. Fine texture. Flowers are pale blue, tiny but pretty, and attractive to bees.

Height and spread: 2-1/2 to 6 feet by 4 to 6 feet. Can be maintained at any size. Moderate growth rate.

Uses: Herb source. Border. Plant 2 to 3 feet apart for sheared or shaped hedge. Containers.

Valued for: Aromatic foliage and flowers, drought tolerance and low maintenance.

Cultivars: 'Collingwood Ingram' grows to 2-1/2 feet high, spreading 4 feet wide. Blue-violet flowers. For shaped borders and edgings, plant 1-1/2 to 2 feet apart. 'Tuscan Blue' is upright to 6 feet high with blue-violet flowers and deep-green foliage. Excellent espalier subject.

Planting and care: Plant from cuttings, flats or containers in any well-drained soil. Attacked by fungus in wet conditions. Full sun. Do not overwater or overfertilize. Prune after bloom. Remove woody branches. Tip-

prune to control form and stimulate growth. Shear any time. Top shearing encourages density.

Salix purpurea
Blue arctic willow, Purple-osier willow
Deciduous shrub
Zones 3 to 8
Native to Europe, northern Africa
and parts of Asia

Blue-gray appearance and tolerance of heavy, wet soils are all this plant has to recommend it. May winter-kill in extremely cold areas. Avoid using the species unless a quick-growing screen is needed for wet areas or for a rough shelterbelt. Dwarfs are best when sheared. Leaves are silvery blue-green, 1 to 4 inches long and narrow. Fine texture. Twiggy winter appearance.

Height and spread: 10 feet by 6 feet, 4- by 3-foot-high dwarfs can be maintained at 12 inches. Fast growth rate.

Uses: Plant dwarfs 1 to 1-1/2 feet apart for border or low, sheared hedge. Plant 3 to 5 feet apart for screen. Shelterbelt.

Valued for: Fast growth, cold tolerance, ability to survive in swampy areas.

Cultivars: 'Gracilis' and 'Nana' are similar dwarf forms, reaching 4 by 3 feet.

Planting and care: Plant bare root, from cuttings or containers in any soil. Full sun to part shade. Shear heavily and often to control rangy

growth. Susceptible to damage from leaf-eating worms.

Santolina chamaecyparissus
Lavender cotton
Broadleaf evergreen perennial
Zones 7 to 10
Native to the Mediterranean

Lavender cotton makes an attractive, gray mound or a neat, boxy hedge. Use dried flowers in herbal wreaths and arrangements. Dried branches hung in closets are said to repel moths. Leaves are small, scaly and silvery gray. Fine, woolly texture. Tiny, bright-yellow flowers are abundant in summer on plants given minimal shearing. Foliage is aromatic and yields a perfume oil.

Height and spread: 2 by 3 feet. Can be held low. Fast growth rate.

Uses: Plant 12 to 18 inches apart for sheared border. Plant 18 to 24 inches apart for shaped, low hedge.

Valued for: Silvery foliage and attractive flowers, heat, drought and poor soil tolerance, fast, tough growth and herbal qualities.

Planting and care: Plant from seeds, divisions, cuttings, flats or containers in spring in any well-drained soil. Full sun. Average to little water. Woody growth can develop. Plants should be sheared periodically to 1 foot high. Do not prune in fall and do not cut to the ground to rejuvenate. Replant if hedge becomes too woody or unkempt. Remove spent flowers.

Rosmarinus officinalis—rosemary

Santolina chamaecyparissus—lavender cotton

Sequoia sempervirens
Coast redwood
Needled evergreen tree
Zones 7 to 10
Native to coast ranges—California through Oregon

Coast redwood is an exceptional, large-scale, sheared hedge or screening plant in a coastal, fog-belt climate. Branches reach to the ground. Tall, narrow, pyramidal form is variable, but uniformly shaped cultivars are available. Looks dry and chlorotic away from coast. Best in fog belt in Zones 9 and 10. Not often grown with success in the East. Natural form in masses dominates and changes landscape character where it is not native. Trees live for centuries. Needles are dark blue-green to light medium green, 1/2 to 1 inch long. Fine to medium texture. Cones are small and round, 1 inch in diameter.

Height and spread: 50 to 90 feet by 15 to 30 feet.

Famous tall tree to 350 feet with great age. Can be maintained at 4 to 25 feet. Fast growth rate.

Uses: Plant 3 to 4 feet apart for sheared hedge. Plant 6 to 15 feet apart for screen. Background. Windbreak. Noise buffer.

Valued for: Stately proportions, fast growth, tolerance of wet conditions and resistance to pests.

Cultivars: 'Aptos Blue' has rich, dense, blue-green foliage. 'Los Altos' has glossy, medium-green leaves that are partially gray on the undersides. Open growth habit. 'Santa Cruz' has light-green foliage. 'Soquel' has soft, dense, feathery, gray-green foliage. It is the smallest cultivar.

Planting and care: Plant from containers in rich soil. Plant tolerates wet conditions but not dry or alkaline. Full sun to part shade. Ample water for fastest growth. Summer irrigation required away from fog belt. Choose cultivars that have uniform color for a hedge planting. Top at least once a year. Shear any time, but never allow hedge to get out of bounds. Side shearing after extensive growth produces stubby branches. Feed occasionally. Old leaves will yellow and drop in summer or fall. Add iron sulfate to soil to prevent chlorosis.

Spiraea
Spiraea
Deciduous shrubs
Zones 4 to 10 as indicated
Species and hybrids originally from Japan and Asia

Spiraea nipponica 'Snowmound' and *S. prunifolia plena* are the most useful spiraeas for hedges and screens. Others spiraeas are planted for their flowers. Medium to coarse texture, except where noted. Flowers are profuse and showy in flat-topped clusters, popular for arrangements. Fast growth rate.

Valued for: Flowers, tolerance of poor soils and city conditions and low maintenance.

Planting and care: Plant bare root, balled and burlapped, from cuttings or containers in practically any soil. Full sun to light shade. Average water. Easy to propagate from cuttings, or replant suckers of *S. bumalda* and *S. japonica*. Cut to the ground to renew. Subject to fireblight.

Sequoia sempervirens—coast redwood

Spiraea japonica—Japanese spiraea

Spiraea x bumalda
Bumalda spiraea
Zones 4 to 10

Bumalda spiraea has dark blue-green leaves with sawtooth edges to 1 to 3 inches long. May have fall color in some locations. Broad, twiggy form unattractive without shaping. Prune or shear in early spring before new growth begins.

Height and spread: Varies according to cultivar.

Uses: Plant 1-1/2 to 2 feet apart for low, sheared or shaped hedge.

Cultivars: 'Anthony Waterer' has deep-pink flowers. Grows 2-1/2 feet high, spreading 2-1/2 feet wide. New leaves are pinkish. 'Froebell' has deep-pink flowers, growing 3 to 4 feet high and as wide. 'Goldflame' has pinkish-red flowers, growing 2 to 3 feet high and as wide. Mottled, copper-colored foliage turns yellow, then becomes mottled again in fall.

Spiraea japonica cultivars
Japanese spirea
Zones (5) to 9

Japanese spiraea grows in a broad, low form. Leaves are dark green, 1 to 3 inches long with sawtooth edges. Prune in early spring before new growth begins.

Height and spread: Varies by cultivar from 1 to 4 feet high.

Uses: Plant 'Alpina' 12 inches apart for border. Plant 2 feet apart for shaped low hedge.

Cultivars: 'Alpina', daphne spiraea, has pink flowers. A spreading creeper to 12 inches high. 'Atrosanguinea' has deep-crimson flowers, to 4 feet high. 'Coccinea' has deep-crimson flowers, to 3 feet high.

Spiraea nipponica 'Snowmound'
Snowmound spiraea, Boxwood spiraea
Zones 4 to 10

Snowmound spiraea grows in a dense, compact form. Leaves are blue-green, 1/2 to 1-1/4 inches long, with rounded, slightly serrated tips. Fine texture. White flowers. The best spiraea for hedges. Shear or prune in early spring before new growth begins.

Height and spread: 2 to 4 feet by 2 to 4 feet.

Uses: Plant 1-1/2 feet apart for low, sheared or shaped hedge.

Spiraea prunifolia
Bridal-wreath spiraea
Zones 4 to 9

Bridal-wreath spiraea has dark-green, glossy leaves 1/2 to 2 inches long. Flowers are white, shaped like round buttons. Fine red fall color. Broadly arching branches make a nice screen. Shear or prune after flowers fade.

Height and spread: 5 to 8 feet by 6 to 10 feet.

Uses: Plant 3 to 4 feet apart for sheared or shaped hedge. Plant 5 to 8 feet apart for screen.

Spiraea x vanhouttei
Vanhoutte spiraea
Zones 4 to 10

Leaves of vanhoutte spiraea are coarse, dull, blue-green, 1/2 to 1-1/2 inches long. Flowers are white. Form is arching or fountainlike. Pruning ruins plant appearance. Lightly shape plants after flowers fade. Best for large properties.

Height and spread: 6 to 9 feet by 8 to 12 feet or more.

Uses: Plant 3 to 8 feet apart for shaped hedge or screen.

Spiraea cultivar

Spiraea cultivar

Syringa

Lilac
Deciduous shrubs
Zones 3 to 9 as indicated

Lilac is synonymous with a certain, pale-violet color, but there are lilac varieties that have flowers in blue, pink or white. Tiny, single or double flowers are clustered on long spikes called *panicles*. Most, but not all lilacs require winter cold before they can bloom. A dwarf species is suitable for low, informal hedges.

Uses: Plant 2-1/2 to 3 feet apart for shaped or sheared hedge. Plant 3 to 5 feet apart or more for screen. Windbreak.

Valued for: Amazingly fragrant flowers, showy, informal screens and cut flowers.

Planting and care: Plant bare root, balled and burlapped or from containers in well-drained, neutral to slightly alkaline soil. Add lime to acid soils. Full sun. Accepts limited drought after plant is established. Best with average water away from the competition of tree roots. Most are susceptible to powdery mildew. A site with good air circulation reduces the risk of infection. Shape young plants early to prevent legginess. Tip-prune as necessary to control growth. Prune once a year after all flowers have faded, before seeds set. Make cuts above the next year's buds. Renew plants by cutting out old and dead wood. Shear hedges yearly after spring growth flush, but this eliminates flowers.

Syringa x chinensis

**Chinese lilac, Rouen lilac,
Persian lilac**
Zones 5 to 9
**Hybrid of Syringa vulgaris and
Syringa persica**

Chinese lilac is often sold as Persian lilac, one of its parents. Dense, arching branches, fine foliage and great flower production make it the superior lilac for screening. Some success in warm-desert areas and in Zone 10 inland from foggy coast. Not adapted for use as a windbreak in the desert. Narrow leaves are dark, medium green, 1-1/2 to 3 inches long. Medium texture. Flowers are single, profuse and fragrant, not quite as large but just as showy as common lilac. Several colors are available. Plant the species for lilac-colored flowers.

Height and spread: 8 feet by 8 feet, may reach 15 by 15 feet. Can be maintained at 3 to 5 feet. Moderate growth rate.

Valued for: Pleasing form, refined look, resistance to powdery mildew, ability to flower in mild-winter and hot-summer climates.

Cultivars: 'Alba' has white flowers. 'Rothomagensis' has violet flowers. It is popular and readily available. 'Saugeana' has lilac-red flowers.

Syringa patula

(S. pabliniana)
Dwarf Korean lilac
Zones 3 to 8
Native to Korea

Dwarf Korean lilac grows as a dense, twiggy form. Single flowers are pinkish lavender.

Height and spread: 3 feet by 3 feet, may reach 8 feet. Can be maintained at 3 feet or less.

Uses: Plant 1-1/2 to 2-1/2 feet apart for low, informal hedge.

Valued for: Dwarf size, flowers right after *Syringa vulgaris* to extend season.

Cultivars: 'Miss Kim' has bluish-lavender flowers, grows to 3 feet high and as wide.

Syringa cultivar—lilac

Syringa cultivar—lilac

Syringa persica
Persian lilac
Deciduous shrub
Zones 5 to 9
Native to Iran and northwestern China, or hybrid of Syringa laciniata and Syringa afghanica

Persian lilac has a compact, arching form and flowers distributed over the whole plant. It is a popular lilac for flowery screens in cold climates. Leaves are blue-green, smaller and more elongated than common or Chinese lilac. Medium texture. Flowers are single, profuse and fragrant, in 2- to 3-inch-long plumes of pale-lilac color.

Height and spread: 4 to 8 feet by 5 to 10 feet. Can be held to 3 feet. Moderate growth rate.

Valued for: graceful, arching form, modest scale and texture and low maintenance.

Syringa vulgaris
Common lilac, French lilac
Zones 3 to 9
Native to southeastern Europe

Common lilac is best as a flowering screen, but can get leggy. Large flowers stand upright on top of the shrub. Common species lilacs are occasionally hardy into Zone 2. They spread by suckers and require little maintenance after plants are established. Good for rough screens or windbreaks. Leaves are dark green, 2 to 5 inches long and heart shaped. Coarse texture. Cultivars are available in many colors. Flower color of species is lilac.

More than 670 named cultivars are available as lilac hybrids or French lilacs. Most do not sucker, and some produce flowers even in areas with little winter chill.

Height and spread: 8 to 15 feet by 6 to 12 feet. May reach 20 by 15 feet. Can be maintained at 5 feet. Moderate growth rate.

Valued for: Giant, fragrant, showy flowers.

Cultivars: Zones 3 to 8, widely available: 'Alba', common white lilac. Grows 12 to 15 feet high with single flowers. An old-fashioned favorite. 'Alphonse LaValee' has double blue flowers. 'Charles Joly' has double, dark, violet-red flowers. Blooms mid-season. 'Ellen Willmott' has double white flowers. Blooms late. Upright form. 'Florent Stepman' has single white flowers. 'President Lincoln' has single, almost true-blue flowers. 'President Poincare' has double violet flowers. Highly rated. 'William Robinson' has double pink flowers.

Zones 4 to 9, including southern California away from coastal fog: 'Lavender Lady' has single, silvery lavender flowers with rich green foliage. Popular and readily available. 'Blue Boy' has blue flowers. 'Mrs. Forrest K. Smith' has light-lavender flowers. 'Sylvan Beauty' has rose-lavender flowers.

Syzygium paniculatum
(Eugenia myrtifolia)
Australian brush cherry
Evergreen shrub or tree
Zone 10 only
Native to Australia

One of the best narrow hedge plants. Probably the most popular hedge in Zone 10. Available from nurseries in clipped columns or fanciful, topiary shapes. Elegant, rich green color in part shade. Flowers or fruit are eliminated when sheared regularly. Useful in limited spaces. Sheared hedges in full sun are bronzy red. Leaves are glossy, medium to deep green with a bronze tint, 1 to 2-1/2 inches long. Fine texture. New leaves in full sun

Syringa cultivar—lilac

Syzygium paniculatum—Australian brush cherry

are almost red. Flowers are subtle, creamy white puffs composed of stamens. Fruit are purple, round and edible. Fruit can be messy when they fall on pavement.

Height and spread: 30 to 60 feet by 4 to 15 feet. Can be maintained at 3 feet by 12 inches wide. Fast growth rate.

Uses: Plant 1-1/2 to 3 feet apart for sheared hedge. Plant 3 to 5 feet apart for screen. Background. Noise barrier. Small spaces. Topiary. Formal shaping. Containers.

Valued for: Tall, narrow form without pruning, ability to be sheared to 12-inch width, fast growth and drought tolerance.

Cultivars: 'Compacta' and 'Globulus' do not reach the stately proportions of the species. Both are popular as hedges, and are adapted to grow in containers. Many other cultivars, including specially selected red-leaf forms with "flame" as part of their name, are available.

Planting and care: Plant from cuttings or containers in average, well-drained soil. Full sun to almost full shade. Little water is required after plant is established. Sheared hedges need constant clipping to look neat. Space plants closely if shearing to narrow dimensions. Cut plants back severely if they get out of bounds.

Tamarix aphylla
Tamarisk, Athel tree
Evergreen-looking deciduous tree
Zones 7 to 10
Native to North Africa and the Middle East

Tamarisk is a rough-looking tree with invasive roots. When trees are grown in alkaline soils, salty secretions from the plant sometimes make it difficult grow other plants nearby. Indestructible and useful in tough conditions, where the tree's appearance will be more gray than green. Accepts shearing. Fire retardant when given regular water. Nurseries rarely carry tamarisk because it quickly outgrows its container. Easy to propagate from cuttings. Leaves are blue-green or gray depending on the salt content of the soil. Scalelike leaves have needlelike appendages. Fine texture. Flowers are creamy or dusty pink in small plumes. *Tamarix aphylla* is not as showy as other *Tamarix* species.

Height and spread: 30 to 50 feet by 15 to 30 feet or more. Can be maintained at 3 feet. Moderate to fast growth rate depending on available moisture.

Uses: Plant 3 feet apart for sheared hedge. Plant 10 feet apart for screen. Windbreak. Background. Noise buffer. Highway screening. Firebreak.

Valued for: Tolerance of alkaline soil, heat, ocean or dry winds, drought, wet situations and low maintenance.

Planting and care: To propagate, make 18-inch-long, 3/4-inch diameter cuttings from existing trees. Insert them 15 inches deep into any soil in full sun. Keep soil damp until cuttings begin to grow. No water is needed after plant is established. For fast, lush growth, dig an irrigation trench the length of planting and water occasionally. Cut to the ground if tree gets out of bounds or after freeze damage. It resprouts quickly from stumps. Difficult to eradicate.

Taxus
Yew
Needled evergreen shrubs or trees
Zones 5 to 10 as indicated

The classic, Irish or English yew hedge has been a feature of great European gardens for hundreds of years.

Syzygium paniculatum—Australian brush cherry

Syzygium paniculatum—Australian brush cherry

Yew is also one of the most popular plants for topiary, formal spatial definition or for shaping in stylized landscapes. Perfect as a background for perennial flower borders. Form is dense and compact, upright, or low and spreading, depending on cultivar. Needles are rich green, flat and shiny, 1-1/2 inches long or less. Fine, feathery texture. Some females bear 1/2-inch, round, red fruit. All parts of the plant are poisonous.

Plants live for centuries. Males must be present with females for berry production. *Taxus cuspidata* and *T. media* are the most cold tolerant.

Nomenclature of *Taxus* is confusing. Growers produce hundreds of cultivars, including golden yews.

Uses: Sheared or shaped hedge. Screen. Background. Barrier. Espalier. Noise buffer. Topiary. Containers.

Valued for: Long life, low maintenance, ability to be sheared or transplanted, and tolerance of shade.

Planting and care: Plant balled and burlapped or from containers in slightly acid to slightly alkaline soil that drains well. Cuttings root easily. Full sun to dense shade. Poor performance when exposed to winds or reflected heat. Not suited to hot areas. Wash down foliage every few weeks during hot, dry weather. Somewhat drought tolerant after plant is established, otherwise average water requirement. Little pruning is necessary. Shear in early spring. Remove feathery, summer growth. For softer appearance but higher maintenance, hand-prune to shape, removing long branches. Plant may be pruned severely to renovate. Fertilize once a year with a complete fertilizer.

Taxus baccata
English yew, Common yew
Zones (6) to 10
Native to Europe and North Africa

English yew has dark-green needles with light undersides. Species is not as popular as its cultivar, Irish yew, the classic, blackish-green, sheared hedge plant. Irish yew is one of the most important hedge plants.

Height and spread: 25 to 40 feet by 10 to 15 feet. May reach 60 by 25 feet with great age. Can be maintained at 10 feet or less. Slow growth rate.

Uses: Plant 3 to 4 feet apart for hedges.

Cultivars: 'Adpressa' is a female with rounded, bushy form to 5 feet high. Often sold as *Taxus brevifolia*.

Irish yew, *Taxus brevifolia* 'Stricta', the classic yew, deserves special mention. Blackish-green needles are striped grayish on undersides. Bears fruit. Slow growing to 10 feet high after 20 years, eventually reaching 20 feet high or more. Accentuate columnar form by binding any spreading branches with dark-colored loops of wire. Hand-prune for elegant appearance. Plant as close as 2 feet apart.

Taxus cuspidata
Japanese yew
Zones 5 to 10
Native to Japan and Korea

Japanese yew grows as a dark-green, broad-spreading, conical form. Excellent for sheared hedges or screens in cold areas. Tolerates city conditions. New growth is soft, yellow-green.

Uses: Plant 2-1/2 to 4 feet apart for hedges. Plant 10 feet or more apart for screen.

Height and spread: 10 to 40 feet by 15 to 50 feet or more. Can be maintained at 4 feet. Slow to moderate growth rate.

Taxus cuspidata 'Nana'—dwarf Japanese yew

Taxus cuspidata 'Nana'—dwarf Japanese yew

Cultivars: 'Capitata' grows 10 to 25 feet by 15 to 30 feet. Can reach 40 feet high. Hold to less by pinching. Forms a broad, dense, upright pyramid. Many decorative fruit. 'Nana' grows slowly to 3 feet by 6 feet. Makes an effective low barrier. May reach 10 feet in 40 years. Fruits heavily. It is often sold as *Taxus brevifolia*.

Taxus x media
Intermediate yew
Zones 5 to 10
Hybrids of Japanese and English yews

Intermediate yew is a popular screen plant. It has dark-green needles with light-green undersides. Cold tolerant.
Height and spread: Maximum size depends on cultivar. Slow growth rate.
Uses: Plant 2 to 3 feet apart for sheared hedge. Slightly farther for screen.
Cultivars: 'Brownii', Brown's yew, grows to 9 feet high, spreading 12 feet wide. Dense, rounded form is useful for 4-foot hedges. Non-fruiting male. 'Hatfieldii', Hatfield's yew, grows 10 feet high and 10 feet wide. Upright, conical form. Widely available. 'Hicksii', Hick's yew, grows 10 to 12 feet high in a columnar form. Narrower and darker green than Hatfield's yew.

Fruiting and non-fruiting clones are available. Plant 1-1/2 to 2 feet apart.

Teucrium chamaedrys
Germander
Broadleaf evergreen shrub
Zones 6 to 10

Germander was once used extensively in medieval knot gardens and as a medicinal herb. Character and texture similar to boxwood when sheared. Useful as an edging in place of boxwood wherever it is too sunny and warm. Leaves are dark green, toothed, 3/4 inch long or less. Leaves may drop in cold winters. Fine texture. Attractive flowers in spikes are purplish or white. Bees love them.

Bush germander, *Teucrium fruticans,* grows 4 to 8 feet high and is useful for larger sheared or shaped hedges or screens.
Height and spread: 1 to 2 feet by 1 to 2 feet. Can be held low. Fast to moderate growth rate.
Uses: Plant 10 to 18 inches apart for border and sheared low hedge. Topiary.
Valued for: Ability to withstand drought and poor, rocky soils, medicinal herbal qualities.
Planting and care: Plant from divisions, cuttings, flats or containers in spring in full sun or light shade. A well-drained soil is essential. Average water. Hardy to −10F (−24C). Shear at least once a year in early spring to keep neat. Spreads by underground rootstalks.

Thuja occidentalis
American arborvitae, White cedar
Needled evergreen shrub or small tree
Zones 3 to 10
Native to northeastern North America

Pyramidal forms of this plant are useful as a narrow, neat hedge. The species and many cultivars turn brown in winter and decline in attractiveness with age. Plant cultivars only. Excellent in moist areas, but not for hot, dry locations. Needles are scale-like in flat sprays. Fine to medium texture. Flowers are inconspicuous. Cones are small and woody. Branches are subject to breakage from heavy snow.
Height and spread: Mature size varies by cultivar. Pyramidal forms are tall and narrow. Can be maintained at 4 feet. Growth rate varies from slow to rapid.
Uses: Plant 2 feet apart for sheared hedge. Plant 2 to 3 feet apart for

Taxus x media 'Hatfieldii'—Hatfield's yew

Teucrium chamaedrys—germander

screen. Background. Windbreak in humid climates only.

Valued for: Planting in humid, cold-winter areas, minimal pruning requirement and small spaces.

Cultivars: 'Nigra' grows 25 to 40 feet tall with excellent, dark-green winter color. Zones 3 to 10. 'Pyramidalis' ('Fastigiata', 'Columnaris') grows as a 25- by 5-foot, narrow pyramid with soft, bright-green foliage. Many nurseries offer plants by this name. Some turn brown in winter. Zones 3 to 6, minimum, depending on nursery source. 'Techny' (Mission), pyramidal form, dark-green color, even in winter. Zones 5 to 10. 'Woodwardii' grows 4 or 5 feet tall, spreading to 8 by 18 feet with great age. Dark-green foliage turns brown in winter. The most drought-tolerant variety. Tolerates low humidity. Useful for low hedges because of its slow growth rate. Zones 3 to 10.

Planting and care: Plant balled and burlapped or from containers. Tolerates a range of soils, but best performance in rich, moist, well-drained soil. Full sun or light shade. Average to ample water. Shear in early spring before new growth begins. Top for neat appearance. Susceptible to spider mites.

Tilia cordata
Littleleaf linden, Lime
Deciduous tree
Zones (3) to 9
Native to Europe

Pleached "limes" have been used for spatial definition in great European gardens for centuries. Beautiful when backlit by the sun. Form is pyramidal with branches to the ground. Old trees have a round-headed form. Heart-shaped leaves are medium to dark green with light undersides, 1-1/4 to 2-1/2 inches long with sawtooth edges. Medium texture. Yellowish-white flowers are edible, small, with spicy fragrance. Bees love them. Inedible fruit are small and round and appear in clusters. Leaves and flowers can be used to flavor salads.

Height and spread: 40 to 60 feet by 20 to 25 feet. Can be maintained at 10 feet. Slow at first, then moderate growth rate.

Uses: Plant 6 to 12 feet apart for sheared hedge. Screen. Windbreak. Background. Pleaching. Canopy when pruned up. Not for hot, dry areas.

Valued for: Long life, fragrant, edible flowers, dense, symmetrical form, tolerance of city conditions.

Cultivars: 'Greenspire' grows 30 to 40 feet high with a narrow form. Straight trunk requires little if any staking. Faster growth rate than species.

Planting and care: Plant balled and burlapped or from containers. Don't buy standards unless you want tree form. Tolerates acid to alkaline soil. Best in rich, moist, well-drained conditions. Full sun to light shade. Tolerates average to ample water. Stake young species trees. Aphids sometimes attack plants.

Tsuga
Hemlock
Needled evergreen trees
Zones 3 to 10 as indicated

These are exceptional, feathery evergreens. Trees live for centuries and make outstanding sheared hedges or screens. Useful on the shady, north side of a building. Cannot tolerate dry winds or city conditions.

Planting and care: Plant balled and burlapped or from containers in moist, well-drained, acid soil. Full sun to part shade. Part shade is essential in hot or dry climates. Ample

Thuja occidentalis—American arborvitae

Thuja occidentalis—American arborvitae

water is required. Can be sheared heavily spring through summer. For feathery look in wider spaces, allow young shoots to grow outward and droop. Top young hedges frequently, until they gradually attain desired height. Space closely for narrow or low hedges.

Tsuga canadensis
Canadian hemlock
Zones 3 to 10
Native to north and eastern North America

Canadian hemlock is one of the best evergreens for a sheared hedge. Graceful, conical form with drooping branches. Needles are dark green, 1/2 inch long with two white stripes underneath. Fine texture. Yellow-green spring foliage color. Small cones hang down from branches.

Tsuga caroliniana, Carolina hemlock, is similar but not as cold tolerant. More dense, feathery appearance with darker color. Native to mountain areas from Virginia to Georgia. Zones 5 to 10.

Height and spread: 40 to 70 feet by 25 to 35 feet, 100 feet high with age. Can be maintained at 4 feet or 20 feet. Slow growth rate.

Uses: Plant 1-1/2 to 5 feet apart for sheared or shaped hedge. Plant 5 to 15 feet apart for a screen. Background. Noise buffer. Topiary.

Valued for: Exceptional cold-tolerance, low maintenance and fine-textured, evergreen elegance.

Tsuga heterophylla
Western hemlock
Zones 4 to 10
Native to western United States, coastal areas of Canada and Alaska

Western hemlock features a pyramidal form and drooping branches. A Western native that is not drought tolerant. Needles are dark green to yellow-green, 1/2 inch long with white stripes underneath. Small cones hang down from branches in profusion.

Height and spread: 125 to 200 feet by 80 to 130 feet. Can be maintained at 10 feet. Fast growth rate.

Uses: Plant 3 to 5 feet apart for sheared or shaped hedge. Plant 15 to 45 feet apart for screen. Background. Noise buffer.

Valued for: Fast growth and fine texture.

Vaccinium ashei and Vaccinum corymbosum
Rabbiteye blueberry and Blueberry
Deciduous shrubs
Native to United States
Zones 5 to 10

Rabbiteye blueberries make an excellent, informal hedge or medium-high screen. Plant early, mid- or late-season varieties for an extended fruiting period and for best pollination. Combine with rhododendrons, camellias and other acid-loving plants. Leaves are medium to dark green. Young leaves are bronzy, 3 inches long or less. Medium to coarse texture. Attractive fall color. Tiny flowers are white or pinkish.

There is little difference between blueberry and rabbiteye blueberry fruit. Plants are also similar. Blueberry is more tolerant of cold. Rabbiteye is more tolerant of warm temperatures and mild climates. Berries are blue and delicious, loved by birds. Eat fresh, in pies, pancakes, muffins or in preserves.

Height and spread: 6 feet maximum. Height and form vary.

Uses: Plant 3 feet apart for shaped

Tsuga canadensis—Canadian hemlock

Tsuga canadensis—Canadian hemlock

hedge. Plant 4 to 5 feet apart for screen.

Valued for: Fruit, attractive form and fall foliage color.

Cultivars: Especially attractive shrubs include: 'Bluecrop', midseason. 'Collins', early to midseason. 'Rancocas', early to midseason. 'Blueray', midseason.

Rabbiteye cultivars recommended for mild-winter areas: 'Homebell', early, hot inland areas. 'Bluebell', random production, large berries. 'Climax', earliest. 'Brightblue', late season. 'Tifblue', early to midseason, requires the most chilling.

Planting and care: Well-drained, moist, acid soil is essential for blueberry. Acid soil is helpful but not necessary for rabbiteye blueberry. Where soil is alkaline, plant in raised beds with peaty, acid soil mix or in containers. Full sun. Both require ample moisture. Roots form close to the surface, so avoid close cultivating. Apply an acid mulch at least 4 inches thick around plants. Add iron chelate or iron sulfate to soil to correct chlorosis.

Remove flowers to prevent fruiting the first two years. Prune in the beginning of the second year by thinning weak branches and cutting back tall, errant ones. Cut back ends of twigs as plants mature to improve form and prevent overbearing. Remove oldest branches. Acid fertilizer helps produce the biggest berries. Cut rabbiteyes back 6 inches before planting.

Viburnum
Viburnum
Zones 3 to 10 as indicated

Many *Viburnum* species are popular for large-scale screening, including the following fragrant, evergreen viburnum species.

V. japonicum, Japanese viburnum, Zones 7 to 10. *V. ordoratissimum,* sweet viburnum, Zones 8 to 10, responds well to shearing.

The following deciduous viburnums make good screens, but are rough in appearance because they produce suckers. *V. lantana,* wayfaring tree, Zones 3 to 10; *V. lentago,* nannyberry, Zones 3 to 10.

The most useful viburnums are described individually in greater detail in the following. These low-maintenance, deciduous and evergreen shrubs are tolerant of poor growing conditions and part shade. All have tiny flowers, in showy, flat-topped clusters that are followed by berries.

Planting and care: Plant bare root, balled and burlapped, from cuttings or containers in well-drained soil. Full sun to part shade. Average water requirement. Easy to propagate from cuttings.

Viburnum dentatum
Arrowwood
Deciduous shrub
Zones 3 to 10
Native to eastern and southeastern United States

Arrowwood is the best deciduous viburnum for a hedge. Numerous, arching, twiggy stems make an excellent screen, even during winter. May be invasive. Screens require no pruning. Shape or shear as desired. Glossy leaves are dark green, 1 to 3 inches long, with jagged edges and hairy undersides. Medium to coarse texture. Flowers are creamy white. Berries are blue-black. Fall color often a beautiful red, but variations occur.

Height and spread: 8 to 12 feet by 8 to 12 feet, 15 by 15 feet with optimum conditions. Can be maintained at 4 feet. Moderate growth rate.

Uses: Plant 2 feet apart for sheared or shaped hedge. Plant 6 feet apart or more for screen. Background.

Valued for: Ability to survive in wet or poor soils and heavy shade. Tolerance to cold and pest-free growth.

Viburnum tinus
Laurustinus
Broadleaf evergreen shrub
or small tree
Zones 7 to 10
Native to Mediterranean region

Laurustinus has an upright form with branches to the ground. Red twigs lend a rosy glow. Needs part shade in desert areas; will not tolerate reflected heat. Tip-prune to shape. Shear any time. Subject to mildew in humid areas. Dwarfs are excellent in containers. Oval leaves are dark green, 2 to 3 inches long. Medium texture. Flowers are pinkish white. Berries are blue with a metallic cast.

Height and spread: 6 to 12 feet by 3 to 7 feet. Dwarf cultivars available. Moderate growth rate.

Uses: Plant 1-1/2 to 2 feet apart for sheared or shaped hedge. Plant 2 to 5 feet apart for screen. Background. Espalier. Topiary. Containers.

Valued for: Tall, narrow form, attrac-

Viburnum japonicum—viburnum

tive, evergreen foliage, tolerance to heat and showy flowers.

Cultivars: 'Compacta' and 'Spring Bouquet' grow to 6 feet high and 3 feet wide. Leaves are dark green. 'Dwarf', 'Dwarf Spring Bouquet', grows 3 to 5 feet high and spreads as wide. 'Robustum' grows 6 feet high and spreads 3 feet wide. Bigger leaves, more coarse appearance than the species.

Viburnum opulus
European highbush cranberry
Deciduous shrub
Zones 3 to 9
Native to Europe, northern Africa and Asia

The species has a rounded form and multiple stems. Glossy leaves are dark green, 2 to 3 inches long, with maplelike lobes. Medium texture. Flowers are pure white. Unique combination of tiny flowers ringed by larger ones. Berries are red and showy, so tart that birds rarely eat them. Fall color varies from orange to red or green. Dwarf cranberry bush is a popular cultivar of European highbush cranberry.

Height and spread: 8 to 12 feet by 10 to 15 feet. Dwarf cultivars are available. Moderate growth rate.

Uses: Plant 6 feet apart or more for shaped hedge or screen. Space 'Compactum' closer. Plant 'Nanum' 1 to 1-1/2 feet apart for border.

Valued for: Tolerance of wet soils or city conditions and showy berries.

Cultivars: 'Compactum' is 7 feet high and 8 feet wide, usually less. 'Nanum', dwarf cranberry bush or hedge viburnum, is flowerless and fruitless with small leaves. Grows as 2- by 2-foot, mounded form that is popular for low hedges. Widely available. Little maintenance required, needs no clipping. Tolerates shade.

Weigela florida
Flowering weigela,
Old-fashioned weigela
Deciduous shrub
Zones 4 to 9
Native to northern China and Korea

Flowering weigela has a rounded form with arching branches that touch the ground. Nice in bloom, nondescript the rest of the time. Best massed in the background. It is not a low-maintenance shrub. It requires hard

pruning annually. Leaves are medium green, 2 to 4 inches long. Coarse texture. Flowers are rosy pink in clusters. Numerous cultivars are available, from white to purple.

Height and spread: 6 to 9 feet by 9 to 12 feet. Fast growth rate. Dwarf cultivars are available.

Uses: Plant 8 feet apart for screen, or closer, depending on cultivar.

Valued for: Profuse flowers, pest resistance.

Planting and care: Plant from cuttings or containers in any well-drained soil. Full sun is best, tolerates some shade. Average water requirement. Flowers bloom on previous season's growth. Cut back after blooming to unflowered side branches. Remove oldest stems. Or, simply cut back entire plant halfway every other year after flowering.

Xylosma congestum
Shiny xylosma
Broadleaf evergreen shrub,
deciduous in cold areas
Zones 8 to 10
Native to southern China

Xylosma grows as a sprawling, loose form. It is most attractive with occasional shearing. Chlorotic, yellow look in full sun or in alkaline soils. Best as a background plant in some shade where it will be more green. Leaves are yellow-green in sun, medium green in filtered shade, shiny, 1-1/2 inches long or less, slightly toothed. Medium texture. New growth is bronzy. Plant suffers heavy leaf drop in cold weather, may be briefly deciduous. Tolerates heat, drought and neglect.

Height and spread: 10 by 12 feet, to 20 feet by 20 feet in 20 years, but may be maintained at any height. Slow, initial growth rate, fast after plant is established.

Uses: Plant 1-1/2 to 3 feet apart for sheared or shaped hedge. Plant 4 to 6 feet apart for screen. Espalier. Background. Containers.

Valued for: Tough, low-maintenance growth in difficult situations.

Cultivars: 'Compacta' is more dense in form and slower growing to half the size of species.

Planting and care: Plant from containers in average soil. Full sun or part shade. Little water is required after plant is established, but best with deep, monthly irrigation. Shape in early spring. Shear or prune out errant branches as necessary.

Weigela florida—weigela

Glossary

Acid—A pH value below 7.0. The opposite of alkaline. Acid soil has a pH of 4.0 to 7.0. Common in soils that have an abundance of peat, leaf mold and humus. See Alkaline and Neutral.

Alkaline—A pH value over 7.0. The opposite of acid. Alkaline soil has a pH of 7.0 to 9.0. Common in chalky or lime soils.

Allée—A parallel row of trees positioned to direct views or channel breezes.

Balled and Burlapped—A method of packaging evergreen plants for sale at the nursery. Their roots are bound in a ball shape, usually in burlap or a synthetic material.

Bare Root—A way in which many deciduous plants are sold at the nursery. When plants are dormant, their roots can be stored and sold without soil, which reduces their cost.

Basal—The part of a trunk or branch nearest the base, as in basal shoots, basal growth or basal leaves.

Batter—The taper or angle of a hedge.

Broadleaf—Plants with leaves that are wide rather than needlelike.

Bud—A small swelling or projection on a plant. The shoots, leaf clusters or flowers that develop from the buds.

Central Leader—The trunk or central stem of a plant.

Conifer, Coniferous—Any of the cone-bearing trees and shrubs, mostly evergreens.

Cordon—A single, straight stem with severely shortened side shoots. The word is derived from a French word meaning *rope, ribbon* or *cord.*

Crown—The top or head of a tree. The main upper branches.

Cultivar—A plant produced by artificial breeding, usually by man. In this book, cultivars are enclosed in single quotes. Example: *Populus nigra* 'Italica'.

Cutting—A section of stem that forms roots for propagation or to be used in making a graft. Sometimes called a *slip.*

Deciduous—Plants that drop all or nearly all their leaves each year, usually in the fall. Examples include *Acer, Malus* and *Populus* species. See Evergreen.

Dormant—The period when a plant has little or no growth. Plants are usually dormant during the coldest time of the year.

Drainage—The movement of water down through soil. If soil is saturated with water, air is forced out and roots perish from lack of oxygen.

Espalier—A tree or shrub trained to grow flat against a fence or wall, usually in a pattern.

Evergreen—A plant that has green leaves throughout the year. Examples include *Juniperus, Pinus* and *Taxus* species. See Deciduous.

Fastigiate—Plants that naturally grow tall and narrow. Example: *Cupressus sempervirens* 'Glauca'.

Force—To cause the branches or shoots of a plant to develop or grow faster or change direction. Forcing is done by selective pruning of other buds or branches.

Form—The overall shape of a tree, shrub or bush. Descriptive terms include conical, globular, irregular, pyramidal, round, spreading and weeping.

Formal—An orderly or regular arrangement of plants in a garden. Includes smooth, precise shearing and pruning of shrubs and hedges to achieve symmetry and balance. See Informal.

Framework—The basic branch structure of a tree. Includes the trunk, primary and secondary branches.

Genus—A group of plant species that are structurally related. A genus is a subordinate member of a family. Example: *Ilex.*

Grafting—A means of propagating. The stem or bud of one plant is induced to grow and become part of another plant.

Growth Habit—Refers to the genetic makeup of a plant, which causes it to grow tall or short, wide or narrow, weeping or upright.

Hardiness—The ability of a plant to withstand cold-temperature extremes. A tolerance of frost or freezes.

Heading—A basic pruning cut. To *head* is to cut the end of a branch, which encourages new growth from buds below the cut.

Hedge—A row of shrubs or trees, usually of the same species. Hedges can grow naturally or be sheared to produce a solid screen.

Hedgerow—A row of plants, usually of mixed species. On a large scale, hedgerows are used to define property lines and to contain livestock.

Hedge, Aerial—A hedge that is an effective screen from fence height and above. The leafy screen begins at fence height.

Hedge, Mosaic—Several similar but different-colored plants interplanted and sheared into one hedge to create a mosaic pattern.

Hybrid—The result of a cross of two parent plants, often two different species.

Informal—Plants growing in a natural shape or form. See Formal.

Leader—A growing stem that is longer and more vigorous than other stems.

Loam—A soil high in organic matter. It is easy to work and has good drainage.

Microclimate—Small area of climate that differs from the general climate. In a home lot, a microclimate is a cool, northern exposure or a warm, southern exposure.

Mulch—Material, both organic and inorganic, laid on top of the soil to conserve moisture, modify soil temperature and reduce weed growth. Common mulches include grass clippings, stone, peat moss and ground bark.

Neutral—Soil that is in the neutral range between acid and alkaline—7.0 on the pH scale.

Rhizome—A swollen, creeping, underground stem.

Screen—Plants arranged in a landscape to block a view. Usually informal in growth.

Scrim—A curtain of delicate greenery that creates a partial veil, adding interest to a view.

Shelterbelt—A combination planting of shrubs and trees used to lessen the influence of climate extremes on your home.

Snowcatch—A smaller version of a shelterbelt, designed to catch blowing snow before it settles where it is not wanted.

Species—A group of plants that have similar, distinctive characteristics. A species is a subordinate member of a genus. Example: *cornuta* is a species of the genus *Ilex.* See Genus.

Spur—Short, slow-growing branches that carry flower buds and fruit.

Strain—A group of hybrid plants producing offspring that are more or less the same as their parents.

Sucker—Shoots arising from buds or rootstock in grafted plants. They are usually removed.

Thinning—A basic pruning cut. Branches are removed selectively to improve the overall stucture of a plant.

Tip-Prune—Cutting or pinching back the growing tips of plants to promote bushy side growth.

Topiary—Shaping a tree or bush into a dense, unnatural form, usually an animal or geometric shape.

Variety—Variations in species that occur naturally without influence from humans. See Species.

Wake—Area of calm behind a wind shelter.

Watersprout—Vigorous, soft shoots that arise from buds as a result of pruning or damage to trees.

Whip—A young, single-stemmed tree. Often used in espalier planting.

Index